TAO TUNING

'the art of flow'

The Temple of Understanding
Volume II

ADRIAN EMERY

Wisdom Press

First published in Australia 2024
Wisdom Press
34 Johnsons Rd
Bilpin NSW Australia 2758
website: www.wisdompress.com.au
website: adrianemery.com
instagram: adrianmoranemery
facebook: adrianemery.author
youtube: AdrianEmery

ISBN: 978-0-6485106-2-8 (pbk)
ISBN: 978-0-6485106-3-5 (ebk)

Cover design and book layout by Publicious Book Publishing
www.publicious.com.au

Printed and bound in Australia on paper from responsible sources

dedicated to humanity
in the hope that we may find
our way back to our rightful place and destiny
enjoying a life of ultimate flow & fulfillment
which is our birthright

Contents

Tao Tuning
'the art of flow'

Introduction

The 'flow' has become the buzzword for the new approach to life. From elite sports to cutting edge management consulting to personal life trainers, it is all about getting into the flow. But what is the flow and what does it mean to be in the flow? As with so many fads and cliches, it is easy to espouse the wisdom with a knowing nod of the head without really understanding what it all means.

Moreover, if the flow is such an enhanced state of being and preferrable place to be, how exactly do we get there and experience it more often, not just in rare moments of peak performance?

I believe that flow is the natural state of our existence. It is not something rare and modern but is as old as humanity itself and is our natural birthright. It is in essence the 'right' or optimal way to live our lives. It is our original and correct state of being which we have unfortunately lost as we evolved into modern day 21st century beings.

Although the state of flow is a natural state of being human, it was only labelled and popularised as such by Hungarian psychologist Mihaly Csikszentmihalyi in his seminal work entitled 'Flow: the Psychology of Optimal Experience' in 1990. In this work, Csikszentmihalyi described this state as one in which people experience deep enjoyment, creativity, and a total involvement with life.

Csikszentmihalyi also explores the ways this positive state can be controlled, not just left to chance and teaches how, by ordering the information that enters our consciousness, we can discover true happiness, unlock our potential, and greatly improve the quality of our lives.

The key ingredients of flow are: doing something that you love or are truly passionate about; that necessitates acute awareness facilitated by a focused attention and serious concentration; presents a challenge in that we need to strive for and reach beyond our current personal standard; is attainable and not beyond our reach but requires concerted effort and leads to personal growth and expansion of consciousness.

Csikszentmihalyi examined the relationship between life, consciousness, fulfillment and happiness. What is important to realise is that this text is based upon countless interviews and studies of many people in diverse countries and situations to determine if there was any correlation between the way we lived our lives and happiness.

Coincidently, at the same time in my life, I was also experimenting with this state of flow exploring deeper states of consciousness in order to optimise my personal experience and overcome the limitations of the ego self. For me this state of flow is being on your path. Your path is the wave that carries you along. Experiencing flow is riding that wave just as any surfer rides the waves of the ocean. It is the Tao of your life. I call this the personal Tao.

I discovered there is a unity or triad between destiny, fate and daily existence. There is an underlying fate that lends power to your life and if you successfully align outer human life and inner spiritual destiny, you ride the wave of your personal Tao. This is the essence of *Tao Tuning*. It is being on your path, fulfilling your destiny and reaping the good fortune that accompanies a positive fate. It is a process of spiritual attunement, much like tuning a musical instrument or tuning a radio or television for clear reception.

In numerous interviews in the book, people express this oneness with life, where they become one with the activity and the resident feeling of separation dissolves. The self merges with the other whether that other is the activity itself, the moment or a larger group of people. Quite often, it is all three. Participants of flow feel an expansion of their being beyond the imprisoned self of the ego. All concerns for the self, all worries, anxieties, fears and limitations disappear. The normal passage of time also disappears.

Moreover, this optimal experience of oneness and joy can transcend the isolation of the self when this flow is experienced with others as in a choir, orchestra, team activity and so on. The self becomes transcendent, and one merges into a larger aspect of consciousness where the normal limited egoic self is no longer dominant.

Over the years, this body of work has continued through many countries, universities, studies and so forth, validating this hypothesis of optimal experience whilst in flow. To be clear, this is not a religious or mystical experience but a fundamental and natural aspect of human consciousness. However, there are techniques and practices required to enter this state of flow. It requires focus, discipline and concentration. One must exclude all interfering distractions, doubts and linear thoughts to enter flow. One must also maintain vigilance whilst in the flow, lest one loses it.

I call this falling off the wave. *Tao Tuning* is an analysis of this state in detail. It is my contention that to be riding the wave of and aligned with your Tao, is a necessary prerequisite to entering what I call the zone of flow which is the space where you are more likely to experience flow, more readily and more often.

In other words, *Tao Tuning* is the work necessary to optimise your life. The state of flow is not just something we experience occasionally in extreme situations such as mountain climbing or elite sports. It is a space available to all of us and is the natural way to live our lives. We need to be spending the majority of our time in that zone rather than believing it is restricted to special and rare circumstances.

Our fate is our personal wave or Tao. Universal consciousness is the divine Tao that permeates all of existence. Step one is appreciating that this universal consciousness is life, is divine and is benevolent. It is the Universal Law that regulates all of the phenomenal universe. The universal law is the impersonal Tao. That law is omnipotent, omnipresent and omniscient.

Step two is the birth of true awareness and the honing of attention. Attention is the lens that must be focused to allow your awareness to perceive reality, to enter the present tense of the now of eternal being. Awareness is the camera that brings that image, that perception, that experience into consciousness. Consciousness is the film, the memory stick, the usb that then holds that experience or perception. Your consciousness is the sum total of your perceptual experience of your journey.

What you focus your attention on, you become aware of, and that awareness then becomes the contents of your consciousness. As you train your attention to focus on the present, on what is, you enter the flow of the universe: The Greater Tao. You enter the flow of your own being, riding the wave of your own personal Tao. You are on your path. Now you may not always be in a transcendent state of flow to be on your path, but you cannot enter the flow if you are not on your path. Not all rectangles are squares, but all squares are rectangles.

When you are on your path your life flows easily and effortlessly. This does not mean it will be without mishap or challenge. The language of life is evolution and evolution works by meeting and overcoming challenge. Evolution is all about adapting to the circumstance of change that life meets on its journey. Csikszentmihalyi is very clear about this point. One must be challenged to experience flow. One must be fully engaged in meeting and overcoming a situation that pits your personal skillset against the task. There is a necessary level of difficulty – not too much and not too little – the goldilocks' balance - so that one knows one can be victorious. There must be struggle without hardship. The goal can neither be too easy nor unattainable.

The process of flow expands one's being and one's consciousness even though to attain flow one must restrict and limit one's being through focus, concentration and personal discipline. This is one of those yin-yang dialectics where one expands via first contracting. Contraction leads to expansion. Discipline leads to euphoria.

In *Personal Sovereignty,* (which is Book I of this trilogy) I explored the ability to be truly sovereign as an individual in this age of conformity and mass social hypnosis. We are all subjected daily to the repetitive narrative of fake news and misinformation that is designed to lull us into conformity and delusion. We need to be able to think for ourselves, to discover our own inner truth and make our own sovereign decisions. It is only in this way that we can ride the wave of our being. First, you must be true to yourself.

It is almost impossible to experience the heightened state of consciousness associated with flow if one is not firstly sovereign. But having aligned our fate, having unearthed our inner being and discovered our core, we then need to be able to execute those decisions resolutely and decisively. Too many of us get caught in lame indecision and irresolute vacillation. Repeated deliberation breeds self-doubt and humiliation because one becomes unable to act. Being in the zone of flow requires decisiveness.

By becoming sovereign, we generate the wave. One must then go out to meet the future as it were, boldly, confident in one's being and one's ability to cope with whatever our destiny brings to us. We need to learn to ride the wave. It is one thing to stand up on the surfboard; it is quite another to ride the wave, especially a big one without falling off or getting dumped. This is the skill of *Tao Tuning*.

It is one thing to experience the peak performance of flow rarely and in extreme situations. It is quite another to set this up as your normal existence and preferred state of being, as your default setting.

We all know those people who possess ample self-assurance and self-confidence, who take the risks and seize the day, who seem to be able to make the most of the opportunities their destiny presents to them. We all know those meek people who never seem quite able to grasp life and make it work for them. They get caught in the paralysis of analysis never achieving anything or fulfilling their destiny.

Tao Tuning is the mechanics and metaphysics of life, the mechanics of staying in the flow. It is the 'how' of how life works. If one wants to be successful in life, if one wants to fulfill one's destiny and spiritual purpose for this lifetime, one simply must master this dynamic and ride the wave of one's destiny.

Now some people just seem to naturally have this ability. But it is a skill that can be honed and improved. It can be cultivated and perfected. The zone of flow is our birthright. It is the natural state of our being when we do not allow the altered negative ego to corrupt that innocence.

As humanity has evolved over eons of time, it has lost this natural state of being and the rational world of the intellect has taken over and we are now caught in the trap of logical thinking. Although, a necessary tool in our arsenal, logic is not the inherent home of human consciousness. We need to get back to what I call the state of intuitive awareness where life is more holistic and present.

We are now caught in the trap of time – the past and the future dominate our minds. The thinking rational mind has taken over. The negative ego has usurped control of the corporate structure of consciousness. We need to unravel this tangle of deceit and break free from the illusion it has woven if we would enter the zone of flow.

Flow is where the entrapment ends, and transcendence begins. Flow is that state where the self is one with life, where time ceases to control our consciousness and we are free to soar into the silence and solitude of personal space. We live within the spacetime continuum. This is the fourth dimension. We are always trading space and time.

Tao Tuning is the science of *LifeWorks* which is my personal philosophy of life. It is the 'how' to the 'why' of Personal Sovereignty. Once we know our destiny, once we align our fate, once we accept our spiritual purpose, it is our responsibility to live our lives as fully and as successfully as possible. There is no limitation in an infinite universe. But there is the finite existence of our lives. This is the plane of duality. You cannot achieve all things and you cannot be all things to all people. You must accept the limitations of being human and the spiritual purpose of your life.

Once we willingly and joyously accept our path, the door opens to the richness of life, not in a shallow material sense but in the exquisite pattern and tapestry of our own being. Life becomes a joyful expression of our inner being. We live life to the fullest, relishing every moment. We begin to own our own story. We know why we are here and have the wherewithal to do what our destiny beckons. We do not shy away from our truth or our lives.

We thrive. We become authentic and charismatic. We become magnetic and supremely successful, enjoying our journey and our good fortune.

Tao Tuning is the science and art of living your life triumphantly, joyously and successfully. It is the ultimate joy of self-expression and the serene contentment of being on your path. It is beyond conditional happiness where we are happy because we have obtained or achieved something. Eventually, that happiness dissipates and evaporates. It is not self-renewing. It requires another fix.

True happiness is not dependent upon an external other: whether that other be a person, place or event. True happiness comes from within knowing you create your own reality the way you want, the way you choose as a sovereign being. You have the recipe, the formula to live your life your way, being true to yourself and being authentic.

Once one masters that recipe, one can bake the cake anytime one likes. One can enter the zone of flow consciously and intentionally. It is an act of volition not chance. However, it is a strict discipline and must be mastered if one wants to take conscious control of one's life and one's destiny.

Good luck and may the flow be with you.
Adrian

The Temple of Understanding

The word temple derives from the Latin word – templum, meaning a sacred precinct or the dwelling place of a god or gods: the house of the deity. In ancient times, the temple was not so much one building as in a church but more of a cluster of buildings with varying degrees of access for different ranks of people or strata of society. These precincts would typically have one main building and many smaller out-buildings. The sacred ruins of Machu Picchu or the Pantheon in Greece typify such a complex temple structure over a vast geographic area.

In modern terms the word temple signifies a place of worship for all faiths as opposed to the words church, synagogue or mosque where each pertains to a specific religion. I am using the word temple in both these senses. On the one hand, it is agnostic in the true sense of the word - not that one is an atheist who does not believe in a Supreme Being or God but rather that it is impossible to know the nature of the ultimate reality from a limited, rational and totally logical viewpoint. So, one does not try to define God but accepts it as an unknowable and ultimate state of being.

In the other sense, *The Temple of Understanding* is a composite structure just as the original Roman word templa (the plural of templum) was a composite structure of buildings. Moreover, just as any building, and especially one as grand as a cathedral or temple, is a complex structure requiring much planning, design and ultimately construction, so too, *The Temple of Understanding* is not just one simple thesis but has many facets to its construction.

The central theme of this structure is that modern humanity exists historically within an all-encompassing and pervasive misunderstanding of who we are, why we exist, where we have come from and where we are going to. This misunderstanding is a virus that has invaded every aspect of our lives, culture and society creating chaos and confusion down through the ages. Like a computer virus that creates havoc with our software or a biological virus that creates ill-health within the body, this virus resides within our meta-belief system or the operating system of our mental makeup.

Like a fish being unaware of the water within which it lives or humanity being unaware of the air we breathe, this misunderstanding has become so pervasive in every area of our lives that we are not only totally unaware of its existence, but vigorously and illogically defend any attempt to shine a light upon that existence and the destructive effects it is having upon our very being and ultimate survival.

It is also my thesis that this misunderstanding is rendering humanity, as the current form of homo sapiens, extinct because the principle of evolution demands that all beings and all species adhere to the Universal Laws of Life through knowing and understanding precisely how life works. This misunderstanding separates us from the flow of life causing blockage and limitation of our energy sources. We have become weak and vulnerable as a species and are no longer plugged into and connected with the divine principles of life.

The Temple of Understanding is not a religious thesis – there are far too many religions in the world already causing enough mayhem, conflict and misery. Nearly all wars, conflict and bigotry revolve around religion which is a direct descendant of this misunderstanding. This temple is not erected to pay homage to any god or gods but to honour life. We may not be able to define or know God, but we can study, know and define life. Humanity is an integral part of life and it is the exploration of our rightful place within the Infinity of Being that this temple seeks to address.

One of the fundamental aspects of intelligence is curiosity – a desire to know how things work. Indeed, humanity has spent most of its history seeking answers to the questions, both metaphysical and physical, as to how life works. But in any epistemology, we need to ensure that our foundations are true and correct. The most important part of any large building or physical structure are the foundations. These must be capable of supporting the eventual structure or it will inevitably collapse. So too, if our founding premises are not correct then the ensuing structure of knowledge will be erroneous opinion rather than justified belief. How do we know if our beliefs are correct?

There is only one sure way and that is the test of time. Similarly, we can only know if a building will survive the ravages of time and weather long after it is built. If our working body of knowledge is correct, we will live and prosper; if not, we will not withstand the evolutionary dictates of time. It is my contention that humanity stands at the crossroads and needs urgently to reassess its fundamental premises or assumptions of how life works because plainly our lives do no longer work.

Whether we examine our lives as an individual human being or as an entire species, something is definitely not working. We are on a collision course with the Earth – the only home we have. We are the only species that wages war on each other to the extent that we endanger not only our own survival but that of the very planet and indeed the neighbouring solar system. As I write, we have two megalomaniac leaders (if indeed that is what they truly are?) threatening us all with their egoic posturing. We are the only species that pollutes its nest to the point where our ecosystem and environment can no longer support us. Our current lifestyle is inherently unsustainable. As individuals, we have lost the meaning and purpose of life, and we seem to be at odds with the process of life itself.

We are fundamentally divorced from reality which leads to the inevitable conclusion that our basic premises are incorrect. They have not withstood the test of time. Life on planet earth is 4.6 billion years old. In that context, humanity is merely a few hundred thousand years old and our particular belief system is but the twinkling of an eye. The overriding paradigm within which western man lives is at most two thousand years old. This is nothing in the grander scheme of things. If we narrow our focus onto the current reigning meta-belief system, it is perhaps at most five hundred years old and the current economic system would be no more than three hundred, born in the Industrial Revolution of the seventeenth century.

So, we can see that our foundations have NOT withstood the test of time. In not even one hundred years, we have created a lifestyle, an economy and a society that is at odds with the basic principle of life, that is inherently destructive on all levels and that is unsustainable. This structure is based upon a set of beliefs that are faulty. And as rational, intelligent beings, we need to urgently acknowledge this fact and make an immediate about turn adapting to the reality that confronts us. This is the dictate of the evolutionary process.

Life on planet Earth has been evolving for 46 thousand million one hundred-year periods. In just one of those one hundred-year periods we have almost destroyed the lot. It is absolute arrogance, insolence and blatant stupidity to not acknowledge that something is fundamentally wrong and what is wrong is our foundation. The basic building blocks of our entire edifice of knowledge are faulty. We live within a monstrous misunderstanding that precludes us from seeing clearly and understanding the sacred processes of life.

As previously mentioned, we do not need to concern ourselves with trying to define or understand the nature of God – the Ultimate Reality. But we do urgently and desperately need to concern ourselves with the nature of life that surrounds us in our own ecosystem or very soon we will not be a part of that life much longer. In this sense life is not negotiable.

One of the intrinsic errors in this misunderstanding is the arrogance of man: that somehow, we are more intelligent than life, that we can bend and dominate life and its natural processes, that we are the crowning glory of creation at the top of the tree of life; that we are the supremely intelligent being on the planet and that life is subordinate to us to do with it what we choose. And nothing could be further from the truth. All forms of life are inherently equal, and all forms of life are beholden and subject to the Universal Laws of Life. These laws do not just pertain to life on Earth but are truly universal, regulating life throughout the omniverse; for we now know that our universe is just one of many and that life is truly infinite.

Again, it is the complete arrogance of man to believe that he is alone in the far reaches of the cosmos and the only 'intelligent' species in creation. Life is far superior to man and life will decide whether the current form of homo sapiens survives or not depending on our choices and our behaviour. Our current trajectory is certain extinction. We need to change our direction, our lifestyle, our modus operandi if we wish to survive. And to make this drastic change we need to change our meta-data fields of who we are, why we are here and where we are going.

This complete software rewrite is essential because we exist within the misunderstanding which as a virus has played havoc with all of our operating systems. We need a complete reboot! This will not be easy, and humanity will be dragged kicking and screaming because it wants to hold onto the comfort zone of the known even if that known is wrong and injurious. Humanity has never given up the *status quo* easily – witness the Inquisition, the Reformation, the Fundamentalist and Fascist mentality that always rules the world. The negative ego holds onto the power it has accumulated. We exist dictated to by our past not our future.

We have a fundamental identity belief that is outdated and outmoded and is no longer serving our evolution or the process of life on the planet. The real question is whether we can make that identity shift in time before it is too late or will the inevitable evolutionary shift to a newer and more noble species of homo take our place. Whether we like it or not the storm clouds of change are upon us now. We will need to go through the eye of the storm in the foreseeable future and we are talking years, not decades.

The real question is whether you, as an individual, will be ready: physically, emotionally and mentally, to ride that wave of change for this will be decided on an individual basis and no one can go through the storm or ride the wave for another. Neither can you do it holding hands! As in any major evolutionary adaptation, those individuals with the required superior genome that is more suited to the emerging epoch will survive and thrive and those that do not mutate will perish and die out.

Obviously, the million-dollar question is: what is the superior and appropriate genome? What are the traits or characteristics that are essential to cultivate to survive into the 21st century and beyond? Moreover, it is not just a matter of following some recipe nor having some genetic surgery to implant the missing gene. We need to redesign ourselves at the core and to do this successfully we need to move out of the darkness of the misunderstanding and into the light of true knowing. We need to establish ourselves with a new identity at our core.

This will be the New Human!

So, the real question becomes – how attached are you to Being You? Can you envisage a totally different way of Being? Are you prepared to give up, to walk away from the structure that you have built around yourself, to dismantle the edifice of you? This is the *Temple of Understanding*. In that temple the old you, the current version of you simply does not exist.

We need to accept that who we are is merely a construct; there is nothing sacrosanct about our definition of being human. It is merely one design and a faulty one at that. But we are attached to the design; we like it even though it really does not work and makes us miserable. We would rather put up with the pain than go to the dentist or doctor or do the work required to make us healthy. Moreover, there is no quick fix here. It requires years of training, discipline and work. We need to fundamentally retrain our brain and the way it works. Our operating system has a virus which makes our thinking process faulty.

Are you attached to your ego? Do you like your toys? Can you exist without your material and egoic accumulations that define who you are? You see you are not who or what you currently believe you are. You are a soul housed in a body. You are a multidimensional being preoccupied with a one-dimensional reality. Even your mind is not just your linear, rational thinking brain. You do have feelings; you do have an intuition; you do intuit; you do have gut knowing and so on. We all experience déjà vu and premonitions. We all work with our sixth sense. We all know these things exist even though they are denied by mainstream media and the scientific establishment.

You are so much more than your currently limited definition. And precisely because we deny these inner riches and wealth of our real spiritual being, we cling to the outer trappings of material and egoic accoutrement: the clothes, the car, the house, the job, the image, the ambition and the social standing. These seeds have been planted for millennia and are now in full bloom. But they are weeds in the garden of our soul smothering the flowers of our real self.

Our true nature can no longer breathe freely but is trampled under the weight of our accumulation. It is so heavy being you! It is unbearable. We are all exhausted from carrying the burden of our negative ego. It will not let us go even for a moment. The eternal and exhaustive inner dialogue of nonsense and mayhem. It is on-going, and it is insane.

We do not need to understand the nature of God. We do not even need to ponder the wanton destruction of the planet. Merely be the witness to your own mind; simply observe the daily ritual of your thinking and your obsession. Witness the haste and the activity that surrounds us - for what? What are we creating as a society? Where is our legacy – what will our great grandchildren inherit? How will they judge us? It will not be pleasing. In a single generation we have squandered the blessings bestowed upon us by the bounty of nature.

The age of mass consumerism and conspicuous consumption. Our current temple has as its altar the greed of materiality and the priest is the alter-ego of our mind. We produce and consume trinkets of triviality. He with the most toys wins. But wins what? What is the purpose and meaning of a life spent pursuing an exterior image that others can be envious of? What are we creating of worth, of sacredness, of lasting value?

Where are our values and what are they? Are we a valued being? Do we value ourselves? Does this question even make sense to you? If I were to ask you: do you really value yourself and how do you do that? If you truly valued yourself would you waste your life, your time, your energy and the precious gift of life in the pursuit of the inessential?

Is your life committed to building something of consequence even if that is serene happiness and inner contentment? It need not be external, although, to accomplish for the good of the world and for others is the highest good and its own reward. More and more studies are now finding that being altruistic creates the greatest happiness. It is not the pursuit of our own pleasure that delivers lasting value but being of service to others. Other studies are also now finding that this is an essential ingredient to living a long and noble life. Those who contribute to society in some meaningful way enjoy robust health into a ripe elderly age. Giving is receiving. Taking leads to emotional bankruptcy and personal depletion.

Life is a gift and it is given freely, but it does bestow upon us the obligation and the necessity to give back. This is a part of the circle of life. All of nature understands this cycle; it is only modern man who has lost the inclination to give but is obsessed with taking. As we deny the inner depth of our true nature with all its spiritual wealth, we crave the trappings of a false idol.

But this is all just a part of the misunderstanding that we suffer under: the grand delusion! We need to redefine who we are and where we came from. If you are on a journey and come to realise you are lost, you must first reflect on when you last knew where you were and where you went wrong. Only then can you find the right path to get you back on track.

Our creation myths are wrong. Our basic cosmology is erroneous. The story of who we are and how we came to be here is a children's fairy story that is filled with improbable events at best and downright misleading lies at worst. We have been misled deliberately to keep us asleep, to keep us afraid, to keep us compliant. A sleeping humanity choosing not to think seriously, not to wake up, not to take responsibility for its destiny and not to take its rightful place in the Infinity of Being.

Far easier to create the antagonists of God and the Devil as the perpetrators of our reality and we the hapless victim in their eternal struggle between good and evil. What a convenient cop out. No accountability; no personal responsibility; no sovereignty.

These are large topics and need detailed analysis if we are to come to a better understanding of who we truly are and why we are here on planet Earth. *The Temple of Understanding* consists of three titles: *Personal Sovereignty, Tao Tuning and BeComing One*. They form the three pillars or foundation stones upon which the temple stands. Each one addresses a separate and specific condition of the misunderstanding.

Personal Sovereignty deals with the ability to be truly sovereign: to make our own decisions, to be free from external influence and thus free to be true to ourselves; to live our lives authentically. To be independent, self-reliant and autonomous; to be a sovereign being. To end the dominance of the altered negative ego and to live holistically with intuition and grace. To experience the real intimacy of sovereign love.

TaoTuning then explores the ability to flow with the cosmic currents of life. To be able to ride the wave of your own personal Tao in harmony with the universal principles of life – the great Tao. To be able to execute those decisions and choices one makes as a sovereign being. And to do this with elegance and panache. To be truly successful and enjoy the life of your choosing: to live the dream without causing injury or harm to any other living being or to life itself; the ability to turn your goals into reality and manifest your innermost desires.

Finally, *BeComing One* puts it all together in a harmonious symphony of life, light and laughter. To be one with the creative forces of life; to be one with yourself – body, mind and spirit. To be one with the Earth and all the myriad forms of life that dwell upon it. To be one with the cosmos. To be congruent and whole. To be at peace and to thoroughly enjoy the eternal journey of your being.

Ideally, the reader should proceed sequentially in the above order for the temple to make sense. After all, we cannot construct a large building or edifice by just throwing stones together: they must be placed carefully according to the architect's design and the engineer's specifications if the building is to survive the test of time and be a pleasing work of art.

We need to redefine our understanding of what it means to be human. We need to evolve into the eighth species of homo and reach beyond the limited understanding and faulty belief systems of homo sapiens. After all, the genus homo has been around for approximately 2 million years; homo sapiens a mere 200,000 and modern man a trifling 2,000!

Evolutionary shifts often come quickly – the dinosaurs supposedly disappeared in an afternoon. Life is forever moving on and survival depends upon intelligent adaptation. Are we, as a species and as individuals, ready for this next shift? How do we know when it will come? More to the point how do we know it is not immanent?

Either way, *The Temple of Understanding* will both prepare you for the coming shift and enable you to live a more fulfilling, enjoyable and healthy life. What could be more important than that?

To be who you want to be – to exercise conscious dominion of your life. To live a truly successful life expressing your inner truth. To free yourself from the dictates of mass consciousness and the conniving of the ruling elite. To be a noble soul inhabiting a healthy body. To be one of the intrepid explorers and adventurers on this grand and glorious cosmic journey. To be a spiritual warrior and way shower lighting the path for others to follow.

To be an early adopter of the evolutionary thrust and become the new human who lives peacefully on planet Earth, communing with Gaia and participating in the brotherhood of man. To be happy and free. To be noble and pure. To have the wisdom to live the life we were meant to live: consciously aware and joyous.

Part I

Wave Theory

Chapter 1

Why?

Mankind has always looked towards the stars and asked why. What is the purpose and meaning of life? Why am I here?

And we have answered that question in so many ways from the most profound and sacred to the most banal and ridiculous. Yet, it is an inherent part of being human; it is an intrinsic neurological process that we seek the answer to why. I have a 2-year-old granddaughter, Mahlia, who asks repeatedly: *'how does it work?'* and the catchphrase of the terrible twos is why. The human mind needs to understand, to bring order or sense out of the seeming confusion of daily life. And as life speeds up in this fast-paced world, where we are all time poor with no time for reflection or understanding, this querying and unrest becomes even more acute breeding anxiety and mental distress.

For those of us fortunate enough to live in a modern, western, capitalist democracy, we live in the most abundant and affluent material society that mankind has created. Yet, we also live in the most spiritually bankrupt, where the search for meaning is becoming ever more important and elusive. For as life speeds up, it seems to lose direction. As we have more external material possessions, we lose the inner possession of ourselves.

We are disconnected from our core, our inner being; we are increasingly disconnected from each other and we are now disconnected from the earth on which we live. Most of us live solitary, isolated lives behind the psychological shell of our negative ego occasionally peeking out to form shallow and unsatisfying relationships with others that do not truly go to the core of our being or emotional needs.

It is not too farfetched nor pessimistic to say that en masse humanity has lost its way. Nowhere is this more apparent than in our relationship with the Earth, our mother, our planetary host, our home and our life source. We are rapidly causing our own extinction and quite possibly that of the planet and all that dwells upon it.

We believe that if we consume more, if we have more goods, then we will be happy. We measure our personal success in life by the amount of material possessions – money, wealth, property, assets, homes, cars etc. that we have accumulated. Those with the most toys wins!

This is an extremely shallow way of living one's life and a sure path to emotional bankruptcy which is why modern man is so unfulfilled. The more we consume and possess, the more hollow our lives become.

One of the most important things a young child does is to create their own unique and personal world view – that is, the new inhabitant of planet earth tries to make sense of life here. The brain needs to make sense, to create order, to understand and it does this by transforming percept into concept. In other words, we perceive via our 5 senses and turn those perceptions into a logical or coherent picture that gives meaning to life. This is called our world view and it is entirely personal and unique for each of us.

From time immemorial different races and tribes have been creating dreamtime myths, religious beliefs, philosophies of life and stories to interpret life, to give it some sense of order and meaning, to create a cohesive structure within which we can live.

Just as we have created ever more elaborate and sophisticated physical structures for our primary need of physical shelter, so too, we have also created ever more elaborate and complex belief systems to house our understanding and to give purpose to our lives; to provide emotional or spiritual shelter.

And just as when we are a young infant, we are fed fictitious nursery rhymes and children's stories to guide our minds to learning, so too, a young and immature humanity created dreamtime myths, parables, creation stories, religions and beliefs to shelter us from the anxiety of unknowing. But these stories were of necessity simple and immature just as a nursery story is filled with fictitious characters and reassuring plots. As the child matures, so too does its understanding of life. We reach intellectually for the truth, for more meaningful and accurate reflections of reality. We forsake the reassuring nursery rhyme for a more scientific and rational depiction of how life truly works.

Yet, for all of our scientific exploration and technological understanding of how everything works from the far reaches of space to subatomic particles, we still hold onto our outworn and outmoded religious and philosophical beliefs about the meaning of life. And it is precisely because these stories no longer satisfy our emotional and intellectual maturity that we feel so bereft of the truth, that our lives are spiritually bankrupt and that we seek shelter in the conspicuous consumption of materiality.

Just as we no longer believe the world is flat or that the sun revolves around the earth or that the atom is the smallest indivisible particle of matter, we need to urgently update our creation myths, the story of who we are and why we are here. It is precisely because we have not done this that we have lost our way, that we stand on the brink of disaster about to commit the species to extinction and probably destroy the planet in the process.

We need a new story! One that is relevant to today. One that is appropriate for the modern world. One that does indeed make sense to our evolved intelligence. One that does answer the core questions of who we are and why we are here. This requires a propensity for the truth: the courage to face things exactly as they are without any self-deception, delusion or evasion. We need to start at the beginning – not with conjecture or childish beliefs but with hard reality of what is before us. For if we have the strength to face this truth, a light will develop from that understanding, the light of intelligence, the light of enlightenment.

We will shine a light on what is with no deception, no illusion, no justification – no excuses! What is, is.

We have evolved enough in our scientific wisdom to put our rational, logical understanding of life and the universe together with our emotional intelligence and our intuitive holistic knowing to formulate new and more appropriate creation stories. Scientifically, we have discovered many things, enunciated many laws which describe and explain to us exactly how things work. However, it is important to remember that these laws of life always existed prior to our discovery and understanding. The laws of gravity, thermodynamics, quantum physics etc. did not begin when mankind discovered them; they have always existed regulating the processes of life. It is just that as we have evolved intellectually, we have been able to observe and understand, to articulate these laws.

So too, on the inner planes of philosophy and cosmology we have a much better and more profound understanding of the origins of the universe and how life has evolved. We need desperately to formulate a new theology and cosmology that is more fitting for modern human. Everywhere we see the decline of established religions as intrinsically these outmoded belief systems fall in on themselves through the law of entropy. Whether it is the paedophilia disaster that is destroying the Christian Churches and making a mockery of their supposed sacredness, or the 'jihad' of some Muslim sects or the fundamentalist fascism of others, traditional mainstream religions have had their day and are no longer serving their purpose of bringing meaning and inner peace to their believers.

As a child, I attended a large Catholic school that was staffed primarily by Christian Brothers. Now, a mere 40 years later not a single Brother remains on the teaching staff, not just because they are in short supply but primarily because no teaching institution today can afford the scandal and risk of trusting young children to the Brothers. If this does not signify the demise of Christianity, then nothing does.

The basic problem is that we have progressed technologically, understanding the mechanics of the outer material world but have not progressed at all in our understanding of the unseen spiritual one. We seek to uncover and discover how everything external works creating more and more material prosperity and affluence, but we refuse point blank to uncover and discover the truth about the real meaning and purpose of life. We love to look outwards but are terrified of looking honestly within ourselves to discover who we truly are and why we are here.

We cling to our childish and immature religious philosophies that have portrayed a picture of a God created in the image of man rather than realising the truth, which is that man is created in the image of God! We still view God as an old man in heaven with a beard and a bad temper – a vengeful being who meets out punishment. We still believe we are born in original sin and that life on earth is a suffering or penance by which we earn our salvation. Whether you adhere to a western-Christian ideology or an eastern belief in karma it amounts to the same thing.

I covered this topic at length in *Personal Sovereignty* and do not intend to dwell on it here in much detail. I merely make the point that it is time to move on; that we need to turn our propensity to uncover, to discover, to understand, to make sense of life from the outer to the inner. We need urgently to recommit to a deeper philosophy of life that inspires, that gives meaning, that nurtures and supports us emotionally and spiritually before we do indeed destroy ourselves, the planet and all that live upon it.

This book is an attempt to do just that. To ferment a debate about the true meaning of life, to stimulate a discussion about a philosophy and cosmology that is more appropriate for modern human with an emotionally mature and intellectually sound foundation.

And it is not that we need to throw the baby out with the bathwater. It is not so much that we need to reject entirely the infantile beliefs of the past for many nursery stories do contain real and good morals – it is just that they are couched in simple and rudimentary terms that are easy to understand by the young child. However, as we grow up, as we mature, we replace the simple with a deeper and more complex understanding keeping the truth of the basic moral intact.

As I explained in *Personal Sovereignty*, the basic problem with our immature interpretation of reality is that we use it to excuse ourselves from taking personal responsibility for our lives. We have created a co-dependent relationship with life that robs us of autonomy, independence and sovereignty. We have made ourselves weak seeking excuses, justification and rationalisation for our erroneous decision making which has led us into this present perilous state where we have become a cancer upon the earth and a real danger to the safety of the solar system.

The problem is not even that we face our own extinction. That would be bad enough. The real danger is that with our immature handling of atomic and nuclear energy we threaten the very life of the universe around us. This is the most pregnant example of how our inner spiritual and psychological growth has not kept pace with our outer technological progress. We have discovered nuclear energy – the building block of material reality - but do not possess the emotional or intellectual wisdom to use it appropriately and wisely. It will only take one deranged megalomaniac to destroy it all!

In many ways, we have become schizophrenic with our advanced, high-tech selves, personified by the ubiquitous smart phone on everyone's ear connected by social media on the one hand, and the emotionally immature and isolated self, seeking shelter in ever more bizarre co-dependent rituals and relationships on the other. It is this intrinsic disconnect that is killing us individually and as a species!

The word yoga means union and its basic tenant is the union of body, mind and soul. In reality, this is the core function of religion: to make one whole! For in wholeness is harmony, health and happiness. In any system, internal separation means dysfunction. The more integrated and harmonious the parts, the more efficient and functional the whole. Whenever there is an internal schism or divide the overall health and functionality of the system suffers.

Modern human is divided within itself. Most of our modern ills whether physical or psychological derive from that inner divide. The increasing incidence of self-harm and suicide testifies to this schism. We need as a matter of urgency to reunite our beings: to become whole, to become one. Any attempt at a retake of religion must solve this inner disquiet and help to make us whole once again.

If we look at any so-called primitive cosmology there is an inherent wholeness that gives purpose, meaning and place: the individual knew his or her place in the Infinity of Being. Life and the universe are so large that it is easy for the individual to feel overwhelmed, to experience the anxiety of separation, loneliness and insignificance. Real religion bestows that sense of significance that empowers and inspires. Religious rituals create bonding, togetherness and unite the individual with their brethren. Ritual creates community. Feeling fellowship with others, feeling one with the larger process of life and the infinity of the universe then no longer threaten but invoke awe and wonder.

We BeCome One! BeComing One we become whole. Becoming whole we are healed.

However, precisely because we have evolved intellectually, this spiritual ordering must make sense to us as mature adults. Humanity is no longer a child. We have grown up and stand ready to take our rightful place as custodians of the planet. The new religion must appeal to our sense of rightness – it must also make scientific sense. It can no longer rely upon myth or blind faith. It must be based in experiential reality. Science has progressed because of the rigour of the scientific process whereby a hypothesis must be proved beyond a doubt by the rational process. The theorem must stand up to the rigour of testing.

So too, a modern theology or philosophy of life must stand up to the rigour of intellectual debate and be proven experientially not just accepted because it is handed down by myth and the religious establishment. The religious institutions have failed us miserably. False dogma, empty ritual, hypocritical posturing and power politics have replaced a sincere and humble perception and appreciation of the divine. Religions have all succumbed to the false gods of mammon, power and greed.

Mankind needs a god, but it must be a real and sensible version not some half-backed concept that locks in stupidity, dependency and abuse. Moreover, it must be totally personal. Gone are the days of one person, whomever that is, telling another what is right and wrong, interpreting, judging or acting as conduit or intermediary. A new religion must allow the individual to exercise their own Personal Sovereignty: to decide for themselves what is right for them. That is precisely why this book follows on from *Personal Sovereignty*. In that book, I argued that it was our outmoded religious concepts that are doing the most harm to our evolution as a species.

However, the individual does need some guiding principles, an ethical rudder or moral compass to assist it in making those right decisions. As mentioned in *Personal Sovereignty*, humanity is not good at making decisions nor at making the right decision. As in any body of science, we further our understanding by observing, uncovering, discovering and understanding the laws of that particular body of knowledge. We then use the knowledge of those laws to build: whether that be a skyscraper, a smartphone or a spaceship. We can only utilise these technologies by first understanding the physical laws and applying them to our purpose.

We do not build a spaceship by ignoring the law of gravity but rather through understanding it to obtain the velocity necessary to escape the earth's gravitational field. Similarly, the smartphone, the world-wide web and all modern telecommunications are based on the understanding of radio waves, transmitters, receivers etc. Modern advances in health are based in our understanding of anatomy, physiology and how the body works. As we further our understanding of how something works, we are able to use that knowledge to master our physical, material world for our own benefit.

So too, as we build a body of knowledge about how the inner, unseen, spiritual world works we will be better able to make our own personal lives work to our own individual benefit. The point is there are definite spiritual laws just as there are definite physical laws of life. We cannot see gravity, but it is there nonetheless, and we cannot ignore it. We cannot see electricity, but it is there nonetheless and if we want to use it, we need to harness its energy and power by obeying its laws. We cannot see electromagnetic waves but if we want to use our advanced technology of smartphones, computers and the interconnectivity of the world-wide web, we need to obey its laws.

We accept these unseen laws without any hint of superstition or myth. In the movie, 'The Gods must be crazy', a coke-a-cola bottle drops from an aeroplane into the dessert and is discovered by a bushman. Thinking it must be a sacred item because it descended from the sky, he embarks on a many-thousand-kilometre odyssey to return it. The point being that to a primitive tribesman a glass bottle is an unknown and therefore mysterious object to which he attributes magical and religious connotations. We just see an empty coke bottle!

We do not attribute mythical, magical, mysterious or religious attributes to gravity, electricity, electromagnetic energy or any other scientific discovery. We merely understand they have become part of our modern-day body of scientific knowledge. Similarly, we need to demythologise religion and our understanding of the spiritual world. It is no different.

It is unseen; it is intangible; it is unknown. But so too were all the above once upon a time. We need a theology, a philosophy and a cosmology that not only works but is based in reality and not in myth. We need to be able to work it individually just as we flick a light switch or use a mouse to drive software upon a screen. We may not know exactly how a car works to be able to drive it. We do not need to know how the mouse drives the cursor to be able to work it. We certainly do not need to know the code language to use an application – we all do it daily.

We need to develop a spiritual understanding that helps us drive our lives, that makes sense of the world, that acts as a moral compass for our decision-making process, that gives us solace in times of personal anxiety, that gives us significance as an individual and that most importantly unites us with life and delivers an appreciation of the divine.

In the end, spirituality is our own individual, personal relationship with God, Goddess, All that Is. It is as unique as our face, our personality, our psyche and our soul. It is yours and yours alone. The roblem with all religions heretofore has been that they attempt to prescribe how we should live our lives by delivering a set of rules, a set of commandments that tell us what we can and cannot do, what is right and what is wrong. And like the 10 commandments, they are set in stone!

Life is forever changing. The only constant in the universe is change. We are all unique. Every moment is unique. All circumstances configure to create that moment as the intersection of time and space. We exist within that continuum. No set of rules can adequately tell us what is right for any set of variables. We need a more flexible and a more mature understanding. As a child, we have a limited, subscribed reality precisely because we need our parents to create a secure environment within which we can grow and develop.

As mentioned in *Personal Sovereignty*, evolution is the expansion from one matrix to another where we experience ever greater freedom, autonomy and sovereignty until we become our own creator. Humanity has now reached the emotional, intellectual and spiritual maturity where it needs to throw away the old outworn and outmoded religious concepts that are strangling its growth and embrace a new way of living. But in order to be able to do this wisely, we need to first uncover, discover and understand the laws of life which regulate our being. These laws are not prescriptive but descriptive. Gravity does not say what should happen but what does happen. Spiritual laws do not proscribe or tell us what we should do; they merely describe how life works.

The better our personal understanding of the laws of life, the more able are we to live our lives wisely, successfully and beneficially. As in all bodies of knowledge, the more we understand and master those laws the more of an expert we become. The better our expertise the more can we exploit, use and transcend those laws for our own benefit. Ultimately, we become the master of life, the master of our own destiny; co-creators with God of a personal life that is heaven on earth.

We do not need to suffer. Suffering is a result of ignorance of the law or a blind and stubborn refusal to acknowledge its supremacy. We are not punished for our sins by a vengeful father but by our sins of ignorance and non-compliance.

Wisdom brings freedom. To drive anything, we need to learn the operating procedure plus the road rules. To drive life successfully, we need to learn the operating procedure for being human plus the road rules for life on planet earth! *Tao Tuning* is that understanding that leads to the mastery of living one's life, here on this planet, successfully, harmoniously and joyously.

Tao Tuning is not a religion; nor a set of rules. If you are looking for a rigid recipe you will not find it here. Give a man a fish, feed him for a day; teach him how to fish, feed him for life. *Tao Tuning* will teach you how to live in harmony with the laws of life, how to make decisions that are right for you given the exigencies of time and space, how to steer your path, how to find your personal place in the Infinity of Being.

Ultimately, *Tao Tuning* is a roadmap to find your way home to yourself, to your own Being, to BeComing One with All that Is!

Chapter 2

The essential Tao

So, what is the essence of Taoism and what is its substantial difference from other major religions or philosophies of life. Firstly, Taoism (pronounced Daoism) is not really a religion. There is no deity or personified Godhead. Tao means '*the way*', '*path*' or '*flow*'. Ultimately, it is a way of living one's life in harmony with the natural principles of the universe, in harmony with nature. Of all the philosophies, it is the most attuned to modern scientific principles including the big bang theory of creation and quantum physics.

There is no God to be worshipped; nor is it a mystical tradition. Most religions originate with one person's interpretation of right living and a set of rules or commandments that prescribe how we should live our lives in order to attain salvation in the hereafter. Think of Moses, Mohammed, Jesus, Krishna, Buddha and so on. No doubt these were exceptionally enlightened people of a very noble stature who understood the complexities and necessities of life and tried to translate their heightened state of perception and awareness into a recipe for life for others to follow.

Most if not all religions are characterised by this state of worship and following! The follower becomes a devotee of both the originator and the religion that grows up around that person.

Unfortunately, this creates and perpetuates a state of separation and striving for the follower who seeks to emulate and copy the formula as set down by the leader. Eventually, this worship of both a Godhead and a 'holy man' robs the devotee of their own self-reliance and sovereignty. We are caught forever trying to live up to and by the recipe or formula as laid down by another. This mimicry results in frustration and a loss of self. Eventually, we become spiritually bankrupt.

Taoism, on the other hand, stresses that there are no rules, no precepts, no commandments. One needs to discover for oneself the path, the way that is right for the self. In that sense, although as old as the other religions, it is an incredibly modern philosophy and very well suited for the modern 21st century human. Indeed, Taoism pushes the individual back upon themself to decide for oneself at each and every instant what is correct and right for that individual given the variables and exigencies of space and time.

And just as Einstein understood that space and time are intricately interwoven and related and do not exist independently of each other, the Tao is the flow that is created by their intersection (more of this later). Moreover, Einstein's unified field is a very eloquent scientific definition of the Tao. So, Taoism is intricately based in science and not mythology or mysticism.

In all religions, God becomes a deified and personified representation of humanity. We have created God as an image of man rather than the other way around. We attribute human emotions and characteristics to God who ultimately degenerates into a subjective and flawed being that humanity then uses (or abuses) to justify aberrant human behaviour; mostly, the killing of other humans in a supposed 'holy war'.

Whether it is the Crusades of the Middle Ages, the Inquisition, the persecution of the Jews in the Holocaust or the modern Muslim Jihad, most wars are justified in the name of religion. Even the Christian concept of saving the savage from Original Sin and converting the new world to Christianity, which has done so much irreparable damage to so many native indigenous peoples and their lands is a testament to the chaos and confusion that result from misguided religious beliefs. Much of the destruction of the planet and our environment can be traced directly to overzealous religious fanatics.

The Tao, on the other hand, is impersonal. Taoism teaches living in harmony with life. The Tao is not a deity or a God. There is no personification. Even the use of the word 'the' as the definite article as opposed to the personified word God symbolises this difference. The Tao is the way of the universe; it is objective, impersonal and universal. It is definitely not subjective, arbitrary or judgemental.

This is probably the key distinction. Most religions are based on a set of rules which if we obey, we are supposedly rewarded by some form of salvation and good fortune but if we disobey, we are punished both in this life and the next. This is an extreme form of subjective judgement with regards to good and evil. Taoism, on the other hand, enunciates behaviour that is appropriate to the given circumstances. It is not that we are punished for our sins but rather that if we behave in keeping with, in harmony with the laws of life, then the flow of the universe, the Tao, works with us, carries us along. If we go against the current, the tide, we meet with resistance and misfortune.

The basic difference is that in all religions there is a set of rules, like the 10 commandments, that we need to learn and live our lives by, much the same as we learn how to read and write, how to spell and do maths. On the other hand, the neonate does not learn how to walk by studying a manual on walking – it is learnt by trial and error. The child first stands up repeatedly and then learns to walk by falling down and getting back up. We learn life by living it.

Taoism has no rules but is a way of life! We need to learn to live our lives in harmony with the laws of life. But we need to do this experientially. There is no Catechism, no rule book, no commandments, no formula and no recipe. This is what scares most people – there is no crutch to lean on except your own innate wisdom which must be developed over time and in space. This is the purpose of being human – to learn.

Taoism is all about one's state of being, one's attitude, one's space and one's place - meaning where is one at in one's mind: what is our attitude towards the circumstance of our life. Are we inherently, intrinsically, in harmony with what is or is there an inner resistance? Are we going with the flow or are we fighting, swimming against the tide?

Ultimately, there is no adequate definition of the Tao. Even Lao Tzu, who represents the father of Taoism more than any other person said in the Tao Te Ching: *'the name that can be named is not the constant name'.* In other words, one cannot define the indefinable. It is like trying to hold water in the palm of one's hand – the more one tries the more one will lose it. The more we try to define God, the more we lose its real essence.

To really understand the Tao, one must live one's life being true to oneself and slowly, gradually, the wisdom, the understanding, the appreciation of its essence becomes apparent. Taoism is most definitely not a religion, nor a dogma, nor a philosophy but rather a way of being mastered by being true to oneself. One comes across the truth by acknowledging and honouring who one is in one's purest form – being true to the self as opposed to learning a set of rules and then trying to live one's life according to those precepts.

In the end, Taoism is all about accepting oneself exactly as one is. This is not a form of complacency or spiritual laziness. Nor is it anarchy or hedonism. Quite to the contrary, the essence of Taoism is a highly disciplined life but not a discipline that is externally generated by living one's life to an externally imposed set of rules. Rather it is the discipline of self-knowing, self-acceptance, self-understanding. Being true to oneself is the strictest discipline for it is not a discipline that one picks up to learn or master, nor a habit one cultivates in order to achieve a specific outcome or target.

Taoism has no objective but to be oneself. This form of discipline therefore is a 24/7 constant. The only rule is that one does not betray one's inner being. Obviously, this is an art that one must cultivate in a world where we are constantly being bombarded by forces and opinions to influence us from without, to get us to fit in with the status quo, to be accepted by others.

Thus, ultimately the distinction is a choice between listening to the outer voice of conformity, tradition and other people's opinion or listening to one's own inner voice, heart and conscience. In this modern world of mass and social media, where we all seem to depend on outside acceptance and validation, being true to oneself is the hardest thing and the strictest discipline.

One of the beauties of life is individual uniqueness. Every leaf, every flower, every face, every person, every day, every moment is unique and distinct. Indeed, we all cherish our individual identity and uniqueness more than anything else. Yet, life also has universal principles that regulate the processes of life. We normally talk of these principles as laws: the law of gravity, the laws of thermodynamics, the laws of physics and so on. Indeed, we use the words *universe or cosmos* to describe an orderly state of existence as opposed to chaos. We all understand that life is an inherently ordered structure. People feel secure and comfortable in a structured world.

Ultimately, all of these individual laws are manifestations of the one universal law: this law is called the Tao, which runs through all of life and all of existence regulating the myriad forms. This law is objective, impersonal and universal in the sense that it does not vary or change according to the person. There is no judgement. There is no God in Heaven meeting out reward or punishment according to our behaviour. All planetary bodies are equally subject to the law of gravity. All material objects fall to earth when dropped – there are no exceptions. This is precisely why it is called a law: it describes what happens!

Another important distinction surrounds the creation myths. In most religions, there are dreamtime stories, biblical parables or mythologies that describe how '*God created the world*'. Whether it be the rainbow serpent or God creating the world in 7 days, these stories have little basis in reality. Nor do they satisfy the modern person's need to know and understand rationally and scientifically how we came to be. We are always expected to accept creation myths in good faith and as an article of faith. If you are a believer, you don't question the Bible whatever version that Bible takes.

Because Taoism has no God there are no creation myths; no childish stories we are expected to take on face value. The Tao is! The Tao precedes the manifest universe. The Tao is just described as the One! The One becomes two and the two beget creation. This is not a dreamtime story; it is an accurate and rational explanation in basic scientific terms. Whether one believes in the Big Bang or not, something existed prior to the creation of the material universe. However, the difference is that we are told that this state is beyond our human mental comprehension.

No adulteration. No childish nursery stories. No dreamtime myths. Just accept the humility of being human with reverence. In other words, accept the finite limitation of being human and realise a limited mind cannot comprehend that which is unlimited and infinite. So, in exquisite simplicity and elegance we are put in our place in the Infinity of Being from the beginning. Just as we need to learn to fully and totally accept our inner selves, so too, we need to accept our standing and position within the infinite universe.

The third and most important distinction is that the principles of Taoism very neatly and accurately describe the workings of the physical world – the mechanics of creation. We are not being asked to accept that God created the world; we are given the way in which the world works. As we master this understanding, we become more adept at living our lives in harmony with those principles. Whereas most religions further ignorance, Taoism advocates wisdom and understanding, developing one's intellectual grasp of how life works, the functioning of the universe, the laws that govern reality.

In many ways Taoism is more science than religion. It is a way of life, but a way based in personal spiritual growth through experiential learning. Taoism is not a body of knowledge that one can study in sacred books, in academic learning. The adept does not become the sage via accumulating knowledge but via becoming wise. This wisdom needs to be earned by engaging with life, reflecting on the truth and furthering one's inner understanding. One becomes more proficient at living one's life. Taoism is incredibly practical. It is all about life: the principles of life, the harmony of nature, the way of the universe, the natural flow of creation.

These laws are not prescriptive in the sense that they do not tell us what we should do in order to gain some personal advantage or spiritual salvation, but rather descriptive in that they merely describe what is and how things work on planet earth. It is totally up to the individual as to whether one chooses to live one's life in harmony with these laws or not. However, the obvious implication is that if one goes with the flow, rather than resisting it, life is more enjoyable, productive and harmonious.

It is interesting that humanity is the only species that insists on going against the tide and vaingloriously attempting to swim upstream!

Whereas religion always has a godhead behind creation, Taoism just posits a universal law. This law runs through all of creation. This law describes what is and how life works. This law then manifests in countless individual applications of that law depending on the specific time, place and circumstance. Thus, ultimately, all laws break down into the essential unified field: the oneness of creation.

Essentially the Tao is a wave. All of creation can be described via the mechanics of wave theory. The terms - *flow, chi, way, path* all describe movement through time and space. The intersection of time and space is the eternal now. In that point there is no future and no past – just what is. We either live in that present or we live in the past or the future. The essence of Zen is to exist within that point: to be here now, 100% focused in the moment of now. There is an Australian aboriginal saying: *now is the moment of your being!* Now is all we have. We cannot hold onto the past and we cannot live in the future. To live successfully, we must accept the limitation of time and space and be here now.

A Taoist sage learns to ride the wave of destiny; learns to align their personal Tao with the universal Tao by mastering the laws of life and becoming an adept surfer of the cosmic waves that run through creation.

Ultimately, the Tao is a wave and operates like any other wave according to the laws of physics. We live in a material or physical universe. This material world is a manifested construct that further adheres to the laws of manifestation. As mentioned at the beginning, humanity has always pondered the beginnings of the universe and the closest we have come to an understanding is the Big Bang. In Taoist terms before creation there was ONE. This ONE is viewed as an impersonal deity, or primal cause. This ONE then divided into two – the polar extremes of creation known as yin and yang.

All of life depends upon cycles to create the rhythm of life, the flow, the chi, the energy that pulsates through creation. If we look at any aspect of the phenomenal universe, it has a polar opposite: day and night, male and female, up and down, summer and winter, hot and cold, light and dark, negative and positive and so on. The original definition of yin and yang was the light and dark side of a hill as shadows were created by the blockage of the sun's rays.

For a current to flow there must be a potential difference. The easiest way to understand the process of creation is a battery: there must be a positive terminal and a negative terminal with a charge differential. When that differential of charge no longer exists, we say the battery is flat and it produces no current. We then need to recharge the battery which recreates the potential difference.

So too, organic life depends upon a male and a female partner to act as polar opposites to unite and form the next generation. We also talk of male and female ends in pipes and other building materials. When we look at planetary and interstellar bodies, we see this same cyclic motion. The planets are held in their cyclic orbits around the sun by gravitational force. Opposites attract and create a polar tension that seeks union. On the simplest level, protons carry a positive charge and electrons carry a negative charge and thus atoms become the basic building blocks of matter by the nuclear attraction of these opposite charges. Different elements combine to form molecules and more complex organic compounds which eventually become life.

The weather is created by the earth's orbit around the sun, the interplay of day and night and the cycle of the seasons. We cannot imagine a world with no day and night or where every day was exactly the same. The beauty of life is its infinite diversity and the uniqueness of every individual being and moment in time.

So, the process of life is intricately connected to this interplay of yin and yang as polar opposites. Yet, it is essential to understand that they do form one continuum and are merely the extreme points of this unitary continuum. This is another important distinction between Taoism and other philosophies of life. Whereas most religions view good and evil as distinctly different aspects of creation in complete opposition to each other and even give them distinct personifications such as God and the Devil, Taoism merely views these polar extremes as two ends and thus aspects of the one being. This is called dualistic monism meaning two aspects of the one thing.

If we examine our own natures, we see this duality within our very characters: we all have positive and negative aspects to our inner selves. We all experience good and bad days. We all have positive aspirations and yet give into self-doubt and lack of confidence. The journey of life is the continuous movement from the negative to the positive: this is called the process of evolution.

The physical, material world requires the potential difference created by this polarity to generate the cyclic waves that underlie all of creation. Time and space intersect to create the moment of now. Eternity is in itself a wave through the time/space continuum. We tend to think of time in terms of past, present and future but in reality, there is only the eternal now which is a wave moving through eternity.

The only constant in the universe is change; this process of eternal change is the Tao as it moves on its journey through space and time. Thus ultimately, Taoism is a philosophy of change. Indeed, one of its primary texts, the I Ching, is called the Book of Changes. This is precisely why there are no rules, no commandments because there are no fixed points. Everything is in an eternal flux of change, and it is the duty of the individual to adapt to those changes just as a surfer must continually adapt and adjust to ever changing forces if he or she wants to ride the wave.

Taoism is all about riding the wave of life. There are ultimately 2 waves: the infinite Tao or wave of the universe which is impersonal, impartial and absolute and the finite Tao or wave of the individual self, which is personal, partial and limited. It is the harmony or disharmony between these 2 waves that creates good or bad fortune. It has nothing to do with sin but one's ability to ride the wave.

However, once again misfortune is not viewed as a punishment for our sins as meted out by a personal authority figure or Godhead, but rather we create our own misfortune through our ignorance by not understanding the universal laws of life that regulate our existence. If I jump off a 10-story building and fatally injure myself, I am not being punished; I have merely ignored the law of gravity. If I stick my finger in the fire and get burnt, I am not being punished; I have merely ignored the law of thermodynamics.

Just as there are these physical laws of life that we know and live our lives by – we do not walk on water, we do not fly in the air, we know we need to eat and drink, so too, there are similar spiritual laws of life that control and regulate our inner life or destiny. As we master aligning our individual, personal, finite Tao with the infinite Tao of the universe, we place our destiny on a firm footing by aligning our actions, behaviour and attitude with the laws of life.

Alternatively, if we insist on swimming upstream, that is, going against the flow, then the all-powerful forces of creation are not aligned, in harmony with us – we are at odds with the universal current of life. It is this misalignment that then creates misfortune, chaos and accidents in our lives. These events are not punishments but merely messages and symptoms of disorder.

Life is a continuous process of discovery and learning. As neonates, we learn about life on planet earth through trial and error. We learn to walk, to talk, to eat, to run, to balance and so on by attempting these tasks over and over again until we gain mastery. Watching any young child under 2 master their biological body is a wonder to behold as they grapple with the conflicting forces operating on their body.

So too, we learn the laws of life through and by trial and error: we become better people from our experiences. As we grow older and more mature, we become wiser, we lose our rawness, our agitation, our restlessness, our arrogance and naivety. We settle down and acquiesce to the laws of life. As a youth, we believe we are invincible and eternal. As we grow older, we realise that neither of these are true, and life becomes more precious.

Taoism is the path of optimisation!

How do we live our lives in the best possible way? Not according to the 10 commandments or any other imposed and prescriptive set of rules but according to what is right for us according to what we want to achieve. In this sense, it is an extremely personal philosophy. We decide where we want to go and what we want to achieve. This then sets in motion the meta-wave of our destiny that we need to meet and ride if our lives are to be successful.

One of the primary tenants of Taoism is the path of least resistance. This does not mean complacency, defeatism or nihilism, but rather that everything happens in a sequential order and that one must be able to wait for the right time. Timing is everything. This is another reason why there are no arbitrary or unequivocal rules, for what is right at any given moment in time will not be right earlier or later.

As any truly successful person knows timing is everything. One must seize the right moment and act decisively when one's opportunity arises, but one must be able to await that right moment. Restlessness and impatience are the liabilities of youth and need to be overcome in order to ride the wave correctly.

Thus, one is not following an externally imposed curriculum or catechism; one is following the wave of one's own destiny as set up by the individual within one's own mind and soul. This presupposes of course that one firstly knows what one wants and where one is going. Taoism is not to be confused with pre-determinism where our fate, destiny or karma is decried by another. The meta-wave of our lives is determined by ourselves and ourselves alone. But this is either done consciously and knowingly or unconsciously and ignorantly.

This is why *TaoTuning* follows on from where *Personal Sovereignty* left off. *Personal Sovereignty* is an investigation of the decision-making process and our ability as individuals to make our own decisions and choices in our own right and on our own: to be the captain of our own ship, the master of our own destiny.

TaoTuning is the exploration of how we ride the waves of life once we have made those decisions; once we have determined where we want to go and what we want to achieve. Decisions determine destiny! But having made those decisions we need to ensure we have the requisite skills, tools and learning to execute the journey correctly.

If we go back to the analogy of the surfer: we have picked the beach, waxed our board and paddled out to where the waves are breaking. As anyone who has ridden a surfboard, snowboard, or skied knows this is not even half the battle. We now need to catch the wave and ride it successfully without falling off. This is where the real work and skill lies.

So too in life, to become truly successful, it is not just a matter of making academic decisions and then wishful thinking. This will get us nowhere but frustrated and despondent blaming others for our lack of good fortune and becoming a victim. No! We need to make it happen – not some academic deity. We need to seize the day. We need to work our destiny by aligning our own personal wave with that of the universe.

That is why I have called this book *TaoTuning*: we need to attune to our Tao. We need to actively align. Just as in any reception, whether that be a radio or television or other media we need to tune into the right channel; we need to tune out the noise and the static; we need clarity of reception if we are to hear and enjoy the message being transmitted.

Each of us is on a unique frequency that is totally our own. Just as we each have our own unique face, fingerprint, personality and body, so too, we each have our own individual and unique wave – our personal Tao. True success in life depends upon tuning into that wave, aligning our personal destiny and our creative efforts with that inner power and energy. This is precisely why sometimes in life, no matter how hard we try, it just does not work and yet, at other times, doors open effortlessly, things flow easily, success comes almost spontaneously.

The time is right! We have generated the correct meta-wave.

Thus, this book is actually a manual for successful living. In Part I we explore the mechanics of wave theory and the laws that regulate wave generation. In Part II we then go onto explore the mechanics of attunement, fine tuning, and reception; understanding the difference between clarity, noise and static. In Part III we then put those 2 analyses together to understand precisely how one generates the meta-wave of success, how one finetunes one's life so that one's destiny and one's fate are on a firm footing. In this way, there is no wasteful expenditure of energy because one knows how to wait for the right time and exactly what effort to put forward to achieve one's desires.

Tao Tuning is a manual to achieve becoming the new human spoken of in *Personal Sovereignty*. It is how we develop those 7 characteristics of Personal Powah, Inner Clarity, Intention, Self-Mastery and Functioning with Dominion, Purity of Purpose, Self-Love and Self-Acceptance, and The Joy of Self Expression.

If *Personal Sovereignty* explored the evolutionary journey of where we got lost and how we created the current planetary and personal quandary we now find ourselves in which threatens our very survival, *Tao Tuning* is a looking forward and recipe for how we can recreate our species to take our rightful place on the planet and take personal dominion of both our own lives and that of Gaia, the Earth, our home and our mother.

Chapter 3

Polarity and dualistic monism

It is essential to understand the dualistic nature of the physical universe or material world in which we live. As Einstein's unified field theory suggests all is one. Taoism says that in the beginning was the ONE and from this ONE became two. Even for the universe to be created initially by the Big Bang, there is the need for polarity. There needs to be this electrical charge or tension of the potential difference between the positive and negative poles for the explosion to have occurred in the first place. Think of an electrical thunderstorm where the potential difference between a highly positively charged atmosphere and the negative charge of earth explodes in thunder and lightning.

Everything in life depends upon polarity: the contraction and expansion of the heart, the cycles of day and night, the rhythm of the seasons, the union of male and female. Life is the pulsation of contraction and expansion creating waves, rhythms, cycles, beats and pulses. Everywhere in nature we witness this eternal rhythm, this universal heartbeat or pulse of life which ultimately is the dialectic of yin and yang.

This concept of dualistic monism can be found in all early philosophies of life from all around the world, east and west – not just in Taoism. Interestingly, the Aztecs held a similar view called the Teotl which is very close to the word Tao! Teotl is the ceaseless, cyclic oscillation of polar yet complementary opposites. It is this endless opposition that creates life in all of its myriad forms.

Thus, complementary opposites create a continuum or field with 2 polar extreme points; these 2 points are termed yin and yang. Now in and of themselves the terms yin and yang have no definite meaning. As mentioned, the original definition was the light and dark (or shadow) side of a hill. However, as all manifest phenomena exist within their own continuum there are always 2 nodes or extreme points that are represented by the yin and the yang of that continuum.

Light and dark, day and night, birth and death, being and non-being, male and female, hot and cold, wet and dry, good and evil, active and passive and so on. In and of themselves neither pole or extreme is seen as better or worse, higher or lower; both are equally essential for the creative process of life, both are equal and necessary. This is the essential difference between dualistic monism and normal religious philosophies which always view the godhead or good as above and preferable to the evil of Satan.

These two opposites are complementary and interdependent. It is the dialectic opposition between these 2 points that create the dynamic tension necessary to generate the wave. The wave is life! That wave is the Tao. If we return to our example of the battery which needs a potential difference to function, we can see the necessity of maintaining this eternal rhythm lest the law of entropy takes over and all of life ceases.

One of the quandaries of life is how does the universe sustain itself? The second law of thermodynamics, which is the law of entropy, basically states that all closed systems eventually return to a state of disorder and run out of energy. Think of a spinning top or the energy you have in the morning after deep and restful sleep as opposed to after a long and hard day's work. Think of your mobile phone or laptop – they all eventually run out of energy and need to be recharged. The energy source must come from somewhere else.

The evolutionary principle of life, however, runs counter to this law. Evolution is the continual movement of life towards ever more complex forms whilst the law of entropy states everything moves to ever less complex forms. Everything in the physical universe eventually runs out of energy and dies whether that is in the space of minutes, years, decades or millions of light years as in the case of a sun or stellar body. Yet, the universe itself sustains itself throughout eternity.

The powerhouse or motor for this continual creation of energy is the dialectic movement caused by the complementary opposites of yin and yang forever oscillating along a continuum that becomes the pulse and rhythm of life. In dualistic monism, life is viewed as a comprehensive whole which is divided into parts so that life can exist and continue on its evolutionary journey back to oneness. The Book of Changes states that:

> *'when opposition represents polarity with a comprehensive whole it has useful and important functions. The oppositions of heaven and earth, spirit and nature, man and woman, when reconciled bring about the creation and reproduction of life.*
>
> *'in the world of visible things, the principle of opposites makes possible the differentiation by categories through which order is brought into the world.'*

Confucius goes still further stating that opposition is the natural prerequisite for union. This statement eloquently summarises the whole principle. One needs the dynamic tension created between the polar opposites to counteract the law of entropy and keep the engine of continuous creation and evolution running. Dialectic opposition is the fuel for life.

Just as a keen surfer needs to develop an intuitive skill regarding the dynamic forces operating – swell, tide, wave front etc. to stay on and successfully ride the ocean wave, the spiritual adept or cosmic surfer, the Taoist sage, needs to develop their intrinsic skill to ride the inner waves of their Tao. In order to do this, we need to examine the fundamental forces of yin and yang and their continual interplay.

Amongst all the infinite pairs of opposites that the yin/yang continuum characterise, the fundamental essential pair to understand is heaven and earth, the creative and the receptive. The first hexagram in The Book of Changes which is a doubling of the trigram: Heaven, The Creative describes the attributes of this quality. The second hexagram, which is correspondingly a doubling of the trigram for Earth, The Receptive similarly describe its attributes.

According to Taoism, it is this pair that lie at the heart of all of creation, all of the myriad forms of life on earth. We will therefore spend some time examining this pair to more fully understand the dialectic wave that generates all of life. We began this treatise with the comment that since time began, humanity has looked to the heavens and asked the meaning of life. We have also argued that *Tao Tuning* is an attempt to define a more appropriate philosophy that is more relevant for today's modern person. It is only fitting, therefore, that we begin our exploration with the Taoist concept of Heaven.

To begin, in Taoism Heaven is NOT the rarefied residence of a personal God. Nor is Heaven an eternal resting place for those good souls who have faithfully followed the will of God and been good citizens of Earth. Heaven is merely an image of the creative power of the universe. It is seen as consistently strong, without weakness, operating throughout time. The yang power is viewed as strong, creative action that initiates the processes of life. All life is seen as originating in and from this primary quality. This attribute is also the movement of time through space and time is seen as the vehicle for making actual what is potential.

The way to success in all aspects of life lies in; '*apprehending and giving actuality to the way of the universe (the Tao), **which as a law** running through end and beginning brings about all phenomena in time.*'

Thus, we see that the creative principle is the Tao, the way or the law of the universe. This is the quintessential yang force which moves through space and time bringing about all of creation by a movement that never slackens and proceeds one day after another and thus endures throughout eternity. The movement is seen as tireless and thus does not fall prey to the law of entropy. The essential qualities of the yang force are strength and firmness, continuous movement and development, perseverance through time and thus success.

On the other hand, the second hexagram describes the intrinsic qualities of the yin attribute: The Receptive, Earth. Whereas the Creative, Heaven, is the male or masculine, strong and firm principle, the Earth represents the receptive, gentle, yielding, devotion of the female principle. The Receptive Earth is seen as the complement, not the opposite of the Creative in that the yin principle completes the yang. This complementarity is seen as nature in contrast to spirit, space as against time, the female as opposed to the male, the outer physical world of the senses as opposed to the inner spiritual world of the soul.

Although both principles are equally important, there is a clearly defined hierarchic relationship in that the creative initiates and the receptive is activated by and responds to this stimulus. The attribute of devotion describes this complementary partnership. It is only when the yin principle abandons this complementary position and demands a position to which it is not entitled and seeks to usurp power or rule that the relationship become dysfunctional and destructive to both.

The Earth connotes spatial reality; in other words, the manifest material world as opposed to the pure spiritual potential of Heaven. The process of eternal life or evolution is the continuous transition from potential to actual, from spiritual to spatial via the dialectic tension created through the complementary opposites of yin and yang, Heaven and Earth, the Creative and the Receptive.

The Creative begets and the Receptive gives birth. The Creative leads; the Receptive is led. Heaven determines; Earth conforms. It is essential to understand this is not to be confused with mythology or any abstract arcane cosmology that is not relevant to daily life. These qualities eloquently describe the process of life and the way to a successful life.

It is also essential not to get caught up in any gender bias. These forces are genderless but are fundamental qualities and attributes of the universe. There is no gender in battery terminals, nor any preferential node. Both are equal and necessary. In fact, Taoism is perfectly clear that we all contain both yin and yang, male and female, positive and negative, masculine and feminine energies in equal measure and stature.

The qualities and attributes symbolised by yin and yang must be learnt and made part of one's own being so that one intrinsically and intuitively knows when to employ and engage either attribute just as the surfer needs to balance the forces of wind, wave and water. The Taoist sage knows how to read the signs of the time and how to respond, how to be led by the situation, how to adapt, how to be receptive.

'how to meet his fate with an attitude of acceptance, he is sure to find the right guidance.'

We return to our original premise of a practical philosophy that describes accurately how life works rather than a set of rules that prescribe how life should work. Success lies in being able to move along the continuum dependent upon the exigencies of the time. For everything there is a season. There is an appropriate time to be firm, active, strong and unyielding, to lead and determine, to beget. There is also a time to be gentle, yielding, passive and guided by fate. It is this totally personal relationship between the universal Tao and one's personal Tao that determines success and good fortune.

One needs to learn to ride the waves of the continuum and we can only do this by understanding and mastering the dialectics of yin and yang. Both need to be engaged; both need to be employed. The Receptive accommodates itself to the qualities of the Creative.

> *'The Receptive has no need of a special purpose of its own; nor of any effort; yet everything turns out as it should. Man achieves the height of wisdom when all that he does is as self-evident as what nature does.*
>
> *'Everything becomes spontaneously what is should rightly be, for in the law of heaven life has an inner light that it must involuntarily obey.'*

There is an ancient Taoist saying: the sage does nothing, but nothing remains undone, meaning that one follows the path of least resistance. One does one's duty, but no more. One does what is required by the situation but does not interfere. One is guided by what needs to be done. One must learn to follow one's inner law and light: this is the path to success.

Thus, the quality or attribute of yin, of following, of devotion, of knowing one's place is an essential aspect of this formula for successful living. We are led by the situation. Our destiny, our fate, our karma, our personal life journey, call it what you will, is a living, breathing thing. It has its own reality; it has its own energy and power; it is the wave of our personal Tao and we need to learn to align, to harmonise, to attune to it. This attunement, to which we will return in Section II, is the quality of the Receptive.

From the ONE becomes the duality of Heaven and Earth and from the interrelation of those two all other beings and life are born and become manifest. This is an incredibly poetic and succinct description of how life works. All of creation comes from the combining of opposites to create new life. This is not a dreamtime myth or children's fairy story. This is a concise, scientific and rational depiction and description of how life works. We can only master this learning through living life, via trial and error, by the observation of what is and what becomes from our action.

We need to inculcate and become these principles; we need to own them within our own being. We need to learn to ride the continuum. It is not that one is completely yin or yang, male or female but both. We need to surf the waves of life and allow them to carry us along just as the surfer rides the wave by harnessing its energy, its power and staying on it, not falling off, not getting too far ahead or too far behind. The consummate surfer blends their effort with the natural energy and power of the ocean wave. The Taoist sage blends their effort with the cosmic wave.

The principles and skills are identical, although one skill is physical, and the other is metaphysical. Eventually, as in any great athlete or practitioner, these skills become automatic and controlled by the autonomic nervous system. The adept cosmic surfer also learns to hand over to their unconscious working instinctively and intuitively.

'through seriousness and fulfilment of duty, character develops richly of itself; greatness comes unsought, of its own accord. Therefore, in all matters the individual hits upon the right course instinctively and without reflection, because he is free of all those scruples and doubts which induce a timid vacillation and lame the power of decision.'

We can watch an elite athlete, especially a professional world champion surfer, and marvel at their innate and instinctive ability to weave, to jump, to turn and ride that wave. But for any of us amateurs who have stalled at the precipice of a really huge wave looking over the edge, we know the scruples and doubts that lame decision and either cause us to pull back or merely fall off the wave.

Similarly, in those really big and important life changing decisions when we do need to seize the day and ride the Tao of our destiny to our future, any self-doubt will cripple our ability to move forward decisively. This is precisely when we need to move into the yang field of deliberate action and begetting while holding onto the guidance of our destiny. Remember, decisions determine destiny.

Inner intention generates the meta-wave of our lives; those grand and glorious waves that seem to swell up from nowhere and propel us into our next matrix, the next chapter of our lives. And we need to be ready to ride that wave for all that it is worth. There can be no lame vacillation, no self-doubt, no hesitation. He who hesitates is lost!

But when we really look back and reflect seriously after the wave has been ridden, we do see exactly where and when we released the initial inner creative, yang energy that begat that wave in the first place. It is just that there is always a time delay, a buffer or cushion between the ideation and the reality and often the wave will appear just when we have given up and forgotten our original intention and desire.

Riding the cosmic wave of one's life is a delicate dialectic process requiring being adept at engaging, employing and becoming both principles. It is never that anything is completely yin or completely yang. Everything is in a constant state of flux moving along the continuum between the two polar extremes. Day is always becoming night and vice versa. We begin to die from the moment of birth. To get stuck on either pole is to fall off the wave!

Creating one's reality is the movement from potential to actual, from spiritual to spatial, from ideation to reality by moving consistently through time to achieve one's goals and objectives. We either struggle vaingloriously to do this on our own swimming against the stream, or we consciously choose to align with the all-powerful cosmic currents and waves of the universe to more easily, elegantly and successfully create our own future.

Chapter 4

Wave Theory 101

To better understand the workings of the Tao, we need to examine wave theory. Waves are an integral part of life; they are not just the waves on the ocean. Electricity, electromagnetic energy, light and sound all travel as waves. Moreover, if we include the pulsation of the heart and blood flow, we can see that all of life and creation are in some way or another connected with this constant expansion and contraction of energy. Nuclear physics has also demonstrated that the building block of matter is not an indivisible physical atom but a packet or photon of energy – a wave.

A wave is basically a cyclic movement between two nodes or extreme points. The simplest wave to examine and understand this is the sine wave which has a classic harmonious curve. We talk about the crest – being the top - and trough - being the lowest point - of a wave. A wave is basically an oscillation. All waves have a frequency or cycle per unit of time. Waves can be incredibly small or incredibly large.

Waves can also travel through enormous distances in space. We talk of outer space and certain stars or galaxies as being millions of light years away. Considering that light travels at the speed of 186,000 miles per second, or 299,792,458 metres per second, that is an incredible distance. Going back to the law of entropy, one can only wonder what energy or fuel powers the wave to travel those distances through space. Again, it is the potential difference or tension created between the node points that thrusts the wave forward and sustains its drive.

Without waves the physical universe could not exist. Waves are the building blocks of creation and the mechanism whereby energy travels throughout the universe. There has also long been a debate as to whether fundamental particles: electrons, protons, neutrons and sub-atomic particles are indeed particles at all or simply waves of energy. Quantum physics now describe these as packets of energy or particle waves called photons and there is only a probability that a particle/wave will exist at a certain place at a certain point in time.

All of matter is eventually energy as described in Einstein's formula: $E = mc^2$ is ultimately a wave of energy. The material, physical universe is composed of waves of energy that appear to our senses and consciousness as matter. But we now know via quantum physics that matter does not really exist at all but merely appears to exist as solid objects. Everything is ultimately a wave.

Just as a projector projects the images on a screen that are really in the film or a television or monitor projects images that are really within the device, external reality or daily existence is a construct of our consciousness. We create the image of solidity. We objectify our perception. Our minds divide the sensory input of our senses and create the image and the illusion of separate physical objects. In reality, matter does not exist. There are just waves in space!

We live in a sea of waves just as a fish lives in a sea of water. So ultimately, Taoism is a 5,000-year-old philosophy of life that coincides perfectly with what science has discovered in the last 100 years. That is why I believe we need to forego our childish and immature versions of religion for one that is more based in the modern, rational, scientific understanding of nature, life and the universe.

As we understand the wave nature of reality not only in a physical sense, but more importantly in an inner metaphysical sense, we can more appropriately form a coherent and intelligent philosophy of life. Ultimately, any religion or philosophy needs to be useful as a guide to right behaviour and daily living. It is my hypothesis that it is the outmoded and outdated versions of religion that are holding humanity back from maturing and evolving into the next generation of homo sapiens; that in our current form as a species we are extinct and thus we have a clear but stark choice, whether to adapt and mutate into a new species that is fundamentally different from our current form or face total extinction and annihilation as a species all together.

Moreover, time is running out for us to make this all-important decision which will need to be made on an individual basis. It is only when a sizeable portion of the earth's population make this necessary transition that a critical threshold will be reached whereby humanity as a whole will transmute.

To survive physically on planet earth, we need to separate and objectify reality, but it is this perception of separation that is now destroying the planet. As we move to a more holistic understanding, perception and theory of reality, we will understand the Oneness of Creation: that all life is intricately linked and that we are the custodians of this oneness of life on planet Earth.

We can only make this transition by embracing a fundamental shift in our thinking of how reality works. We cannot see electricity waves or sound waves or the electromagnetic waves that now enable us to use smart phones, computers or the internet but we certainly use them daily to live our lives. In fact, the whole of modern life and the technological comforts we enjoy are dependent upon the functioning of waves.

In terms of spiritual causality, we need to adjust to wave theory. We need desperately to understand the inner unseen connectivity of things rather than limit causality to direct physical cause and action. Two waves intersect and as a result form a third wave that is a mathematical equation of the first two. Human beings are complex emotional and mental creatures who put out different and sometimes opposing waves. All thoughts and emotions are vibrations or waves. These waves go out into the universe and create our future. Our brains are continuously transmitting waves into the ether that then come back to us as our destiny and fate.

Often, we cannot directly see the causal connection. Quite often, these events come from a seemingly unrelated space, and we view these events as accidents and ourselves as victims not realising that the waves we have created and generated by our thinking and our attitude and sent out into the world in our past are merely returning to us to create our present:

> *such experiences are not merely effects produced by the external world, but logical consequences evoked by our own nature.*

It is all a question of logic and causality. We flick a switch, and a light comes on. We click a mouse and a cursor on a screen moves. To a primitive person these events are a-causal and not connected, but to modern person we understand the inner, unseen, causal connection even though we cannot visibly see the electrical waves operating. Modern science is learning how to move physical objects by transmitting mental electrical waves via complex headsets and computers that then direct matter.

Wave theory is essential to understanding life. Mastering wave theory is essential to self-mastery and living one's life successfully. If all of life and all of creation can be reduced to waves, then humanity as an intelligent species needs urgently to grasp this phenomenon. Most waves cannot be seen but we can see the visible effects of the invisible. Even a wave on the ocean cannot truly be seen until it reaches the shallows and breaks. As the sea floor shallows the wave becomes more pronounced upon the surface of the ocean.

We know that a tsunami or tidal wave follows from an earthquake and that this wave can travel thousands of miles, causing massive destruction even though we cannot see the wave until it reaches the shore. So too, we often unknowingly unleash massively destructive waves into our lives that at some point in the future precipitate calamitous events. Similarly, we may generate profoundly positive waves that then manifest as seemingly serendipitous good fortune. Either way we need to understand the way waves work and that all of reality both in the outer physical world and in our inner personal destiny and fate are the result of waves.

Waves travel through space and time. Waves have an amplitude, a frequency and a life cycle. The amplitude of a wave is measured by the distance between the two node points similar to the diameter of a circle. The frequency is measured by the number of oscillations per unit of time. Some waves, like light waves seem to travel infinitely, whereas other waves may only travel short distances and last microseconds.

There is also a distinction between what is called the carrier wave and the content or data being carried by that wave. We are all familiar with the difference between the sound quality of AM and FM radio; we are all familiar with the transition from analogue to digital television and so on. We live in a digital age. These terms refer to the carrier wave. The content – being the sound or the image – is identical but the wave carrying that message is not. There is a superior quality to FM sound and to digital images. Science is now hypothesising that we actually live in a digital world composed purely of data or packets of information which we then interpret as reality.

Thus, it is not just the wave itself that is important but the data or message it carries. It is said that light waves are particles or packets of information. In other words, the light waves travelling through the universe carry information and instructions that feed our consciousness just as radio waves, television waves and other electromagnetic waves carry data that is then deciphered or translated back into sound or image by a receiver configured appropriately to translate the incoming vibration.

We say that we feel the vibe of a place or a person referring to the vibration that emanates from that source. A vibration is a wave! Waves travel as vibrations. We can get good or bad vibes and some of us are more sensitive than others to these waves. Similarly, there are those who are more sensitive to what is called psychic or unseen vibrations from the spiritual world. There have been numerous experiments conducted throughout the world where one person will transmit a message – data – and another person in a separate room will receive that impression. Moreover, these experiments have been conducted with all sorts of intervening materials, such as lead etc. and varying distances to better understand the strength, nature and character of these waves.

To be sceptical of these waves because they are unseen, and we do not understand their nature is archaic and stupid. 100 years ago, we did not fully understand electricity, yet the modern world has become totally reliant upon this wave of energy. 50 years ago, we did not fully understand the full scale and use of electromagnetic waves, yet our lives in terms of computers, smart phones, the internet etc. have been radically transformed by its use. Quantum physics now understands the sub-atomic world is composed of probability waves and not indivisible solid particles.

It is also interesting that 100 years ago, Einstein postulated that gravity was a wave. It is only in the last 12 months that science has now verified this point. It will be interesting to witness, how in the next 100 or even 50 years, science discovers how to use and benefit from this particular wave theory.

Waves exist all around us. More and more of biological and physical life is being reduced to waves. More and more of modern civilisation is becoming dependent upon the understanding, mastering and use of waves of various kinds. Nearly all modern scientific discoveries come down to our investigation and understanding of waves.

On the inner planes emotions are waves; thoughts are also waves. We all operate on our own individual and unique frequency or vibration. We can feel these waves or vibrations when people approach us, particularly when in a highly emotional or agitated state. We can all feel anger, hostility, love and kindness. Some people just attract other people and animals by their vibration whereas others repel. We all intuitively and instinctively know these things, yet as a species, we are in denial about their scientific reality. We stubbornly refuse to build a more coherent, logical and rational base for our religious philosophy of life based in this knowledge. It would be as if we reject electricity or electromagnetic waves simply because we cannot see them and thus believe they are evil.

Originally, we needed wires to transmit and carry these waves as in the original telegraph, telephone, radio and so on. Then came the transistor radio, the cell phone, the smart phone and now we are all connected via Wi-Fi meaning wireless frequency. We are becoming more knowledgeable at transmitting and receiving wirelessly! Eventually, we may be able to transmit electricity without the necessity of poles and wires.

All of life on earth depends ultimately upon the sun for warmth, energy and information. These rays travel to earth as a wave. Cosmic rays or waves permeate outer space bringing life, energy and data to the planet. In the end, waves are the way the universe exists and communicates. Humanity's knowledge of this all-important subject is still in its infancy. Most science fiction in terms of time travel, space travel and so on presupposes a more intelligent understanding and use of wave theory.

5,000 years ago, Taoism understood the significance of waves in the life of the universe and the life of the individual. The Tao is the ultimate wave! That wave moves through creation. You could say that wave is God; but this definition of God is not personal or subjective: it has no personification. It is definitely not an old man with a beard living in Heaven. It is universal. It is omnipresent and manifests in countless and myriad other waves.

Taoism is an attempt to understand and translate that wave theory into a practical and utilitarian way of life. The Tao is the way – the way of the universe, the way of life. It is the way the wave works. Hence, the words: *way, wave, flow, Tao* become interchangeable, and all refer to the same thing. In the west, we use the term God. In different religions, different words are used but usually with the understanding that one cannot adequately define or capture that essence. Indeed, many religions postulate that one should not even refer to the name of God.

In the Tao Te Ching, it says: '*the name that can be named is not the constant name*'. The Bible says: '*in the beginning was the Word and the word was with God.*' In Islam, the word or name of God, Allah, should not be spoken of lightly. There is this universal understanding that the more we try to verbalise or objectify the nature of God, the more we lose its essential essence. Christ said: I am the way, the truth and the light meaning these three things are the same.

Dualistic monism is based upon the intuitive understanding that the material universe is in a constant and dynamic state of change and this change is the process of Life. Everything moves through cycles and seasons according to the law or wave of its own being.

The symbolic representation of this wave theory is the logarithmic spiral and its three-dimensional counterpart the helix. It is also interesting that this pattern exists everywhere in nature from the coils of a seashell to the structure of immense galaxies in space. The spiral links the two ends of polarity in beginning and end, periphery and centre by showing they are but two ends of the one continuum. It also depicts the contrary movements between these two poles of yin and yang.

The logarithmic spiral also depicts another important distinction between yin and yang and the process of creation and evolution, in that density or contraction is a characteristic of the centre whereas acceleration and expansion are characteristics of the extremity. This process of dualistic monism or dialectic materialism gave birth to physical matter under the process of contraction. The process of evolution is the ever expansion of life into more complex and sophisticated forms. This is the ever-expanding evolutionary journey home to where the Big Bang of creation begun.

Contraction and expansion are the forces or fuel for life. The heart contracts and expands which pumps the blood through the body. From the smallest subatomic particle to the farthest reaches of space and interstellar bodies, all of life exists within this rhythmic motion of contraction and expansion. The human body and indeed all biology is based on the contraction and expansion of the autonomic nervous system. The autonomic nervous system controls the functions of the body and divides into complementary opposites: the sympathetic system is the emergency awakening or activation of the heart, blood, energy and output to stimulate activity whereas the parasympathetic is the closing, recovery, contraction of rest.

While we do not necessarily view either the spiral or the forces of expansion and contraction as waves, in essence, they are. So too, the swirls in one's fingerprint, the spiral growth pattern of hair on one's head, the helix of the genome, the spiral shape of the early foetus, the spiral pattern of certain plants, shells and so on all testify to the universal design principle of the dialectic of yin and yang. These opposing forces fuel the constant expansion and contraction of the universe which then translates into the propelling motion of the wave. We can see these waves throughout the whole of creation and as a fundamental principle of life.

To summarise: in the beginning, pre-creation, there exists The One. This One then becomes two – the poles of yin and yang which have a dialectic tension between them expressed as a potential difference. This potential difference then sets up a wave or movement between the two polar extremes based on the constant expansion and contraction of the universe and all within it. This wave is the Tao or the Law of the Universe and is invisible and everywhere. This energy wave exists on an extremely high frequency that cannot be detected physically but can on the inner psychic emotional and intuitive planes.

This wave then descends into the lower vibrations of physicality which become the positive and negative particles and photons of subatomic matter and light and give birth to the material plane. This is the contracting process of materialisation which began with the Big Bang. Life then ascends through ever increasing expansion to ever more complex forms of molecules and biological life through the process of evolution.

Humanity is the pinnacle or extreme point in the materialisation process of nature and the beginning of the return journey to the infinity of the One from which the whole journey began. In this way, the principle of dualistic monism depicts both the materialisation and evolutionary processes of life as the original contraction and expansion of the universe.

We began our discussion with the principles of Heaven and Earth or the Creative and the Receptive. It is essential to realise that these are not to be taken literally as real spaces or places, as in most other religions, but rather a metaphorical principle. Heaven represents the ultimate expansion of the centrifugal mode and Earth represents the extreme contraction of the centripetal mode.

It is also essential to grasp that all of the scientific discoveries made in modern times, including Einstein's Unified Field and wave theory of gravity totally support this representation of the universe. As modern science discovers more about the workings of the universe, this dialectic interpretation is validated. We do not need to rely upon blind faith or childish parables or dreamtime stories to build our religion or philosophy of life. Empirical science validates the wave nature of the material universe in which we live and the overall evolutionary processes of life. The dialectic forces of yin and yang are the driving forces of life generating waves, cycles and rhythms that then manifest throughout the physical universe.

We thus arrive at a philosophy or cosmology grounded in experiential reality and backed by empirical science. As humanity matures both rationally and emotionally, it can discard the superstition, the irrational, the illogical and the denial that has blinded it for too long and led to an immature co-dependent relationship with the forces of creation that has stymied its evolution and its ability to assume its rightful position as custodian of the planet and thus be welcomed into the intergalactic federation of evolved cosmic beings.

Chapter 5

The One Law

We need to return to our previous discussion concerning prescriptive and descriptive laws as it is essential to fully grasp this distinction, as a fundamental platform of an emotionally mature philosophy of life that truly enables us to live our lives more fully, consciously and nobly.

Anyone who has been the parent of a young child, especially around the age of 2 (the terrible two's) or a young puppy knows the importance of training and discipline. If we do not succeed in setting meaningful limits and boundaries, if we do not establish firm foundations and correct protocols, the child or pup will become a menace not only to itself but to others.

Discipline and order are an essential part of a successful life. But so too are strong will and fierce independence. The whole purpose and challenge of intelligent education, child rearing and animal training is to get this dialectic balance correct. Once again, we see these two opposing yet complementary opposites. We have the expansive force of self-expression, curiosity and wonder that lead to personal growth and psychological development on the one hand, counterbalanced by the contracting force of needing to fit into the family dynamic, society and be a part of humanity.

We cannot have ultimate unfettered freedom and neither do we want oppressive repression. It is the same in the development of strong character. We do not want unbridled licentiousness and self-indulgent myopia but neither do we want excessive asceticism or self-denial. We all face this dialectic challenge every day of our lives.

Indeed, we could say that the truly successful human being is the one who finds this rare balance maintaining a healthy and wholesome natural curiosity, love of life and expressing their creative urges as well as fitting into society and playing an integral role in the development of humanity. History is littered with extremely creative souls who just could not get this balance right and ended their life in misery, frustration and often sadly suicide.

The two opposing forces of yin and yang rule our lives; if either gets out of control or we go to either extreme, we lose control of our lives and fail to achieve fulfilment as a highly evolved human being. Discipline is necessary; but so too is personal freedom. I have discussed this quandary at length in *Personal Sovereignty* and so do not intend to dwell deeply on the subject in this book. However, it is essential, for the purpose of our discussion to understand this polarity in our personal lives.

Whether we like it or not life is constrained. We all have limits, boundaries and parameters beyond which we cannot venture. Human beings cannot fly; nor live underwater. We need to eat and drink. We need to observe certain mores to fit into the society within which we live. To be truly successful at life we need to observe these limitations and make them work for us, not be in a constant war fighting the laws of life.

Laws are essential if there is to be order and the universe is an extremely ordered place. If there was no order, there would be chaos and living beings do not fare well in chaotic circumstances. We need order and stability to grow and thrive. Indeed, as we enter this age of uncertainty and disorder, the incidence of anxiety and social unrest is becoming the true pandemic.

Ever since people came together in nomadic tribes, humanity has grappled with this need for discipline, order and a set of rules so that people could live together in peace and harmony. History is also the sorry tale of those people who have willingly broken those rules, unleashing destructive forces creating disorder, mayhem and chaos. The eventual result is always injury and suffering whether of the one or the many. But even within this framework of order there have been many diverse and varying attempts to solve this dichotomy of individual personal freedom within the constraints of a functioning healthy social system.

As argued in *Personal Sovereignty*, the modern, western, democratic, capitalist model is probably the closest humanity has come to solving this equation. We need firm boundaries within which the individual is free to explore and express their innate individuality. Returning to the upbringing of the young 2-year-old or the young pup, we do not want to totally destroy their free spirit. We do not want to beat them into submission. We do not want to repress or destroy that natural effervescence or joie de vivre. But neither do we want a troublesome, selfish, myopic uncontrolled being; this simply does not work. We have all witnessed the overly indulged and spoilt child who spoils life for everyone.

There must be balance between these opposing forces of love, joy, enthusiasm and free spiritedness and discipline, control, order and strength.

The whole outcome of wave theory is that waves operate according to cosmic natural law. Starting with the Big Bang of original and ultimate expansion, the material universe is the constant pulsation of the rhythm of life forever in systole and diastole, expansion and contraction. This rhythm then manifests as the wave or Tao of the universe. The point being that this wave is a universal law running through and regulating the physical universe.

However, natural laws are not prescriptive; they do not dictate what should happen but describe what does happen: it is an expression of the way life works. Things do not drop to the ground because they are told to but because this is what happens naturally. Natural laws therefore require no effort; they describe the path of least resistance.

In humankind's quest to regulate individual behaviour, to create an ordered and harmonious social structure, we have created what is called prescriptive laws that proscribe or tell us what we should or ought to do: drive on the right or left-hand side of the road, stop at a red light, pay our taxes, not steal, not kill and so on. These prescriptive laws vary from culture to culture and society to society and are as varied and diverse as the world of human.

We can divide these laws into 3 broad categories. The first would be the religious laws of how one should live one's life in order to be a good moral person and enter the kingdom of heaven. The 10 Commandments are a good example but every religion, every philosophy of life has their own version. Indeed, Christ simplified these rules into one: love one another as I have loved you or do unto others as you would have them do unto you.

Second, there would be what one would call the mores of that social system depending upon the historical epoch, culture and society. Nudity is a good example of how in some societies, there is a healthy embrace and acceptance of public nudity whereas in others it is an affront and may even be illegal. In some societies, one can only have one spouse whereas in others polygamy is the norm. In most societies, these mores or customs have been encoded into the laws of the land.

The third would be the legislative requirements of specific laws that these days tend to cover every aspect of our daily lives as we become ever more controlled and dominated by legislation. One would shudder to think of the criminal, industrial, workplace, residential, development and so on and so on laws that now regulate every facet of our lives. Legislative laws prescribe what we can and what we cannot do in every behaviour and activity of modern life.

Whereas the capitalist democracy has given us the most amount of personal freedom, the governments of the modern western world have constrained this freedom under the burden of an ever-increasing legislative overlay. What we say, how we dress, how we build our homes, how we work, how we drive – whatever activity you want to think of, there is a prescriptive law to tell us what we can and cannot do. Even if one goes to the beach: swim between the flags, dogs must be on a leash, no dogs between certain hours etc.

The unfortunate consequence of this legislative overlay on the life of the individual has left the modern person with a jaundiced and lopsided relationship with and understanding of the function or rule of law. We resist and resent their ever-present burden and struggle to regain our hard won but easily lost personal freedom.

As also mentioned, religious laws are outmoded, old fashioned, childish and immature and no longer serve the current spirit and evolution of humanity. Everywhere we see this struggle between the individual and the rule of law. Even the biggest issue facing the world today, the 'jihad' or holy war of terrorism is no other than a conflict of ideologies and religious viewpoints and laws of life. To the fundamentalist, modern, free, western society betrays the laws of Islam and must therefore be punished in not too dissimilar a way that the Christian missionaries went out to civilise the native world and bring them under Christian law three hundred years ago.

Any populous will rebel against excessive legislation particularly if those laws are seen to be unjust, undemocratic or favour the few. But we have thrown the baby out with the bathwater. We have rejected all laws rather than understand the discernment between descriptive natural law which merely describes what does happen and prescriptive man-made law which tells us how to behave.

In other words, natural law describes the path of least resistance; it explains to us exactly how life works. If we live our lives in harmony with these laws our lives work, our destiny flows, and our fate meets with good fortune. We call this good karma!

This is the path of least resistance and thus requires the minimum of effort to achieve our desires. On the other hand, prescriptive laws invariably require effort. We need firstly to be aware and as we all know ignorance of the law is considered no excuse. In this modern era with its infinite array of legislative requirements it is functionally impossible for any human to know and understand all the nuances and interpretations of these laws. Thus, the explosion and dominance of the legal profession in our lives.

We learn natural laws very quickly as a young child. We learn that fire burns, that things fall to the ground, that being wilfully selfish, stubborn and out of control lead to misery. We learn how to relate – that good will and harmony work better at building successful relationships than animosity and ill-will. We learn that hard work, integrity, honesty and doing the right thing lead to a more harmonious and pleasant life than laziness, dishonesty and misbehaviour.

We all have a conscience! That conscience is our inner rudder; it tells us instinctively what is right and wrong not because we are following some external rule, law or precept but because we know it in our being.

The problem with this plethora of modern laws is that it teaches us to distrust our inner being plus it creates so much noise or static that the still, small voice of our conscience can no longer be heard. We have rejected natural law for the profanity of man-made laws.

Although the One Universal Natural Law of the Universe, the Tao, does manifest in countless other physical laws of life and creation, these laws are not complicated nor in conflict with each other. Our bodies work. The solar system works. The law of the jungle works. Nature in all its profusion and diversity works. Nature in the wild, whether that be the animals in the jungle, or the plants of a rain forest, do not have a manual or set of rules to dictate their behaviour. They exist as is; they obey the law of their being; they live in harmony with universal natural law and function in simplicity.

Natural law does not complicate! Natural law does not need overlay upon overlay of legislative dictates telling animals how fast they can run, how much they can eat, who they can play with and what they need to put aside for their retirement fund. Yet, without this legislative complexity nature works!

The essence of Taoism is this natural universal law that regulates and directs life along the path of harmony and least resistance. It describes the process of life. The highest wisdom is apprehending and learning this law and then living one's life in harmony with its essence. The crucial distinction being that this is not academic or arcane book learning. There is no Catechism, no Bible, no 10 Commandments. One learns directly from life. One hones one's inner being. One learns to still the thinking mind and pay attention to one's soul.

In this way, there is no outer conflict and hopefully no inner conflict. For the essence of Taoism is also that this Universal Law manifests as the individual personal law of our being: unique, individual, and personal. This individual law describes who we are and how we operate; it does not dictate or tell us what we should do rather what is best for us at any given point in time given the circumstances of our reality.

Like the 10 Commandments, man-made prescriptive laws lack flexibility and invariably provoke resistance precisely because these current circumstances are not sufficiently taken into consideration. Witness the unfairness of a long-time abused wife who eventually retaliates and kills her abusing and violent husband. She is charged with murder. Consider the defending father protecting his family against an armed and aggressive intruder. He is charged with murder. We now have innocent soldiers obeying instructions who are being charged with manslaughter to appease the political correctness of an irresponsible war.

I may be driving safely at 4 am in the morning with no traffic on the road and be exceeding the speed limit that is set for peak hour traffic during a busy day but be guilty of speeding. I may have obeyed all the legislative procedures and legal professional advice in terms of my tax or superannuation contributions to then have the legislation retrospectively changed and I am outside the law.

One of the major differences between natural and man-made law is that natural law is eternal and does not change. The laws of gravity, thermodynamics, nuclear physics and so on do not chop and change. We live in a stable and consistent universe. Without the interference of man, nature works eternally and without falter. There is no pollution, no waste, no unfairness, no discrimination.

On the other hand, legislative requirements are always changing depending on the political agenda of the government. More and more, citizens are realising that laws are there not to serve the people but to serve the political elite. Legislation is becoming more onerous, complex, unfair and difficult. Life is becoming more and more regulated.

The recent events of Brexit and the increasing election of the outsider is the people's voice of rejection of an elite that has taken the imposition of these man-made prescriptive laws to the limit. Remember, the basic principle of dialectics is that anything that goes to an extreme will bring about its opposite. The western world is experiencing the paradox of the populous vote against the establishment's hold on power.

If we consider that planet earth and thus its natural law is 4,600 million years old, we can sense the stability, the continuity and thus the security of life on earth compared to the extremely narrow window of an election term where politicians are taking an ever-decreasing short-term view as to their own re-election rather than what is best for society. Similarly, the greed of short-term gain and profit is totally destroying the long-term viability and stability of this order.

Natural, universal law is there to make life work for all. The sun shines equally on all beings. Nature supports all creatures great and small without distinction or favouritism. Thus, humanity needs desperately and urgently to come to terms with the concept of natural law. Laws must be fair. Laws must honour the individual. Laws must be there for all equally. Laws must further life. Man-made prescriptive laws are necessary to regulate society but must mimic and be based upon universal principles. That we are out of sync with life, with nature, with the natural ebb and flow of creation, with the Universal Tao is evidenced by our modern ills from personal ill-health to global pollution.

Society has gone too far in imposing this legislative overlay of prescriptive laws telling us what we can and cannot do. And as most of these man-made laws do not resonate with this universal principle of life, the individual is losing its connection with its inner self and the law of its being. It is this law that tells us what to do; it is this law that guides us to do right with instinctive certainty. It is this law that knows our past, our present and our future. It is this law which is our path, our way, our wave, our destiny, our fate and our energy. It is this law which is our personal Tao!

As we attune to this inner law, we become more whole; we heal the internal division within our being; we grow in spiritual stature, in self-confidence, in character and in rightness. We just know intuitively, instinctively what is right for us. We no longer look without to others for guidance whether that be an ideology, a religion, a theory or a person. We become more self-reliant.

We go within, into the quiet of our inner heart and soul to make our own decisions; to determine our own destiny; to generate the wave that then becomes our good fortune. We do not seek another to tell us what to do. If we return to the teachings of Christ: love one another as I have loved you; do unto others as you would have them to unto you – there are no rules. It is rather a way of living one's life.

All the great mystics and teachers have just lived their lives humbly, simply, at peace and in harmony with natural law. None have postulated great or complex rules but have tried to demonstrate the way of life. It is usually the followers who have created the religion, the philosophy, the dogma and these have become more complicated and divorced from the truth down through the ages. One has only to look at the hypocrisy of Rome and the epidemic of paedophilia in the Christian Churches to see these people do not live the teachings or way of Jesus, nor are they in harmony with what is right.

Unfortunately, the more prescriptive laws society makes, the more we diverge from the path of oneness. For it is always one person's interpretation passed onto others. I am telling you what to do; how to live your life. I become the authority. Every individual must become their own authority – the author of their own lives. It is your story! It is your script. It is your play. It is your life to be lived your way, being true to yourself and no other.

We are afraid that if we follow the dictates of our own being we will be wrong; we will be humiliated; we will be wild. The emerging 2-year-old and the young pup do have a wild untamed streak and yes, we all need the confines of limitation, but we must not surrender our innate individuality in the process of our education and upbringing. Your individuality is your most precious and sacred possession. It is the divine gift of life.

Your being is your law; your law is your being. They are two sides of the one thing – your personal Tao! To obey your inner law is not to be dictated to by any form of injunction, belief, theory or thought. It is not a matter of the thinking rational mind. It is deeper. It is the inner core of your being. It is you. This law merely describes who you are and what is your optimum path. You still must choose whether to follow its promptings or go the way of your ego. This is the gift of free will.

Your inner law does not compel you. It has no coercion. It never uses force. But it is the optimum path for you to achieve what is best for your personal, spiritual growth. The question always is whether that is our choice, or do we get distracted by external transitory appearances. As the noise of the external world creates distraction, confusion and static we lose the attention, the focus and the discipline required to heed the dictates of our own being.

As our lives are dominated by more and more man-made laws which tell us what we should do, we lose our inner authenticity betraying who we really are for an artificial construct conforming to external legislative compliance. This distinction between natural and man-made laws is an inherent part of both Japanese and Chinese cultures, particularly the older more traditional way. In Japan, the word, kata, means rules or the proper way to behave oneself. It is distinct from legislative laws in that kata is equal among all Japanese whereas legislative laws are viewed as arbitrary and designed to suit individual purpose thus being biased and subjective.

In ancient China, there was a code of honour which bound the higher classes to behave according to tradition and inner values rather than a set of laws which pertained more to the lower classes. This tradition of honour and a higher code was also prevalent in many cultures and societies such as the Knights of the Round Table, the European Aristocracy and so on.

Unfortunately, in the modern world this inner code of honour has been replaced by the outer rule of law and humanity has lost this innate connection with its inner voice or conscience of what is right for the individual not because of fear of the legal process but precisely because it was the right thing to do.

It is the fundamental thesis of Taoism that we all do know right from wrong and that if we follow our inner core values and code of honour, we will do the right thing naturally without external coercion or manipulation.

Thus, two things have happened over the last hundred years. The first is that the legislative overlay has replaced this inner code of conduct. We now do what we are told to do by external man-made laws, not so much because we believe it is the right thing to do but because we are circumscribed by the legislative/judicial/legal system. We have eroded our inner guidance system.

Second, as this legislative overlay becomes more onerous, subjective and unfair, we have lost our inherent respect for the rule of law. This means, if we can get away with it, we will break the law. This is seen in the explosion of organised crime, multi-national company tax avoidance and the advent of terrorist activity throughout the world. People will avoid or evade a system of law that they view to be unjust, subjective and biased to the few.

The breakdown in law and order throughout the western democratic world, the crumbling of our education system, the fundamental belief that legislation is designed to raise revenue for the government as opposed to really organise society (eg. speeding and parking tickets), and the wholesale disrespect and disregard for man-made laws in general, all testify to this widening gulf between legislation and the people at large.

These are natural consequences of the shift from natural to artificial laws. We have lost our way; the way that is the wave, the law of our being, our Tao. Each and every species has a way, a path it must follow to survive, to thrive and to prosper. Once a species loses this way it inevitably becomes extinct, just as once an individual loses that inherent connection with its inner law it meets with misfortune and quite possibly death.

For the law of our being is our inner guidance system, our moral compass, our rudder and our best and closest confidant in the difficult process of living our lives, finding our way in life and making our own decisions. We are cast adrift at sea in a raging storm of conflicting emotions, desires, opportunities and temptations without a keel or a rudder to keep us on the straight and narrow.

If we have the courage to face ourselves exactly as we are, both as a species collectively and as individual human beings, it is obvious we have lost our way. We are at war with each other, the world, the planet on which we live and inwardly with ourselves. We live in a perpetual state of conflict, tension, dis-ease and confusion. Most of us do not know who we are or what we truly want. We no longer live based on our inner reality but based on whatever is fed to us by the social machine of mass media, social media, advertising and other external cues. We urgently need to regain this connection with our inner navigational system if we are to find our way back to a way of living that is in harmony with natural law. No species can continue to survive at odds with the ecosystem and biosphere within which it lives.

For these ecosystems are highly complex and regulated according to natural law. Although each species within that system and the ecosystem itself have their own inherent law of their being, these laws are all in harmony with each other like the individual instruments in an orchestra. Together they play the symphony of life. This symphony is an incredibly delicate and delicious melody of peace and harmony that has its own inherent order.

Once any being or species steps outside of this score, they begin to play out of tune creating discord, violence and disorder. They begin to collide with the other players on the chess board creating chaos and mayhem. This is the fundamental cause of ill-ness and dis-ease: we are no longer congruent with the law of our being. We become dysfunctional as a human animal. We become discordant in the symphony of life, the music of the spheres, the Word of God. We are out of step and out of tune!

Chapter 6

Permissible Zone of Variance

The wave is our way, our path, our route to success; the path of least resistance to achieving our inner most desires and living our lives authentically. It is not an externally imposed law telling us what to do or what we should do. There is no God in Heaven meeting out punishment. There is no heaven and hell waiting for us in the afterlife to either reward or punish us for the conduct of our behaviour here on earth. There is no entity saying thou shall or shall not – it is totally up to you.

Our behaviour is either aligned with, in accordance and agreement with the inner law of our being and thus leads to good fortune or it is contrary to who we are at our core and thus leads to misfortune. The easiest way to understand this is to consider the rules of the road. If we stick to our lane, if we drive with intelligence and excellence, then we get to our destination safely. If we obey the road rules, being mindful of the other cars and drivers around us, we will travel without incident or harm.

However, if we fall asleep or get distracted and fail to pay attention, wandering all over the place, particularly meandering into another lane, we will inevitably collide with another car and cause an accident. This is misfortune as it creates inconvenience, delay, possible bodily injury and most certainly damage to one's vehicle. If we fail to obey basic road rules, such as stopping at red lights or overtaking dangerously the likelihood of danger increases.

However, within our lane there is a margin for error. In other words, we can wander a little, as long as we hold our vehicle within our designated lane. Once we cross the median line, the risk of collision increases. So too, in life, our Tao or the law of our being is not fixed and rigid – we have what I call permissible zones of variance within which we can wander, experiment and vary without coming to harm.

As opposed to rigid man-made laws which do not allow for much exception or experimentation, the Tao is a living wave and is based upon the principle of change. The eventual goal is evolution and growth, and this growth depends upon trial and error: learning from life, learning by making mistakes, like the baby getting up each time it falls as it learns to walk.

We need to return to wave theory and understand the dialectic relationship between the opposing forces of yin and yang as the extreme nodes or points of change. The fundamental principle of wave theory is that the energy travels continuously along the continuum of the wave path between the two extreme points turning at each node and travelling back towards the centre and then onto the other node. This oscillation is the key to the eternity of creation and the overcoming of the law of entropy. The potential difference between the two nodes sets up the dynamic tension that constantly pulls the wave between the two extreme points.

In other words, nothing in nature travels in straight lines; everything moves along the continuum of its path, its wave, its Tao. As mentioned previously, every wave has both an amplitude and a frequency. The amplitude is the measure of the distance from the mid-point to the node point. The larger the amplitude, the higher the energy. The amplitude is basically the height of the wave. The larger the amplitude, the brighter the wave.

In life, the larger the amplitude, the greater the permissible zone of variance. Going back to our analogy of the road, the wider the lane the less likelihood one will wander into an adjoining lane. This is the basic difference between an old country road and a modern freeway: the lane width is always larger in the more recent construction. Anyone who has travelled on quaint old country roads has experienced the danger of narrow winding lanes.

As an individual, it is advantageous to live one's life in a wider lane, allowing for greater zones of variance and less likelihood of collision. The consummate art of the accomplished Taoist sage is not to go to the extreme point, just as the test of a good driver is not to touch the median line. If we push anything to extremes in life, we invariably encounter resistance. The art of living successfully is to stay within one's zone on a smooth trajectory without lurching from one extreme to the other. This is the zone of flow where we are more likely to experience peak performance.

We all know people whose lives lurch from one catastrophe to another or who always seem to be living close to the edge in chaos and confusion, provoking and encountering resistance, calamity, disaster and danger. It is almost as if these people need that edge to stimulate their adrenalin and make them feel alive. The whole concept of living on the edge, extreme sports and the introduction of the word and concept of the 'extreme' in our modern vocabulary testifies to this tendency to live on the edge.

The Taoist concept of the path of least resistance is that one lives within one's lane; one knows the permissible zone of variance and never pushes things to the extreme but turns just short of the node point. In nature, we see this cyclic change when things go to extreme. An extremely hot day will produce either a thunderstorm or a cold front. Severe droughts bring on floods.

In the life of the individual, extreme diets bring on the opposite of binging; excessive asceticism provokes an indulgent reaction whereas extreme self-indulgence brings about regret, guilt and dis-ease. Anything that goes to extremes brings about its opposite and the turning point is invariably not smooth or harmonious.

The wise Taoist, on the other hand, is like the skilled and experienced skipper who goes about carefully, with forethought, preparation and caution avoiding the dangers of the rocks or becoming becalmed because one has gone too close to the headland. The goal is to live one's life elegantly with the minimum amount of turbulence, upheaval, mishap or violence. One wants to sail in calm waters making headway on one's path but not provoking misfortune by pushing one's life to the extreme.

We cannot travel on a straight and narrow highway; this is the false rigidity of a fundamentalist approach to life. We need a certain degree of latitude to learn, to grow, to make adjustments, to weave, to generate our own wave. A straight line is not a wave. Straight lines do not endure through time; they have no momentum; no internal energy to carry them forward.

We need to generate and harness the energy of the wave. The law of our being needs to express itself as a wave and for this it needs amplitude. It is in our best interest to achieve the optimum balance between too large an amplitude where we are wasting too much time in excessive oscillations and too small an amplitude where we have not given ourselves enough room to move and thus generate energy.

For example, a person who is following no fixed path or who is always changing their direction, path, intention or lacks character with no firm values or principles will create a zone that is too wide and thus wasteful in terms of energy and trajectory. On the other hand, a person who is too strict, too narrow in their outlook on life or lacks compassion, empathy and emotional intelligence will set up a narrow zone that does not facilitate growth or expediency.

This is the fundamental distinction between the classic religious philosophy of life that hands down a strict set of rules, laws or commandments by which we must live our lives with very little leeway, and Taoism which says we all create our own reality, we generate and set up our own wave, our own zone, our own trajectory according to the law of our own being. As we become better surfers of the Tao, we become more adept at designing this wave. In the final analysis, this is our fate and our destiny. It is our life and our choice, not something imposed from without but rather something designed by ourselves in harmony with who we are at our core.

This is not based upon blind faith or a co-dependent acceptance of an artificial and external code of conduct but rather a scientific, rational and logical understanding of how life works. It is based in experiential reality, but just as any elite surfer or athlete will know it is not just science; there is also the component of art. The master in any field, whether that be sports, art, music, science or any other discipline of life combines the skill of years of training with the intuitive overlay of flow.

The master practitioner always makes the effort look effortless; operates in that zone of being that, in fact, is now called the zone. But one does not automatically arrive at that zone without years of training. It has been scientifically quantified at 10,000 hours. Research shows that to become highly proficient in any field of human endeavour, we need to put in at least 10,000 hours' practice and training to reach that zone of artful elegance where the mastery takes over and the conscious mind gets out of the way.

We can see, even in the modern use of these words: the zone, the edge, extreme, the way, that humanity is fundamentally realising this opportunity for self-mastery in many areas of life. What we now need to realise is that we can adopt this framework, this model, this vehicle for life in general which is the whole rationale underlying the personal growth movement of positive psychology, personal training and living one's life optimally.

Taoism goes beyond this to the realm of spiritual supremacy: that we can indeed live our lives according to the law of our being, creating the optimum path for personal growth and self-development, generating our own wave within that zone that carries us along on its energy to achieve the life we want and to operate as a spiritual being at our personal best with no outside rules!

If we look again at current surfing world championships compared to 10 or 20 years ago, we see an extraordinary growth and development in the skill of the sport. Whereas originally the surfer merely rode the wave, we now witness the surfer riding up and down the face of the wave optimising the physical relationship between wave, surfer and board with the whole thing becoming much more fluid, acrobatic and artistic.

We can compare the old large wooden surf boards of 50 years ago, to the outmoded religions of the past. They fulfilled their function of carrying the surfer on the wave but lacked the finesse and flexibility afforded to a consummate surfer by modern lightweight fibreglass boards. Traditional religions did give us a moral vehicle to travel upon on our life journey, but they lacked individual flexibility fostering a one size fits all attitude depriving us of our innate inner wisdom. This was appropriate in the childhood and adolescence of humanity's evolution but no longer. We now need the flexibility of a medium or vehicle that allows us much more flexibility and personal ownership of our path.

Now this does not mean a lessening of personal responsibility or a dilution of a moral or ethical code of conduct. Quite to the contrary. As we adopt a more personal philosophy, the way becomes stricter in that we need to listen to and obey the dictates of our own being. In many ways, this is a lot harder than merely following an external set of rules for we need to be true to ourselves; we need to be in constant contact with the law of our being. This is the ultimate discipline! The highest good is being true to the self.

For there is no formula. There is no recipe. There are no rules. There are no gurus; no masters to follow. Each one of us needs to design our own path, to set our sails on our own tack, to understand the path we are on, to learn at any given time what is the permissible zone of variance, for this changes constantly with the weather of our lives. At times the zone narrows when we are in transition, danger or turbulent waters. At other times, we have broad lanes of smooth sailing when the force is with us and we need to make full use of the propitiousness of the time. At times, we do not know and need to tread carefully; and yet, at others, we need to be bold and take risks lest we lose the opportunity for action.

Taoism is not a passive philosophy of life and certainly does not preach pre-determinism. It holds us individually and totally responsible for creating our own reality in this world by being astute and responsive to the demands of the time, by constantly listening and adjusting to the prevailing forces, just as the master surfer must continually adjust to ride the wave. In Taoism, we are co-creators with the universe. It is our spiritual challenge to align our individual personal wave or Tao with the Universal Tao. This is how we align our fate, our destiny and generate good fortune, optimum outcomes for personal well-being, health, happiness, freedom and prosperity. Personal success here on earth is both the goal and the reward for mastering this skill and developing one's own pathway.

If we go too far and cross the line of demarcation between lanes that signifies the extreme point, then the universe pushes us back onto our path, not because we are wrong, malevolent or bad people but precisely because we are going the wrong way, just as another motorist in an adjoining lane will toot us to warn us that we are wandering and in danger of collision. Collision, resistance, misfortune are not punishments but merely signals that we have gone too far, are outside our lane or pathway and are in danger of going the wrong way for us.

This is not per some arbitrary external set of rules but according to the optimum path we have set up. Permissible zones of variance are not artificial constructs or religious precepts; neither are they prescriptive laws we must follow under pain of sin. They are rather the extreme points or nodes of the personal wave we have set up and are on. If we go beyond this extreme point, we will no longer be on our path and forfeit the energy-wave inherent in our trajectory and will need to generate a new wave. This is akin to the surfer falling off the wave. The energy of the wave will no longer carry the board or surfer along.

We see this often in life when we take the wrong turn, break someone's trust or make a really stupid decision that causes us to lose our momentum. Or we may become totally self-indulgent losing ourselves in distraction, desire or negativity and fall off our path. In Taoist terms, calamity and severe misfortune whether personal, financial or ill-health are the natural consequences of going beyond the extreme node point, crossing the line and leaving our designated lane. We even refer to people as going too far, crossing the line, betraying our trust or confidence. We have all witnessed people on self-destructive benders that last too long and end up destroying their reality. These people need to start again to rebuild their lives including the trust, friendship and confidence of those around them.

We all have a path - a way that is appropriate for us. That path expresses itself as a wave that has a specific amplitude and frequency. That amplitude is the distance between the midpoint and the extremity of the wave. Once we go beyond that point we are no longer on our wave and forfeit the carrier energy of that wave: our reality collapses. Like any surfer, we need to get back on our board, swim back out to where the waves are breaking and get on another wave. In life, this is misfortune! We have forfeited the favourableness of the situation.

It is essential to grasp the significance of permissible zones of variance, understand how they work and become adept at both designing an optimum amplitude to achieve your objectives plus recognise the absolute amplitude you are in at any given point in time. To become a master surfer of the Tao this is a necessary and requisite skill.

Chapter 7

Composite Waves

To really understand and master this skill we need to return to wave theory, particularly how two or more waves intersect and become a composite wave as this is the essential way to change amplitude. An important characteristic or property of waves is their ability to combine with other waves which can be either constructive or destructive. Two or more waves can come together constructively to generate a composite wave of higher amplitude. In other words, the energies of the two waves are said to be in phase and thus augment each other building a stronger wave with more energy.

On the other hand, the original waves may be out of phase and thus lead to a composite wave that has less energy and less amplitude. In this case the original waves compete with or negate each other. We have all experienced this in life where two or more people can come together, and their energies combine synergistically to achieve more than the sum of the parts. Two people working harmoniously together can usually achieve more than double the work. On the other hand, if people are in conflict or discord, their combined energy will be destructive and produce less output.

If two original waves both have an amplitude of X and are in phase the resultant composite wave will have an amplitude of 2X. If the two waves are out of sync, then the two amplitudes will counter-affect each other neutralising the resultant wave to zero.

It is important to realise that we do generate our own waves with our inner intention and the law of our being. However, if I set up conflicting intentions that generate waves that are out of phase with each other, the resulting composite wave will have a weak amplitude and result in a weak manifested reality. If on the other hand, my inner intentions are harmoniously aligned the resultant generated waves will combine to produce a composite wave with more energy and thus greater amplitude. This will manifest a stronger reality.

It is obviously advantageous to learn and master this technique of generating positive harmonious waves that are in phase and that do not counterbalance each other out of existence. The simplest way to view this is to understand that all thoughts and emotions are waves going out into the ether or universe that generate our future. Moreover, all thoughts and emotions are either positive or negative and thus generate either positive or negative waves. Positive waves will combine to produce a positive wave of higher amplitude; negative waves will combine to produce a wave of a higher negative amplitude and positive and negative waves will tend to cancel each other out.

Let's say I want to manifest a life partner and put out to the universe via desire, thought and affirmation that I want a loving partner; but let's also say I have an inner fear of intimacy and being hurt or disappointed. I have set up a positive wave of expectation and a negative wave of fear and anxiety. Moreover, as the first wave succeeds bringing me closer to my desired goal of personal intimacy, my second wave of fear will become stronger and thus potentially jeopardise my chances of success.

I have created conflicting waves that are out of phase and will eventually neutralise each other. When the attempt at intimacy finally fails because of these countervailing waves, the second wave of inner distrust and disappointment will be reinforced with a greater amplitude and my primary wave of expectation of success will decrease. Over time the negative wave will win out.

This is why many people who experiment with affirmations actually end up with the opposite of what they intend because they have not done the inner work of personal processing to uncover and dismantle the potency of the negative emotion which eventually sabotages the primary good or positive intention or desire.

Similarly, many people cannot make up their minds decisively as to what they truly want to do, which path they want to follow. It could be as simple a decision as the purchase of piece of clothing or as complex as a career path or job. If we cannot make up our minds, ruthlessly and unequivocally, oscillating between two opposing choices or alternatives, we may secretly put out to the universe that we want both and want the universe to decide for us or we may just be unable to choose.

This will also result in two waves that counterbalance each other resulting in weak manifestation: we may lose both options because we did not choose decisively setting out a clear intention and thus generating one strong wave with high amplitude. Or we may manifest one but be riddled with self-doubt as to whether we made the right choice thus setting up a third negative wave after the fact. This negative wave will diminish the power and amplitude of the primary intentional wave.

It is essential to realise that wave theory rules our lives! Waves are scientific facts of life and the universe. They are impersonal and absolute. They function according to wave theory. We need to master this theory if we would master our lives. As human beings, we possess biological bodies and need to follow the laws of life intended for our physical bodies: food, water, rest, sleep, shelter and so on. As incarnate beings on planet earth, we equally need to follow the laws of manifestation to generate and create a life that is harmonious, successful and to our design.

We have emphasised that waves are the fundamental building blocks and messenger-medium of the universe. Waves are the way life and the universe work. To become successful at life we need to successfully master generating positive and harmonious composite waves. Taoism is not an arcane and academic book learning; it is a living philosophy of life that enables us to live our lives successfully. As we become more adept at riding the cosmic waves of creation, our lives become easier, more successful and more enjoyable. We manifest what we want without effort! We ride the greater cosmic waves to success and life becomes fun. There is far less angst, fear and anxiety.

There are two essential ingredients to this success: focus or single mindedness and understanding how to harmonise composite waves. In many ways, these are polar opposites on the yin/yang continuum. Yang is the centripetal force of contraction: the primary masculine principle of Heaven, the Creative – firm and strong intention, unyielding: that ability to decide on a certain path and stay focused on that path and outcome without wavering, without getting distracted or side-tracked. Highly successful people have this single mindedness.

Moreover, meditation, martial arts, elite sports, professional dance and drama and being at the top in any field of endeavour requires this single-minded dedication and passion. Truly successful people have that rare ability to both discern what they truly want and possess the personal discipline to renounce or sacrifice other pursuits and paths that distract from that focus.

This ability to stay focused is a necessary prerequisite of success and an application of the yang principle. However, as in all things, if we go to extremes, if we become overly fixated, rigid and obsessed with that single focus, we often lose sight of the greater beauty of life. Too often, high achievers do not enjoy a harmonious and balanced life sharing their success and joy with their loved ones. Many forsake love and joy for this single-minded focus on success. Focus is not obsession! To become obsessive is to cross the yang boundary or node point and thus forfeit the yang energy.

Life is never simple and certainly not unitary. As complex beings, we all have many conflicting desires and intentions; we are made up of many parts. Indeed, the beauty of life is intricately woven into its tapestry. Truly successful people do not live lives that are only focused on one objective; they have that ability to enrich their lives by enjoying the banquet that life presents before them.

The ability to be a multi-dimensional being is essential to true spiritual success; we need to be able to harmonise the conflicting pressures and paths of our lives into one cohesive whole. We thus also need to master the centrifugal force of yin which allows us to gain a broader perspective, to create rich and varied lives that encompass health, wealth, family, career, sports and hobbies and whatever else makes up the tapestry of our lives. Truly successful people prioritise these many and varied aspects of their lives determining when and how much to focus on each giving each sector its due attention and focus without becoming lost or distracted. Unsuccessful people, on the other hand, seem to lurch from one desire or path to another without ever achieving any true success in any endeavour. Jack of all trades; master of none.

This is where the yin force is allowed to go to extremes and one is forever tossed hither and thither by one's conflicting emotions, desires and distractions. One does not possess that central force of unity and strength that enables one to harmonise the waves. The waves one generates are out of phase cancelling each other out resulting in weak manifestation and a life of turbulence. One is no longer in control but allows the winds of fate to carry one's life along. Candle in the wind! Many people welcome this distraction or diversion precisely because they do not really know what they want and secretly hope life will somehow lead them along the right path finding their good fortune via some magical serendipity. Synchronicity and serendipity are not the same thing!

Once again, we see this essential need to balance and harmonise the polar extremes of yin and yang if we would generate and ride the wave, the chi, the path of our Tao successfully. If one goes too far into the pole of contraction, one's life becomes overly fixated and narrow, often ending in a dead end when that particular phase or cycle comes to completion as it must. If we have put all our focus and attention into merely one aspect of our lives, we are robbing our lives of the beauty and joy of a well-rounded holistic life. If we allow ourselves to be carried by the currents of the wind, we are blown all over the place and end up frustrated and bitter because we have achieved nothing of significance.

Both extremes lead eventually to emptiness. Only by successfully mastering this opposition and learning how to generate composite waves that are in sync and phase can we enjoy the fruits of a life that is rich, full and varied. Composite waves are a fundamental aspect of being human more than any other animal. It is what makes us human. We do not live to merely eat or survive. We do not live to eke out an existence. Abraham Maslow's Hierarchy of Needs points to the divine complexity and beauty of the human condition.

Moreover, we want and need different things at different times and everything has its season. Whether we use the time cycle of a lifetime, decades, years, months, weeks or days there are always cycles within cycles and seasons within seasons. These cycles are of themselves waves within our fate and destiny and we need to learn to harmonise our creative output with the demands of the time. Time is an essential variable or instrument in the Taoist's arsenal. As we live our lives and evolve through our personal cycles, it is essential that the waves we are generating change according to the time and our personal evolution.

What we want and desire as a child, as a teenager, as a young adult with a young family of our own and as an elder of the tribe are hopefully all different. To be stuck in adolescence or childhood never moving into emotional maturity is a very sad indictment of a life not well lived. Our lives change and so too do our desires, hopes and dreams and what we want to create with our lives. Thus, the waves we are generating are in a constant state of evolution and progress. Moreover, as we are successful in life realising our inner dreams and desires and bringing them into fruition, we necessarily move onto greener pastures. It is only the unsuccessful who are continually caught in unrealised and frustrated time loops.

It is not just that we want to harmonise the composite waves of our lives at any given point in time but that we also want their generative power to kick in and manifest sequentially. A truly successful person will know and anticipate the ending of a major life cycle and will commence the intention and generation of their next cycle way before that end comes, so one is not left stranded on the beach like a whale. Understanding composite wave structures, cycles, amplitudes and rhythms is an extreme skill that can only be learnt through the trial and error of living our lives with attention: paying attention to our inner most thoughts, desires, wants and intentions and then watching how those waves manifest in the reality of our daily lives.

Most religious doctrine places the individual in a co-dependent and subservient position relative to the Creative force whatever form that takes whether that be the Christian God in Heaven, the Buddhist and Hindu gods of the East or the Allah of Islam. All posit some form of pre-determinism where the individual is beholden to the Godhead for his or her salvation and the execution of their lives.

On the other hand, Taoism is extremely modern and applicable to the current evolution of humanity in that it stresses and teaches that it is the individual's own efforts that determine their reality. Life is not happenstance but is an art and a science that must be learnt and mastered. Indeed, the whole purpose of life is mastering this process so that one can consciously create the life that one wants – this is eventually the only definition of success that makes sense.

My life must be authentic. It must be truly my own personal creation not according to my upbringing, background, tradition or heritage. Not according to what someone else wants for me but according to my own innermost truth: what is right for me according to the law of my being, my Tao.

It is this law that dictates my being. It is this law that manifests as my destiny, my fate, my karma. The closer I can align my destiny and fate with my self-generated waves the better. It is not just a matter of harmonising the composite waves of my own creation but more importantly of learning how to harmonise my own consciously generated waves with that of my own personal Tao. We will return to this all-important skill later but merely need to introduce the concept now as an essential function of composite wave theory.

What is essential to grasp at this point is that human beings are a complex mix of conflicting thoughts, emotions, desires and intention and these various factors go out into the universe as diverse waves. If there is no attempt to coordinate these diverse emanating waves our resultant composite wave will lack strength, amplitude and cohesion causing confusion and weakness in our outer lives. To create a truly successful life we need to acknowledge and master the focusing force of yang and the embracing force of yin to weave a rich tapestry that encompasses all aspects of life that are important to us as individuals. Using the analogy of a beautiful rug or tapestry we need both the horizontal and vertical axes to create the picture.

Moreover, once skilled, we can consciously coordinate these disparate waves to generate a much stronger composite. For example, if we have no work-life balance, focusing all of our energy and attention on our career, we will become exhausted and alienate the loved ones in our lives. This will eventually cause our work life to fall apart as we will lose touch with our essential humanity ignoring other people and becoming overly fixated and arrogant.

If, on the other hand, we set up harmonious waves for work, family, recreation, personal growth, leisure and so on, we will enjoy a more balanced and harmonious life furthering our success in each of these essential aspects of life, being able to achieve more without either exhausting ourselves or becoming alienated from others.

This is not revolutionary and is self-evident but how many of us truly possess the scientific knowledge of how to do this well without sacrificing one for the other. Sometimes, we merely oscillate, putting all of our attention into one – say work – for a period and then focusing on another – say family – when disaster demands it. This is a result of going to the extreme and crossing the line of permissible zone of variance. The wall or line of demarcation forces us back into our lane just like the honking horn of our fellow motorist or the complaints of our spouse. We have gone too far, and our Tao forces us back onto our path, onto our wave but we have lost momentum, and it is a very clumsy way to live.

Those people who enjoy a fulfilling career path, a loving family, a healthy sport or activity and a passionate hobby live rich and rewarding lives where the energy from one aspect fuels and augments the others. I work hard because of my family; I enjoy my time with my family because I have a fulfilling career. I am able to focus on my work while at work but focus on my sport or hobby when I am away from work. Thus, rest and activity become complementary. Invariably, health, wealth and happiness come from an accurate allocation of time, energy and attention between the competing yet complimentary components of a successful life.

Essentially this comes from learning to ride the wave of our life, successfully balancing the polar opposites of yin and yang.

Part II

The Attunement Process

Chapter 8

The continuum of time and space

One of the more complex of these polar extremes to understand is the time space continuum. We would not normally consider these to be polar opposites or even part of the same continuum as we would for hot and cold, up and down, male and female, dry and wet and so on. But Einstein's theory of relativity depicts a new way of looking at the physical universe where the old absolute concepts of time and space as distinct and separate properties are replaced by the continuum of what has become known as spacetime. Einstein unified space and time and made them relative to each other like all the other yin/yang polarities. Space and time became extreme node points of one continuum that curved and folded about itself.

This is the now famous Theory of Relativity where the entire physical universe was viewed as relative with the space/time continuum forming the boundaries, but within those boundaries human consciousness still sees time and space as absolute and distinct identities. Nowhere do the ancient concepts of Taoism and the modern concepts of nuclear science merge more than in quantum physics, relativity theory, the unified theory, string theory etc.

Einstein himself had a keen sense of the mystical and unknowable nature of the universe but insisted that eventually the human mind would decipher these at present contradictory aspects of creation. Indeed, many scientists at the forefront of Quantum Theory, Chaos Theory and Relativity Theory eventually turn to ancient spiritual texts to explain the workings of the universe as the outcomes of these theories paint a picture of reality that is both bizarre and strange to normal human consciousness and that the nature of the universe is still a long way from being understood by the rational mind.

But whether we do understand it or not, we do all live within the continuum of space and time and time has become our chief nemesis in this fast paced, time poor, modern world. We all complain we simply do not have enough time! We all perceive time as speeding up. We all seem to live in a world that is going increasingly faster with us getting left further behind. No matter what age, occupation, country or demography, this is now a planetary phenomenon. Could it be, as Einstein predicted, that the speed of time has indeed changed and that we merely need to adapt?

If we examine the concept of the calendar itself, we can immediately see that time or more accurately the human measurement of time is not so fixed at all. Calendars fall roughly into three main types: solar, lunar and lunisolar. The modern western Gregorian calendar is solar, whereas Buddhist and Islamic calendars are lunar. Wikipedia lists over 50 different types of calendars dating back to prehistoric times with varying lengths for years, months and weeks.

Yet, we all assume there are 24 hours in a day and that at least this is a constant. But apparently, this is not so either. There is a difference between what is called sun time and clock time. Sun time is based on the cycle from the highest point the sun reaches from one day to the next. However, this is not always 24 hours exactly. At different times of the year, it varies 15 minutes either way giving a total variation of half an hour! Another complicating factor is the Precession of the Equinoxes, which is the gradual movement of the Earth's rotational axis in a circle relative to the stars once every 26,000 years.

Hence, we can see that time is not as absolute as we would like to imagine. Moreover, psychologically we have all experienced episodes where time seems to have stood still while waiting for some important event or news or alternatively has speeded up when excited. There are also periods when time just does not exist, and we seem to exist outside of the continuum. Time is therefore relative and not absolute. One of the core attributes of flow as testified by many is this apparent stepping outside of time as one becomes one with the task. One is no longer within the human clock but transfixed by the intense focus and identification with what one is doing. The flow participant is freed from the tyranny of time. This is also the essence of zen meditation – a freeing of the spirit.

Moreover, time should be our servant and not our master. As we have all become time-poor, humanity does seem to be at the beck and call of time rather than the other way around. *'I do not have enough time'* is a statement of this predicament as if time is something we do or do not have enough of. It is undoubtedly true that time is a rare and precious commodity and that we need to consciously become more aware of our personal use of time and more responsible. But we do have all the time in the world to achieve whatever it is we so desire if we understand the true nature of time and particularly how to integrate it into our wave theory of reality.

Like Einstein's theory of relativity, it is all relative to the way we think!

Thought is a process in time. Thinking is electro-neurological activity in the brain. It takes time to think. The perception of time is relative to the speed of thought. Once we become agitated, fearful or restless and lose our inner composure, time definitely speeds up. Once we return to inner peace, tranquillity and stillness we seem to regain time again. Time and perspective are another of these inner continuums.

We do live within the space/time continuum, and we do need to learn to ride this wave like all the others. Waves move through space and time. Indeed, one could say that the movement of the wave through space is time. As mentioned, we speak of stars and galaxies being many millions of light years away and use this time as a measure of that vast distance.

The gift of life is the gift of time. We are given a certain amount of time on planet Earth: to be incarnate physically on the Earth. We are all aware of this passage of time as we grow, mature and eventually die. Ultimately, death is nothing more than the cessation of that passage of time – we have run out of time on this planet. This is where the concept of not having enough time comes from: what we would like to achieve or experience before we die; the proverbial bucket list!

Yet, it is all a trick of the mind. Meditation is the stopping of thought and thus the cessation of time, particularly the past. Past, present and future are also concepts in time; not time as measured by the clock so much as time measured by the passage of our lives. When time becomes our master, rather than our servant, we spend most of our precious time lamenting the past and fearing the future.

We dwell on the past, going over and over in our minds rerunning the movie or thinking how we could or should have done things differently: '*if only I had of......*'

Memory is a function of the past whereas imagination is a function of the future. Life is a function of the present. All meditation and mindfulness techniques ultimately break down to living in the here and now: being present in the eternal Now. It is only in this present tense that life exists. Modern man spends far too much mental time or thinking in either the past or the future and ignores or wastes the precious present.

When we say, time is precious what we really mean is life is precious and we can only live life in the present. That is not to say one should not reflect on the past to learn nor imagine the future to create one's life the way one would like it to be. After all this is precisely how we generate the wave. But these need to become highly disciplined mental activities directed and regulated by the higher conscious mind.

To truly live our lives successfully, we need to engage both our faculties for reflection and introspection and our propensity for positive imagination, but this is certainly not wishful or fearful thinking nor dwelling on the past in some vainglorious attempt to change it. The only way to ride the wave of the space/time continuum is to be at their intersection point which is the present. It is precisely this intersection that is the point of personal power from which one generates one's future reality.

The secret of mastering time is to truly live in the present moment, totally aware and fully conscious of what is occurring now. Not to have sections of our consciousness, our awareness, locked in either the past or the future. We can change the past by learning from it; we can create the future by moving solidly on our path. If we are truly on our path there is nothing to fear; there is no need for anxiety, apprehension or impatience. If we are truly on our path, there is nothing to regret. It is all a part of the process and necessary to get us to where we are Now.

We live within the security and sanctity of our own Tao. In this way time becomes our ally, our tool, our instrument and our friend. We use time wisely to move forward carefully to achieve and manifest our lives. We stay on the wave of our reality. Just like the surfer, we cannot move faster than the wave nor can we get left behind. The trick to surfing is staying on the face of the wave; keeping up with its pace and momentum; not getting dumped by moving too far forward or getting left behind by moving too far back.

It is exactly the same with one's life, one's wave, one's Tao. We must learn to keep abreast of our destiny and our fate. We cannot pre-empt it by moving forward prematurely through impatience and restlessness nor can we get caught up in fear, doubt and anxiety and miss the crucial moment of action. We do need to seize the day, but we need to ensure that day is ours!

It is the harmony of this movement, the alignment of one's effort or output with the energy of the wave that is the mastery of time. One uses time to make actual what is potential; one understands the function of time and thus masters it.

> 'Here is shown that the way to success lies in apprehending and giving actuality to the way of the universe (the Tao), which as a law running through end and beginning, brings about all phenomena in time. Thus, each step attained forthwith becomes a preparation for the next. Time is no longer a hindrance but the means of making actual what is potential.'

In simple terms, what this really means is that there is a natural rhythm or tempo to our lives – this is the wave of our Tao, the law of our being. But as in all things, this rhythm or tempo is not always the same. Just as there are seasons within nature, there are various seasons within our lives. The pace or frequency of the wave is not always the same; it speeds up and slows down. There are cycles of activity and rest, there are cycles of achievement and reflection. There are times to wait and other times to act. There are times of danger that require caution and times of clear sailing when it behests one to make the most of the propitiousness of the time.

The only constant in the universe is change and as any surfer knows only too well, the waves do not come consistently, nor are they all the same size. Indeed, some break smoothly and some dump! In our lives, we need to be able to wait for the right opportunity to act. If we move prematurely, we will be dumped. If we hesitate when the time of action has arrived, we will see the wave move on without us. In both cases, we forfeit the energy and momentum of the wave.

Thus, time is no longer an academic or absolute measure of interval. It is a living thing and like all living things relative and has a rhythm of its own. Mastering time means coming to know one's own destiny; consolidating one's fate on a firm footing; being at one with one's Tao, riding the wave. Mastering time is mastering the relationship between one's daily reality in the here and now and the unseen wave or energy of one's Tao. In this way time becomes the surfboard that one rides into the future.

Another way of viewing this is the analogy of a stairway. One is reminded of that song: '*she's building a stairway to heaven*'. Time becomes that stairway. We need to climb one step at a time ensuring we do not skip any crucial stages nor get stuck halfway up. Time becomes the ladder of one's life upon which we climb. One is also reminded of the children's game of snakes and ladders. How many of us climb the ladder only to slide down the snake before reaching our objective? The essential point to grasp is that one's understanding and thus perception of time needs to drastically alter from an externally imposed and thus arbitrary phenomena, over which one has little or no control, to a malleable tool or instrument at one's disposal.

However, as in all tools, if we do not know how to employ or use them, we are unlikely to achieve our objective and quite likely to get hurt. Time has become humanity's nemesis precisely because we have lost control of its use. We no longer know how to use and master time. Time is no longer our ally but our foe. As we clutter our lives with more and more conflicting desires and distractions; as we spend more and more time dwelling in the past or anticipating the future; as we lose the ability to focus in the present, in the here and now, and become scattered in too many diverse directions, we fall off our wave and forfeit its momentum. We have lost our way; our energy and time is no longer with us.

On some inner level we are aware of this estrangement and feel that time has become our foe precisely because we are no longer in alignment with our destiny. We are no longer climbing that stairway to heaven but slipping down the slippery slope of the snake. We are all aware when we get lost or distracted. We all know when we waste time whether that be merely hours or days or a complete lifetime. We all know when we are estranged from the law of our being. We feel vulnerable, alone, at odds with our selves. There is something wrong even though many of us are not aware enough to put our finger on it. But nonetheless there is this pervading sense of unease which eventually becomes dis-ease.

The adept Taoist sage or surfer develops a highly attuned sense of this alignment and knows the first imperceptible signs of divergence; they do not wait to fall off the wave but adjust immediately. They do not wait to ram the wall of permissible zone of variance or push their reality to extreme but ride their wave carefully, constantly adjusting, adapting to the nuances of time. Time is the medium of the message. In Marshall McLuhan terms, the medium does indeed become the message; another yin/yang continuum of medium and message. In Taoist terms, this is called the meaning of the time and it is the highest skill and art of the Taoist to be able to read this message and adjust to the demands of the time.

Time does indeed become one's ally in that it brings one the message of what is happening in one's external daily reality. Whether we like it or not no man is an island; there are always other influences operating in one's life. It is the ability to negotiate these influences wisely and correctly that bestow good fortune or misfortune. Misfortune is not a punishment for our sins or some form of bad karma but rather a misreading of the message; a maladaptation to the movement of the wave.

The I Ching or Book of Changes is composed of 64 hexagrams with 6 lines (thus the word hexagram) in each hexagram. Each hexagram describes a particular chapter, epoch or time in our lives. Each of the individual lines within a hexagram then describes the flow or movement of the chi or Tao through that particular life situation which is described by the hexagram. Thus, there are 64 x 6 or 384 distinct and specific time situations or zones that one encounters along the way and each of these situations has an appropriate response to most wisely deal with the situation presented if one wishes to remain within the zone of flow.

As we become more adept at facing life and interpreting the meaning of the time or being able to read the message, our innate ability to flow improves. There are times of peace and times of standstill; there are harmonious times and discordant times; there are times of progress and times of regression; there are times for patience and times for courageous action; there are times of intimacy and times of estrangement. All the nuances of life are described, plus the best way to deal with the meaning of that particular time or set of circumstances.

Change is the message of time and time is the medium of that message. How we adjust and adapt to that change determines the relative peace or calamity we face in our lives. But one message is loud and clear: it is pointless going against one's fate. It is folly to fight against the inner flow of one's destiny. One needs to ride the waves and not get dumped and lost in the white water. Our success in riding the flow of our wave determines our ability to operate in the peak performance of flow.

The I Ching is a totally radical depiction of the movement of time; not as in a calendar or a clock but as a barometer of the meaning of the passage of time; exactly what situation does one find oneself in at any given moment. It is the relevant chapter in the story of one's life that is important; not the chronology of the clock. Just as a wine connoisseur can tell the date, time and place of a particular wine from its bouquet, taste and appearance or an antiquarian can pinpoint the maker and place of origin of an *objet d'art,* the Taoist sees the moment of the time as a unique set of circumstances leading to the meaning of that moment. Time is viewed as the movement of the Tao, the flow of the wave.

We have become so psychologically trapped by our conventional measurement of time: the date on a calendar or the hour of a day that we forget to view time as the movement of our lives. When we ask what time is it, we always answer with a chronological definition rather than a psychic perspective. It is 2pm on Tuesday the 8th of March 2022 for example, rather than a time for reflection or a time for consolidation. We no longer examine where we are right now on our wave and thus ignore the beauty of the journey. We totally miss what is going on now because we are transfixed by getting somewhere by such and such a time. Thus, the clock has taken over our lives, particularly the 9 to 5 work clock.

Each and every moment in time is the juxtaposition and interdependence of both external objective events and inner subjective psychic states of being. It is the ability to match, harmonise and synchronise these two states that is the key to a prosperous and beneficial life, to being in the zone. The one is the outer state or situation confronting the individual; the other is one's inner psychological state of being.

This state, space or attitude is viewed as being all-important. If we approach a given situation or set of circumstances with the wrong attitude, we will fail to meet it appropriately. The goal is to adjust one's stance, viewpoint, position and attitude to match and mirror the prevailing external forces, just as the surfer must adjust their physical stance and posture to match the prevailing forces of wind, wave and water.

One's state of being is viewed as one's adjustment to the external life situation. The reason it is called the Book of Changes highlights that the crux of the adjustment is not to get overly fixated with any specific set of circumstance or detail but to view its movement through time. One is not concerned with the transitory but with the eternal law operating beneath the surface. Change is not viewed as something chaotic, happenstance or meaningless and thus dangerous to be feared, but rather as a meaningful and connected whole. Change is the expression of the eternal law of the Tao. It is our job to understand that whole. What exactly is going on in our daily lives from a spiritual, larger picture perspective.

What happens in our external daily lives is a projection, image or out-picture of inner psychic processes or states of being that precede this reality. Just as in quantum physics, the mind or expectation of the scientist influences the eventual outcome of the experiment, our inner psychic states influence the changing landscape of our lives. In some way, the outer is an image of the inner projected onto the screen of daily reality. The means of this projection is time, just as the projector at the theatre is the means to project the movie onto the screen.

Think about an old-fashioned reel in a movie theatre. The moving picture is really a set of stills shot sequentially one after the other on the magnetic tape. As these stills are projected in time at a certain speed, they form the moving picture on the screen. In the same way, we set up images in our minds. These images or projections exist within our imagination first and then out-picture on the screen of our lives. The medium by which this is achieved is the vehicle of time. Time becomes the vehicle whereby the potential within becomes the actual without.

As we become more adept at mastering time, we master the process of manifestation; we become better at manifesting the life of our dreams. But we still need to adjust to the mechanics of time. Things evolve. Things happen sequentially. We need to keep pace with the rhythm and tempo of our own creation depending on the strength or amplitude of our generated waves. It is only by engaging honestly with the reality we have created that we can become cognisant of what lies within.

If we view time as a foe to be battled, if we believe we do not possess enough time or that time is against us, then quite obviously, this mechanism of manifestation will be disturbed and diluted. We will be generating an interference pattern that will lessen the phase or amplitude of the resultant composite wave. Our manifestation ability will be thwarted by our anxiety.

The significant point to realise about all this is that in this philosophy of life, we do indeed create our own reality by our own personal efforts, output and psyche. Thus, time becomes a tool or instrument of that creation. In all other traditional philosophies of life, one is to some extent the victim or at the behest of superior external forces whether that be God, the Devil, or any number of other religious deities that exist around the planet. Almost all cultures and peoples have their own version of an external deity or force that controls our personal life and destiny.

In this sense, we live in a cued universe where some other, external power, exerts an invisible influence on our life journey. Time is not a vehicle we are in control of. It is like being a passenger in a car being driven by someone else: we are not in control of the vehicle. This facilitates and furthers this feeling of being a victim to time or that we do not possess enough time. Historically, what has happened is that the self is no longer the master of time and time has become the enemy because it is viewed as being in control.

Once we regain control of our destiny and our lives, we regain control of time as an ally, a friend, a tool and an instrument by which we do create the future of our lives. But the point of power is in the present – not in either the past or the future. We must be centred in the now, totally alive, alert and aware in the present tense to be able to fully take control of the vehicle. It is much like driving. We must keep our hands on the wheel and steer the car even if we do have it on cruise control. We must be alert and not fall asleep. We must maintain vigilance and remain alert to the conditions of the road as well as the behaviour of those other drivers on the road. If we fall asleep, even for a microsecond, we forfeit that control and inevitably have an accident.

It is significant that all experiencers of flow state this as one of its overriding characteristics.

In Taoism timing is everything. We must maintain vigilance and be mindful of the conditions of the time. We must adjust constantly to those conditions moving in harmony with the chi or flow of the wave that is our personal Tao. The vehicle is this intricate interrelationship between the self and the movement of the wave not unlike the synchronicity that must exist between surfer, surfboard and wave. All 3 elements exist in a continuum, a delicate dance of being. This is the vehicle of our destiny.

The wave has the origin or source of its power in the past just as any wave upon the ocean is created by terrestrial forces of the past be they tide, storm or tempest. We sit in the present on the crest of the wave aligned with that power which takes us into the future. There is this continuum between past present and future. If we spend too much time dwelling on the past or anticipating the future (worry, lament or fear) we forfeit the power inherent in the point of now. The more we worry about the future, the less personal power we possess to determine it. We fall into being the victim of time and not its master.

It is interesting that in one sense we all have the same amount of time – 24 hours in a day, but what we do with that time varies immensely from person to person. It is abundantly clear that different people achieve enormously different outcomes with the same amount of time, so it is this interrelationship between the individual and time that is of the essence.

We all seek success. We all want wealth, prosperity, health and happiness. We all want what is best for our lives and there are an infinite array of formulae and recipes to achieve that success however one defines it. What is essential is how we live our lives on a daily basis. The day is the ultimate unit of time in that it is discrete and begins and ends with the movement into and out from sleep. We cannot not sleep – it is an essential part of life and ingredient of healthy living. The day becomes our finite unit of measure. We either use each day to build our lives or we waste it. The saying *carpe diem* – seize the day, emphasises this truth.

If one is walking all one can do is to put one foot in front of the other; the step becomes the definitive measure of distance, hence the original measure of distance being the foot or 12 inches which came from the Roman army's march through Europe. The 'foot' was the average size of a soldier's foot. We just take one step at a time. The longest journey begins with a single step!

So too, one lives one's life one day at a time and it is this appreciation and perception of the preciousness of the day that seems to be the primary determinant of success. Successful people fully utilise the day. Unsuccessful people tend to waste it. Each and every day is precious and essential. Even if one is having the day off, it is essential to relax and really optimise one's use of that time to recharge, recuperate and reenergise.

As any surfer knows, you can only ride one wave at a time and ride that wave for its duration or until you decide to turn off it (assuming you do not lose balance and fall off). Similarly, the day is the discrete wave we ride in our lives. How often do we thank God when we get into bed and go to sleep especially after a long and hard day? Sleep brings a finality and an end point, a natural mark or measure of completion to the tempo of time more than any other measure (hour, week, month, year etc.) Similarly, the Christmas-New Year period signifies the ending and beginning of the yearly cycle which also marks the rhythm of time.

If one would master the manifestation process and make time an instrument of one's biding, one must master the day as the vehicle and measure of time. Just as one can only take one step at a time, one can only live one's life one day at a time and truly optimise each and every day. In that way one does secure one's future and one's success.

The Tao of one's life, one's personal wave manifests in one's day. So, the self only needs to examine today to ascertain how one's life is working. In this sense, it does become incredibly simple. We waste far too much energy looking at the big picture of our lives and not focusing on the important step of the day. If today is successful; if one lives a meaningful, enjoyable and successful day, then one's life will be successful. If today is confused, chaotic, haphazard and fraught with accident, one's life will not be successful.

We return to the concept of permissible zones of variance. If one stays within one's lane, driving conscientiously and safely, it is unlikely one will have an accident. If one is wandering all over the place it is only a matter of time before a collision occurs. Of course, all this presupposes that one is on the right track, that one is on the right road going in the right direction for even if one travels safely, living one's life one day at a time but going in the wrong direction, one will not achieve success or arrive at one's destination.

Different people experience the day differently. We all have good and bad days. We all have days when we achieve a lot and other days when we look back and do not seem to have achieved anything at all. It is said the most productive day is the day before going on vacation because of its finality. Taking time and the day for granted seem to be the biggest danger. One does need to seize the day with both hands and ride that wave to its optimum.

Every surfer knows that the surf is different every single day. One just needs to go check it out. Every Taoist knows the wave of one's life is different every single day and needs to be ridden differently depending on its nature and the conditions of the time. Time becomes not only the vehicle but also the messenger. Time tells us what is going on. If we are alert, aware, awake and sensitive to the conditions of the time we will be receptive to the nuances of our personal Tao. Every day is new. Every day is original. Every day is an opportunity to ride the wave of one's life.

We need to plan our day. We need to begin each day with awe and reverence for the great gift that life is. We need to end each day with gratitude. This is real religion. This is that truly religious attitude to life – not a belief in a mythological being who has power over us but a deeply appreciative and devout emotion that connects us with the gift of life; a religious awe in the face of eternity, an awakening of the perception of the common origin of all beings, an awareness of the Oneness of Creation. In the end this is the only definition of God that makes sense.

Religion can no longer be confined to the church or mosque or synagogue or temple of whatever nature or definition. Religion must be a sincere appreciation of the sacredness and interconnectedness of all life and all living beings. It cannot be sectarian or factional. It cannot condone killing or jihad of whatever nature. It must connect us deeply with the well-spring of life, the divine sacredness of existence. Each day must be sacred and lived as the divine gift that it is.

In the final analysis, it is our own personal relationship with our own life that is important and that is the key to our destiny and our fate. It is this relationship that determines our personal Tao or path. It is whether we resist that path through denial, through excuse and justification or whether we accept our fate, our destiny and arrive at a oneness with the flow of its being. In this oneness, there is that peace that passes understanding that all religions talk about. There is a contentment and a centeredness. In Taoist terms, we are what is called central and correct. In surfing parlance, we are on our board, on the wave and riding it successfully. All forces are in balance and harmony.

We can either vaingloriously try to swim upstream or go with the flow. It is an entirely personal choice and a choice that must be made every single day when we first emerge from sleep and regain consciousness of the day. It is in that transition from sleep and the dream world into the light of early morning that we establish our relationship with the day. In that moment is the seed of all that is to follow. We either allow the brain to be distracted by the innumerable impressions that flow in from the world – the hustle and bustle of daily life, or we maintain composure. We remain focused and calm. We still the mind and achieve psychic balance. This is true meditation. This is the open window to the zone of flow.

We discipline the mind to acquire that seriousness and clarity needed for coming to terms with exactly where we are at on our journey. We know the day is important and our next vital step on our personal path. We know that in that sacred moment we are creating the day to come and thus securing our future. The first moment is the seed of the day. If the day is the unit of measure of our journey, then the first moment of consciousness, each day, is the vital determinant of a successful day and hence a successful life.

One's relationship with the day is the truly religious act! It must become a ritual one performs every morning in the temple of one's heart and mind – in the altar of one's consciousness.

Unfortunately, too many religions have become divorced from daily life. I can go to Church on a Sunday and commit any number of sins during the week. Whatever religion I adopt, it must become a way of life. It must be a philosophy of life. I must act consistently with my beliefs and the teachings of that faith. Any religion is useless if it does not become meaningful in the moment of my day-to-day living; if it does not truly become a guide to my every action.

The beauty of the wave is that we cannot fall asleep. We cannot put our religion away when we want to commit a transgression, or we just want to be lazy. It must be a living, breathing relationship with all that is, with life, with creation. It is eternal and always there. It is the way we live our daily lives, and this is precisely why the day, as the unit of measure, is so important. We track our progress daily. We ensure each and every day we are on our path, not getting lost, not getting distracted, not taking a detour. We do not relegate religion to Sunday or Saturday or any other holy day. We treat every day as sacred, as important and as a necessary step along our path just as every step is important when walking.

Chapter 9

Earth School

If the day is our basic unit of time in terms of one step at a time, then a lifetime is the appropriate measure of the journey. We began Section I with the perennial questions of the meaning of life – why am I here and what is my purpose. These deep inner questions that we all ask at various times in our lives and answer on a deep inner personal level. Moreover, these are the questions a religion or a philosophy of life need to help us answer. In times of need, it is often our faith or belief in an afterlife that sustains us and gives us that hope and strength to carry on.

However, in this modern age, the old religions are failing to provide this context and meaning. From this perspective, our cosmology provides the backdrop, the context, the meaning that gives us purpose, surety and solace. Certainly, those people with a firm faith seem to possess a sturdier frame and attitude than those who lack any philosophy.

As mentioned in *Personal Sovereignty*, the basic problem with most religions, both east and west, is that they posit life here on earth as a means to some end in another – whether that other be the Christian Heaven, the Buddhist Nirvana, the Islamic Heaven and so on. In this way, human life on earth is robbed of purpose and beauty for its own sake; it seems we need to suffer here in order to earn our salvation. Life on earth is viewed as a sufferance, a punishment, a penance one needs to endure in order to get somewhere else or to be rewarded in an afterlife.

I believe this is why humanity en masse is now turning away from traditional religions and precisely why we need a modern practical spirituality (not a new religion) that restores dignity and meaning to life here on earth for its own sake. One of the fundamental precepts of

Taoism or Zen is that one should do each task for its own sake as time and place demand and not with an eye to the result or the reward. This concept, called innocence is at the heart of satori or the enlightened life.

'Before enlightenment chop wood carry water; after enlightenment chop wood carry water.'

What this saying means is that what we do each day, the tasks of life do not change as we evolve only our inner attitude towards these tasks change. We no longer resent, resist or reject being here but embrace life fully, being in the moment of now. Be here now is another way of saying the same thing.

In modern parlance, one is mindful. In the end, being mindful means being present, not thinking but being at-one-with the moment of one's being; being here and now; being fully present, cognisant and mindful. Interestingly, whereas we in the west call it being mindful, the ancient eastern texts call it emptying the mind. To truly be mindful, one's mind must be empty; we must enter that state of no-thought where the mind is at rest, complete and content with all that is. There is no inner resistance; no wanting, no forces operating internally to upset the flow. We become tranquil, at ease, at peace with ourselves, our life and the world about us; there is no disquiet. This is the zone of flow.

I call this BeComing One!

Mindfulness and having an empty mind are another of these yin/yang dialectics. In order to be mindful, the mind must be empty of thought. Thinking must cease! This is probably the hardest continuum to master and is another of the major distinctions between the old traditional religions and modern spirituality. Most religions rely upon obedience to an externally imposed set of rules which require thought. Taoism requires one listens intently to the inner core of one's being to ascertain at any point in the space/time continuum precisely what is correct for the self. This requires extreme degrees of mindfulness, focus and self-discipline.

If we continue our analogy of life being a metaphorical journey and each day being one step and a lifetime being the whole journey, we need to ensure we are on the right journey lest we will be walking in the wrong direction. Thus, we come back to the original question of life – how do we know we are on the right journey; how do we know where we are going; how do we know what our life is all about? For it is all very well to practise mindfulness, to be aware, fully present in the now and living our life conscientiously according to the inner dictates of our being. This is the microcosm of the eternal NOW!

At the other end of the continuum is the macrocosm of our lifetime. We need to know our journey; our life needs to make sense to us; to satisfy our inner sense of meaning and purpose. Some people just know this from an early age – having that certainty of purpose, direction, career path, spouse and so on whereas others need to search to find their path.

Your personal Tao is your path, your life story, your wave and your journey. It is your fate and your destiny. This path needs to be in harmony with the greater forces of the Tao of the Universe for there to be alignment between the two and for the permissible zones of variance to work. In other words, we need to be on the right road as well as being within the right lane. There is no point in driving along meticulously and impeccably if one is not on the right journey; if one is going the wrong way.

But this implies there is a right and a wrong path for any human being which looks awfully like either pre-determinism, karma or just plain old-fashioned religion. How does Personal Sovereignty truly operate if there is a right path for us and where does this path come from? Is it imposed from without by some external being or deity or does it spring from within our own inner being?

In many ways, we are just rephrasing our original questions regarding the meaning and purpose of life, but it is this rephrasing that is important for we are not relying upon an external source to tell us what is right for us. We are asking the same questions but from a radically different perspective and sometimes it is this ability to rephrase, to re-contextualise, that provides the opportunity for growth and understanding. Often when we look at something but from a different angle we arrive at a different solution.

As Einstein famously said one cannot solve a problem from the same level of consciousness on which it was created. We need to evolve; to change perspective to arrive at a new vantage point.

It is the thesis of this book that the old perspective no longer supports us or gives our lives meaning and that therefore we need desperately to find a new way of looking at life; a new philosophy that reshapes, recrystallises and renews our understanding of what life is all about and why we are here.

We need to attune to our own destiny, to our own fate, to our own path and this is the second key component of *Tao Tuning*. This ability to attune or tune into our own frequency, just as we must tune into the correct frequency of any electromagnetic signal to receive a clear message. Think of tuning your radio to a particular station or fine tuning your television to pick up the channels. We all know that if we do not hit on that correct frequency then the signal is clouded by static and distortion. The message is not clear and there is nothing worse than listening to a radio or watching a television where the image and sound are not clear and in sync.

Indeed, we can compare this thesis to the recent changes from analogue to digital television, from AM to FM radio or even to the various generations of mobile phones and so on. Each of these technological advances provide clearer, stronger, more robust carrier waves to facilitate better image and sound quality. No one would prefer to go back to AM radio, analogue television or earlier generation mobile phones.

Moreover, in this highly interconnected digital world, where we have all become increasingly dependent upon mobile and internet reception, we know the frustration of having none. When we do not have strong and fast connectivity, we become frustrated, moody and anxious. That electromagnetic reception has now become part of our security and comfort zone, so to be without it is disconcerting. Similarly, inner reception of the cosmic currents of Taoist messages is just as necessary for our inner peace of mind and tranquillity. If we have no spiritual reception, we quickly lose direction.

A more modern philosophy of life needs to provide a clearer, stronger and more robust carrier wave for the meaning of life. In each of these cases, the content of the message has not changed; the quality of the carrier wave and hence reception has. Life has not changed; the meaning and purpose of life have not changed. Taoism does not represent a new religion in terms of prescriptive laws; it is certainly not advocating a new way of life or a new set of commandments that one must learn. Rather it is advocating a different orientation so that we can receive a clearer message as to what our lives are all about and this reorientation is a move from looking externally without for one's answers to a looking within to one's inner being to find the true meaning and purpose of one's life.

The mindfulness movement does not advocate doing anything different but doing the same things differently: paying attention, being aware, being present while one is living one's life. The old traditional religions preached going away to a monastery to practise this sacred life; withdrawing from the hustle and bustle of life to focus on some after life. The basic principle of Zen is to remain in life but to be fully present; to give oneself totally, 100%, to the process of life, to what is going on but not to be swamped by it. To not become distracted by daily reality.

This is not to be confused with hedonism or nihilism. It is certainly not a philosophy of eat, drink and be merry for tomorrow we die, with an outright denial of any spiritual context or purpose. Rather it is that in the discipline of living one's life with focused attention one attunes to its inner meaning. Our life, our destiny, our fate guides us on our path and leads us to our spiritual fulfilment. The answers do not come from without – whether that be from a dogma, a catechism, a guru or any other source. The answers must come from within; one must attune to the small inner voice and be true to the self.

Thus, there is this relationship, almost a business partnership, between the self and one's destiny. They must be aligned and work together cohesively. And they each have their specific function; it is another of these dialectic continuums. The self is concerned with the outer reality of daily life – with the microcosm of each daily step, the detail of life on earth. This is the function of the positive ego as explained in *Personal Sovereignty*. One's Tao, or soul, is concerned with the big picture, the macrocosm of the destination of the journey of a lifetime, the spiritual context. It is this context that provides the backdrop, the larger meaning and purpose, the why behind what we do.

A truly successful and enjoyable life results from this dynamic business partnership between one's positive ego and one's Tao. Both have their specific role and function to play. Both are important and form the two polar nodes of this continuum called being human. It is called the New Spirituality where we embrace our personal sovereignty taking responsibility for our personal behaviour and becoming accountable for the impact of that behaviour on the world about us.

We are all becoming more aware of the importance of Why! It is not what we do or how we do it but why that is important. What is our intention; what motivates us; why is it important to us as a human being. Once again, it is obvious that some people have a clear definition of their personal why while others do not. Successful people know their why; know their destiny; know the meaning and purpose behind what they do. Every action is designed to fulfil that why so there is an elegant efficiency and simplicity to their lives rather than a haphazard waste of time, energy and effort.

It is this why that supports your life. It is this why that nourishes you, that gets you up in the morning, that provides the daily discipline to perform at your personal best, to achieve, to move on. That is precisely why this partnership is such a vital prerequisite to a successful life. As in all things it is a delicate balance. If the why gets out of control, we become obsessed, overly focused on the destination and burn ourselves up like a meteor consuming our energy in our overzealous passion. We become the arrogant zealot. On the other hand, if we do not know our why we will become too easily distracted and forego our path similarly losing our energy in irresolute vacillation. We become the indulgent narcissist.

We can be the meteor burning ourselves up in a manic trajectory or a Catherine wheel burning oneself up in a spiral going nowhere fast!

The why provides fullness, stability, self-containment, joy and contentment. Knowing our why is like having a rudder, a moral compass that furnishes strength of character and strong will. No why and we become empty, morally bankrupt, open to indulgence and distraction.

Think of any journey – physical or spiritual. If it is something we want to achieve then getting to that destination becomes the fuel for the journey and as we progress, as we get closer to the goal, we become more determined to see it through. If, on the other hand, we are just wandering aimlessly, without a clear direction or destination in mind, it is that much harder to stay focused and we will almost definitely get lost, distracted, despondent and give up.

Life is a journey. Your personal life is the most important journey you are on. Everything else comes from that journey. It is essential that that journey makes sense to you; that you know precisely where you are at on that journey at any point in time and what is your destination. Your destination is your destiny; your destiny is your destination. Both are your personal Tao. It is this destiny that generates the wave; that gives you power and momentum; that carries you along just like an ocean wave carries the surfer. Without this alignment between self and fate, life lacks meaning, purpose and rhythm.

Fate lends power to life. The essence of Taoism is to align the two assigning the right place to life and to fate bringing the two into balance and harmony and thus putting one's fate on a firm footing. This is that dynamic partnership that is so essential to creating a joyous, harmonious and successful life. We all know and experience those days when we ride majestic, powerful, flowing through life with no interruption or misadventure. We are in the zone of flow. And we all know those other days when nothing flows, everything seems to conspire against us and we are just blocked.

This is the essence of the wave. If the chi is there you ride the wave victorious; if not, you do nothing! It is not wisdom but folly to insist on catching waves when either they are simply not there, or the surf is too treacherous to go into the water.

The basic problem with traditional religion is that it invalidates life on planet earth. Whether one adheres to the concept of Original Sin or the wheel of karma, or any of the other multitude of religious doctrines, life on earth is viewed as a penance or a preparation for some other time and place. Nowhere does traditional philosophy or religion demonstrate the sanctity of life and emphasise the great gift that it is. Surely, if we start with the premise that life is a burden or a suffering, it is extremely hard to create a philosophy of life that is joyous, exciting and optimistic. If we denigrate the sanctity of life at its core, is it any wonder that people have such little respect for the oneness of life and the importance of every living creature?

The whole point of mindfulness or Zen is the absolute sacredness of the moment: that we exist within the eternal now and that being 100% in the present is the ultimate discipline and the ultimate reward. This is flow. We do not exist in order to get somewhere else in another place and time; rather we exist to be here now. The promise of eternity is only valuable if that journey is an enjoyable one. No one wants to exist forever in either purgatory or hell or even heaven. Life is to be enjoyed. The whole purpose of life is to learn to accept its sacredness and its joy. We need to learn to receive the gift of life.

If we exist in either the future or the past, if we exist to achieve something somewhere else, we forfeit the moment and just as the point of power is in the present, so too, is the point of enjoyment. To truly enjoy the wondrous journey of life, one must be on the wave living one's life fully. If we have an ulterior motive of doing in order to achieve or be or even become, we cannot be true to our inner nature which can only exist in the present.

If we return to the concept of being receptive to the voice of our inner being, of attuning to our path, our destiny and our Tao, we must be present to listen. Imagine listening to an exquisite piece of music or a running stream or the sound of the waves lapping the shore. We must give it our total undivided attention to really appreciate and savour that moment. If our mind wanders, thinking of either the past or the future, we forfeit being with that music, we lose the experience and the enjoyment.

In this modern, fast paced world we have lost that centeredness: that ability to pay attention to the present, to give the moment its due desert. This is precisely why we find time speeding up and that we do not have enough time. If we exist within the eternal now, we have all the time in the world; we have eternity. This is an incredibly hard concept to get our heads around for we live in a world that is now so dominated by time, by doing, by deadlines, by having to achieve certain goals by a certain due date, that time has indeed become the master and we its slave.

Our normal daily lives are taken up by the busyness of life: we get up and must go to work. The whole artificial concept of working for money in a way that totally dominates our day has effectively corrupted our relationship with time, with that unit of measure - the day. If we do have a day off, there is so much to catch up on in our personal lives that we are still on that treadmill. Occasionally, maybe once or twice a year, we take vacation and very occasionally within that short interval we do experience the stillness and the sanctity of the day, of the moment, of the eternal now.

Ask yourself a very simple question: if there are 31.5 million moments in a year (60x60x24x365) – how many moments do you experience totally in the NOW? In any one day, if there is approximately 60,000 excluding sleep, how many do you truly experience without mental chatter and distraction?

The prevalence of social media has worsened this phenomenon, in that many people can now only validate their experience by posting it on-line. They are not really there in the moment. It seems we can only experience life through the lens of a screen or monitor and not firsthand by direct sensory perception. This distorts and messes the whole percept/concept continuum and makes us live our lives second-hand, seeking outside validation from mass consciousness rather than from our inner consciousness. We become so distracted by posting the event, we totally miss its sacredness.

This is why people crave wilderness and why preserving what little wilderness remains is so vitally important. It is not just the biodiversity of life that exists within the wilderness, but its living presence. We can sense the immediacy of life. We can hear the sounds of silence. We can feel the chi and pulsation of the rhythm of life. The greater Tao exists in nature. We exist within its divine embrace. This is precisely why one feels so recharged, rejuvenated and refreshed after spending time in nature and the more pristine, the more we are invigorated.

Again, if we use that example of being on a wonderful nature hike or trek, there is little point in the exercise if we are not fully present to the moment: being aware of that wildflower, that bird song, those smells of the forest and so forth. The point of the hike is not just to get to the end but to enjoy the experience, otherwise there is little point in doing it. So too, in the journey of life, staying in the moment to enjoy the wonders of the trip is essential.

And this is the fundamental difference between traditional religion and the new spirituality. Although, both posit life as a spiritual journey, the former views life on earth as a means to an end – which only exists after death, while the latter views living life fully in the present as the purpose. We do not attain salvation by abstinence and a denial of life here on earth; we attain enlightenment by fully embracing life in the eternal now. Life is not a means to an end; life is the end in and of itself.

Life is the divine gift, and the essence of that gift is eternity. We do not need to earn a hereafter, to work for a mythical end point, to strive for salvation, to struggle against our baser natures. On the contrary, we do need to learn to go with the flow; to graciously accept and receive the great gift that life is. It is given freely with no strings attached. That may sound simple enough but is in fact the hardest thing to achieve, for we must silence the disquiet of the thinking mind. We must exercise the daily discipline of mindfulness: being in the present and attuning to our inner voice.

The point of the journey is this acceptance: to become more fully who we are; to be able to express our inner divinity 100% of the time and in all situations that we encounter. There is no doubt that as we travel our own individual path, we do encounter challenges, hardships, problems and issues. There is also no doubt these events are sent to test us, to teach us, to assist in our personal development. Evolution is the undisputable quality of life. Life never stops evolving. Life and evolution are two sides of the one prism. Evolution is an inherent aspect of life.

Returning to the analogy of the surfer, we do need to master riding the waves of life. Some days the sun is shining, the water is glassy, and the waves roll in almost perfect. Other days the weather is stormy, the sea choppy and the waves treacherous. We need to learn to adapt, to respond appropriately, to not lose our cool and to know when not to go in the water.

It is not that in foregoing traditional religion we forsake all personal discipline, morality or spiritual aspiration. Quite to the contrary, the discipline becomes more real and immediate. We acknowledge and appreciate life as the teacher. We develop a more profound respect for not only the sanctity of life but also its role as our mentor. Life is the message and the messenger. Life becomes the voice of our destiny. As mentioned before in terms of the motion picture being a projection from a reel, we project our lives upon the screen of daily reality.

Hence, we do not need to refer to any arcane or academic book, bible, koran or any other set of rules. We do not need to learn to live our lives by rote. We do not need to listen to any other external source. We do need to pay full attention to what is occurring in our daily lives. We do need to be fully present, cognisant and aware of exactly what is going on. We do need to be engaging in an intelligent conversation, dialogue and partnership with our lives. This is a living, breathing, dynamic philosophy of life that is here and now, in front of us every moment of every day, confronting us with the truth of who we are and who we are becoming.

Religion is not a garment we put on, on a Saturday or Sunday or any other holy day and then take off so we can deceive ourselves and commit whatever offence to life we may choose. True religion is not temporary or hypocritical. True religion is having a genuine, sincere and consistent religious respect for and appreciation of the sanctity of life and especially one's own personal life.

The real gift of life is not just that we are alive; that we breathe, eat and are physical. The real gift of life is that your life is personal. Just as each and every face, body, personality, leaf, flower and creature is unique, the sacredness of life is that your life is unique to you and depends totally upon how you live it. You are the writer, the producer, the director, the actor and the stage designer. You create your own reality, and that reality is your life. Your life is the stage upon which you act and have your being.

You are in a synchronistic and symbiotic relationship with your life. In traditional religion, to some extent or another, you are the victim of forces beyond your control. Other deities, gods, devils and so on control your life and your destiny. The truth is you control your destiny by your actions, behaviour and attitude. Decisions determine destiny. It is ultimately your decisions and choices, your attitudes and beliefs, your thoughts and feelings that are the stage props that build your set.

Taoism is a practical science of life that teaches you how to become the prime mover in your life; how to build this co-creative partnership with life so that you and you alone determine your destiny. This is an incredibly powerful and meaningful shift in perspective that is not academic or abstract. It is also not difficult to learn; one merely needs to pay attention to the permissible zones of variance. Life will tell you when you are going the wrong way for you.

It is like those large red signs on freeways upon re-entering from a rest area – YOU ARE GOING THE WRONG WAY! Life is extremely clear in its messages and direct. This is not a game of hide and seek. One does not need to retreat to a cave or a monastery. One does not need to spend a lifetime studying ancient wisdom and one certainly cannot learn to master life from a book. One could read every book on the planet about surfing, but if one does not go in the water and get wet, one will not become an accomplished surfer. One can read every treatise on flow, but if one does not engage fully, directly with life one will never experience the joy of peak performance. Like the toddler learning to walk by falling over, we learn to surf by falling off the board and getting back on it. We master life by living it fully not by running away into a false ascetic rejection of life on planet Earth!

Life is intelligent. One of the peculiar predicaments of modern western man is that he or she thinks that intelligence is the prerogative of humanity. We deny and devalue the intrinsic intelligence of other creatures – both animals and plants – and fail to appreciate the immense divine intelligence of creation. Precisely because we have separated God from creation and created some mythological being in Heaven, remote from life on earth, we have taken divine intelligence out from life. But life is God and God is life. God is all there is. Divine Intelligence is within everything: every cell, every atom, every particle, every photon and so on. Everything has and is divine intelligence.

Your life is inherently intelligent. One could say our lives are more intelligent than us because life has not been corrupted. We have! Your life is your constant companion. Think about it. In your quieter moments; in your reflective introspection; in times of great sorrow and great joy; when you are quintessentially you - you are with life. Your life!

Your life is the outer manifestation of your inner psychic and spiritual journey. It is your destiny and your fate out-pictured on the screen of daily reality. What happens, what occurs is what you attract, what you create, what you write upon your tablet. Religion is not reserved for the church or temple. Religion is not a part of life; religion is life. People who are truly religious, of whatever persuasion, live their faith. It is real and all-encompassing. It involves every aspect of their lives; it permeates every decision; it determines who they are as people. It is immensely personal and real. It is not academic or abstract.

Even in classical religion of whatever guise, a saint is one who lives their faith totally.

Taoism is the science of living one's life in harmony with the descriptive laws of life. It is living a balanced whole life. It is acknowledging the divine intelligence of creation and the divine benevolence of the universe which means life is on our side. It is not against us. It is not hard. Life is not meant to be a struggle. Life does not suck!

Just as time is your ally, life is your travelling partner on this glorious journey of evolution. The goal is to evolve; to become more of who you are: to BeCome One by integrating all the various aspects of your personality, psyche and soul; to become God.

Now in normal traditional religious terms this is blasphemy. To aspire to become God, to even make such a statement is the height of arrogance and stupidity. We are mere mortals and stained by sin. We cannot even think of such a thing. But if God is everything and everything is God and if divine intelligence resides within every aspect and particle of creation, then we are divine at our core just like everything else.

When we say to become God, what is really meant is to express our inner divinity; to realise our oneness with life; to personify the sanctity of life, to really and truly appreciate the divine gift that life is. It is not to usurp the place of God but rather to humbly accept our place in the Infinity of Being. Even Christ said no more than the birds in the trees; I and the Father are one. To assert one's divinity does not put one above creation but to be a part of it. What humanity does now is absolute arrogance. We believe we are above nature. We believe we can kill, plunder, rape and ravage the earth. We believe we are at the top of the evolutionary tree and that nature is beholden to us.

We pollute; we destroy. We take and take and fail to live within the rhythm of life. This is true arrogance; not to humbly realise that we are divine and that that divinity places extraordinary obligations upon us to behave correctly and appropriately, taking personal responsibility for the consequences of our actions upon the fabric of life.

If our personal life is our life partner, then life in its expanded and universal sense is the measure of our success: to be one with Life; to tread upon the planet without causing grievance, without causing injury, without causing offence. This is the ultimate quest. Our destination is not some mythological place in a future tense or afterlife; our destination is Oneness: to be able to live our lives in complete harmony with the Universal Law of Life – the Supreme Tao. God, Goddess, All That Is.

To be fully aware, alert, present. To be so at one with all that is that there is no karma, no discordant waves, no resistance and no retribution. If we return to the concept of composite waves and we acknowledge that we do indeed create our own reality by the waves that we generate, it becomes paramount that we are not sending discordant waves out into the universe that then return as misfortune in our future.

In separating ourselves from creation, in creating the victim myth of traditional religion, in abrogating our manifestation power to an imagined external deity, we have robbed ourselves of our Personal Sovereignty. We are no longer able to take control of our destiny. To truly do this, we must accept that we do indeed have that power and that responsibility.

If we are sending out both positive and negative waves, the composite wave generated by their mixing will create a distorted reality. There is interference between the projector and the screen, and the image will be interrupted by the static produced. We will not have a clear picture. We will not be able to accurately hear what life is telling us. We need to disentangle the waves to ascertain the forces operating.

In this way we purify our output. But we need the screen of life to reflect for us what we are projecting. This is the inherent beauty and simplicity of this system. There is no intermediary; there is no one else to tell us, to inform us, to interpret for us. We need to do the work ourselves. This becomes the process of life. Life is the message and the messenger. Our daily reality, our fate and our destiny reflect back to us exactly what we have created.

We only need to face our lives with uncompromising truthfulness; we need to have the courage of being brutally honest with ourselves and acknowledging that we indeed have created whatever is confronting us. We also need to know that we and we alone can change it. For it is only when we possess this courage and this honesty that life will show us the way, that a door will open, that the path to success will reveal itself.

But it is only after we have done this due diligence, after this reflection and introspection, that we can proceed on our way and embrace our destiny. To try to evade the truth; to exist in denial and blame another, whether that other be another person, life, destiny, God, call it what you will, will only result in failure and humiliation because we will be generating more discordant waves causing more future chaos in our lives.

Thus, as in all things, the Why becomes extremely important. It is a prerequisite to success. If we do not know our why, we exist within a psychic fog of unknowing and lack of clarity – it is extremely hard if not impossible to find our way. And remember our way, our path, our chi, our destiny, our fate and our Tao are all one and the same thing. They are all facets of the one prism which is the law of our being. Clarity and chaos are dialectic opposites. The former leads to inner peace and contentment; the latter to confusion and anxiety.

Yet, we are where we began endeavouring to answer the question of the meaning of life: why we are here. And in so many areas and issues of life we can only come upon a clear definition by beginning with negation of what something is not. We have argued against the old traditional definitions and historical religious answers that all tell us the answer is out there somewhere in some holy book or place – that we must go on a physical pilgrimage or seek out a guru or master or study some arcane text to discover the meaning of life, the answer to our why.

Taoism tells us to merely look intently at the life we are living in minute detail: to study the screen of our daily lives and in that projection we will find the answer. Life itself holds the key! In many ways, this is a lot harder for there is no one to help us, no one to rely upon, no one to interpret for us, no one to tell us what to do. This honesty is incredibly confronting and can be overpowering.

This is precisely why the book *Personal Sovereignty* precedes this one and it is necessary to understand and master its concepts to truly find your Why. You need to be able to make your own decisions; you need to be able to totally rely upon and trust your own perceptions, your own conclusions, your own answers. It is life and only life that can tell us, that can guide us. It is our own personal relationship with life; it is our own inner voice, our own inner being, the law of our being that talks to us and gives our lives meaning and purpose.

Unfortunately, too many people would like to define their purpose in terms of the outer world: what they become and achieve out there on the planet, how they are seen or perceived by others or by the many roles we all play in our personal lives. However, your real purpose is much more personal and private. Your true purpose is to realise and manifest your divinity: the fullness of your being; to become the totality of your Self.

It is not that we are here to be a great doctor, teacher, mother, writer, artist or any other role, although these roles that we adopt and play out in our lives are extremely important parts and stepping stones along our way. But these are all merely temporary and transitional facets of our being. In the fullness of time all roles come and go. Time marches on and the inevitable waves of life give to us and take away all these things. People also come and go. We are born alone, and we will die alone no matter how close we may become and how much we may love and be loved. In this sense our lives are our own.

We all do have important parts to play on the planetary stage. Each and every one of us does possess unique and rare gifts and needs to give these gifts to the world. Each and every one of us is a unique piece in the gigantic cosmic gig saw puzzle that is human life on planet earth. Each and every one of us is here to love and be loved, to develop meaningful relationships and play our part in the unfolding drama of life on earth and many of us define our purpose by fulfilling these roles.

But these roles are not our purpose; they are a manifestation of fulfilling that purpose. They are a symptom and not a cause. At each point along the journey of life we will be playing another role: we will be children, parents, scholars, teachers, lovers and combatants. We will have various jobs and careers. We will be many things to many people. But we cannot define our purpose by these transitory roles. We need to go deeper, lest when a particular chapter reaches its conclusion, as each and every chapter will, we will once again be faced with the same question – why? Who am I and why am I here?

If we define ourselves too narrowly or too dependent upon one set of circumstances, we will become reliant upon that reality and when it passes there is the danger that we will lose that definition of ourselves. This is why many people, when they lose a loved one or their career ends, find it very difficult to continue on their path; they feel they have been robbed of their identity precisely because they have defined themselves in terms of that particular set of circumstances.

I am the CEO; I am the boss; I am the nurse; I am the mother; I am the movie star; I am rich and famous; I am the husband, wife, lover. I am the top athlete and so on. We define ourselves in terms of our external achievements and relationships. These definitions do not answer the fundamental question of why we are here and only lead to spiritual and emotional bankruptcy when their duration in our lives ends. Many successful and famous people end up either emotionally destitute or committing suicide when their day in the sun comes to its conclusion. They have no alternative definition or purpose.

The meaning and purpose of life cannot be answered by any definition of what I possess or what I do in the world but only rather by who I am as a human being, as a soul. It is my personal evolutionary journey of progressive perfection to become more of who I am, to become more fully me. The roles I play in my life are chapters in the novel of my life, but they are not the book. My life must make sense as a connected whole and it must make sense to me. There must be a moral to the story. That moral is the meaning and purpose of my life for this lifetime.

When you discover that moral, that essence of the story, everything shifts. It is one of those singular moments when you stand in the centre of the intersection of time and space and view your life from the perspective of eternity. It is no longer dependent upon, nor defined by, any temporary set of variables; it stands beyond the temporal and becomes firmly planted in the eternal. You exist beyond this lifetime; you become your soul. You know yourself as an eternal being. You understand who you are and what your journey is all about. You become free from the fear of death for you know truly the spirit never dies, only the vehicle of the body.

This is a very humbling experience because you recognise and acknowledge your frailty, your imperfections, you know exactly where you are on your personal journey to perfection. Through the meeting of your divinity, you also face your humanity and understand the spiritual journey you need to embark upon to become more fully who you are so that you can more fully express that humanity and that divinity for they are but two sides of the one coin. Your purpose is to become God! As mentioned, this is not an act of arrogance but one of extreme humility for it is a recognition of the Oneness of Life and that we are all One. Oneness is all there is. This realisation places immense obligation and duty upon us; this is real religion! We see all that separates us from life and fully grasp that we need to transcend that separation.

No one else can make that journey for us. This is not something that can be learnt in books or put off till another life or an afterlife. This is not something that can be denied or avoided, although it can be delayed. It is a necessary journey. We all need to BeCome One. We all need to face our separation, our isolation, our alienation, our selfishness, our loneliness, our cupidity and our arrogance. There can be only one purpose to real religion and that is to feel the fullness of life, to appreciate with awe and wonder the oneness and interconnectedness of life and every living being; to feel the sacredness of the moment as the divine gift that it is.

True mystics and religious leaders have experienced this sanctity and tried to communicate its preciousness to us, but we have bastardised its essence turning their teachings into base rituals devoid of meaning.

Every being must make this journey to oneness for themselves. There are no shortcuts and no alternatives.

We can define ourselves for so long by an identity we form along the way but eventually all external definitions will fade and fail. BeComing One is not an academic nor intellectual pursuit. It is an inner spiritual journey that gives your life meaning and purpose. It just is. It is the ultimate discipline.

I remember reading once as Krishnamurti tried to describe this state of oneness. He compared it to sitting by an open window; one must wait for the breeze to blow in – one cannot force it. He describes it as grace; one must be able to wait but one must have the window open! In other words, one must make the necessary preparations and do whatever the self needs to do to eliminate that sense of separation but in the end, it is the Grace of God that must come of its own volition.

Humanity has defined itself erroneously. We have come to view ourselves as one very minute part of who we really are, and in the narrowness and shallowness of this limited perspective we have lost view of our grandeur and magnificence. That is why life lacks meaning and purpose. Imagine one is embarking upon a grand and glorious adventure – a cruise through Europe or a trek through the Himalayas and then halfway through the journey one loses memory and perspective and defines one's trip in terms of the next port or the next leg of the trek. One would lose the grandeur of the trip. Worse still, if we merely focus on the hardship and the pain of putting one foot in front of the other and do not look at the majesty of the mountains, the trek loses all significance and joy.

We have allowed our egoic part – that part of us that deals with daily life on planet earth and physical survival - to become the be all and end all of who we are. We have negated our larger essence – our spirit, our soul, our higher self and consciousness and lost perspective of our spiritual journey. We cannot find the meaning and purpose of life on the egoic level. It only exists on the Taoic level. The Taoic level is the level of our soul journey back to oneness.

We return to the dialectic of the universe and the yin and yang of creation. The One became Two and the myriad beings came into being from those two. This is the Big Bang, the creation of the material universe and the descent into physicality and separation. We have erroneously defined this descent as an act of defiance, as the Original Sin of Adam and Eve, as the rejection of the Will of God, as the wheel of karma and thus erroneously defined ourselves ever since.

The descent into matter and separation is merely one pole of the binary universe: the centripetal half of the universal pulsation of life. It is just as essential and necessary as the contraction of your heart. But it leads into its opposite – the centrifugal expansion of evolution and the return to oneness from which we came. Life on earth is not some form of punishment but rather an opportunity to consciously create your own godhead willingly and knowingly. If we view ourselves as minor egoic beings, we simply cannot discover or uncover the greatness of who we really are; we cannot appreciate the grandeur of the spiritual journey we are on and we cannot adequately define our purpose. We simply do not understand our Why!

Any attempt to define the meaning of life from a shallow perspective simply will not work and will leave us spiritually bereft. If the purpose and meaning of life is to BeCome One, then the meaning and purpose of our individual lifetime must be defined in terms of our current state of separation and what we need to do to achieve that oneness, to heal the rift and seal our soul.

If we use the analogy of a sculptor chiselling at a block of stone to create a masterpiece, the work is defined in what is taken away by the sculptor and what is left behind as the work of art. We need to chisel away those parts of our being that cause separation leaving only the state of oneness. We all have our doubts, our fears, our greed and our conceit. We all have an ego that views itself as separate, as better than or less than. We all live within our egoic shell of separation just as we all live within our biological skin that defines our body and its boundary.

These borders are necessary for survival on planet earth, but we certainly do not end at our skin and neither do we end at our egoic shell. Boundaries are a part of physical life on earth, but they are arbitrary and should not determine our definition of ourselves. Objectification is a part of the human neurological process and the formation of language and thought, but it is not an accurate representation of reality as nuclear physics has shown us. There are no objects – only densities of energy appearing as matter. Just as the sculptor removes the parts of the block that are unnecessary for his or her masterpiece, we too, need to chisel away at what is unnecessary and inessential to our pure being.

All forms of intense meditation are the practice of removing the egoic definition of the self so that one is left with the essence of our being – our inner law. The essence of mindfulness is to enter that quietness of no-thinking and timelessness where we become one with the universe, with whatever is happening or whatever we are doing. We lose that sense of separation and become one with the chi or flow of the universe. Our personal Tao and the Universal Tao merge and become one. We are home and complete! Most of us have experienced this state of transcendent oneness when completely absorbed in a sport, hobby or artistic act when both time and space disappear, and we merge with the activity. Our egoic sense of separation dissolves and our consciousness expands into oneness. This is the state of flow.

Many practitioners achieve momentary glimpses of this state of Nirvana, Samadhi or enlightenment but to live permanently within this state of oneness takes considerable time, work and effort just as the creation of the statue of David took Michelangelo considerable time, work and effort. We all have our personal baggage. We all have our personal story. We all live within our own psychic prison. We are all blocks of stone becoming magnificent works of art.

But we need to define for ourselves the purpose of this lifetime and to do this we need to examine our story, for our lives present to us what our personal journey is all about.

Chapter 10

This is your Life!

If you want to discover your life purpose look no further than your life's story. In that story is written all you need to know – you just need to understand the language of life. We have all seen the television series 'This is your Life' where the presenter reads the person's story and brings on stage relevant friends, family, colleagues and so on.

Your life is a narrative and a play. You are the writer, director, producer and main actor. You have chosen your parents, your siblings and written the broad outline of the plot before you were born. As a soul, you set the blueprint, the basic narrative and direction. To be sure it is not set in stone and there is ample room for movement, ample opportunity to ad lib, for spontaneity and adjustment as you go, but the basic theme remains the same none the less.

It is a bit like jazz. There is the basic melody and chord structure but then plenty of scope for improvisation. Nothing is more exciting than watching and listening to masterful jazz musicians improvising off each other – making music. We could call it the 'jazz of life.'

All mysteries need codes to be deciphered and the mystery of life can only be opened once we firmly accept this quantum leap in understanding. Life is not one lifetime. Life is not predetermined by an external deity or power. You are on a soul journey. Your soul is on its journey back to oneness. Earth is a school within which we learn specific lessons on our journey to oneness.

The soul sets up the basic plot and theme – the moral of the story. The soul chooses the main players in your drama – your parents, your siblings, your lovers and your life partners. The soul sets out the basic narrative in terms of events – where you are born, what is your heritage, genetics, genome, demography and so on in order to create circumstances to facilitate that lesson.

Think of planet earth as a university of life. Before we enter university, we choose a faculty – engineering, science, medicine, economics, law and so on. Within that faculty, we then major in certain electives according to our preference and what we want to become. And just as there are a finite number of faculties, so too, there are a finite number of meta-lessons to be learnt on earth. However, each student customises their learning according to the electives and options they choose. No two students will follow exactly the same curriculum. And no two souls follow the same spiritual path to oneness.

We are all unique individuals. Each one of us has our own unique story, our own personal journey, our own unique lessons to learn. Many studies have been done on biological twins that share the exact same lineage, genome and upbringing. Yet, no matter how close, no matter how similar and joined, at some vital point their personal stories diverge. As they get older their individual stories become unique.

If we examine our life story from this perspective of asking why, we will soon discover our personal Why. Why would I have chosen these parents? Why would I have chosen this particular time and place, this epoch even, to be born in? Why did I choose these siblings, these friends? Why did I set up my life the way it has been? Why did I choose this path? What is it teaching me?

Look at the difference here! There are no victims; there are no accidents; there is no unknown why did this happen to me. There is no unfairness, no malevolent universe, no past bad karma, no punishment, no suffering. I consciously chose this path to learn specific lessons and these lessons all revolve around qualities of being – to become a better person; to become a fuller person; to achieve and reach the fullness of my being.

Now I know and appreciate that this is a quantum leap in understanding but give it time to settle in, give yourself time to digest and contemplate. Do not reject the concept out of hand and dismiss it entirely for whether you like it or not, it does put you back in the driver's seat, in the seat of control. For if you are the writer, director and producer you can rewrite the script, you can change the movie, you can rearrange the actors and the stage set. You are in charge. You hold the power.

Moreover, if you take the time to truly examine the story of your life you will find it revolves around a neat set of variables and circumstances that repeat themselves on various octaves and in various patterns, but the basic theme remains the same. Have you ever noticed the patterns repeating: the same kinds of people, relationships, events, playing out over and over? Have you never felt you are in the same movie but in a different time and place? Have you never noticed the patterns in your relationships, the same behaviour, the same fears, the same neuroses, the same mistakes? The same thoughts going round and round in your head.

Deja vu is a reality!

If you truly have the courage to face yourself exactly as you are, you will notice the life lesson emerging when you were a young child, and then an adolescent, a young adult, a mature person and even in old age. The lesson remains the same – we merely play it out on various octaves and in various scenarios to give us many perspectives and to give us many opportunities to master the lesson completely.

Indeed, our external success upon the stage of life, on the planet, in daily reality is completely determined by our success in learning and mastering this inner lesson. If we evade, avoid, resist and fail to negotiate that learning, our daily lives fall apart. It is not that we need to master the lesson all at once, but we do need to engage with the learning. If one enters university, one does not graduate or master all the subjects in the first semester. It takes time and diligence. It is also sequential. One lesson precedes another. We cannot just skip to the end of the book.

These lessons are life lessons, and it does take a lifetime to totally master that aspect of the self, of the soul that one is working on. But one must be engaged in the learning. One must accept the challenge. Those people who intuitively know what their life is all about just seem to go about living their lives successfully, becoming better people, working on their character, their self, their soul - honing who they are. These people use time to build their lives and create good in the world. They live authentically: being true to themselves; honouring the inner law of their being.

Your unique gift to the world is your life lesson. As you master that lesson life sets up the opportunities to both perfect the learning and give the gift of that learning to the world. These are but two sides of the one coin – another of these yin/yang continuums that one must master. Often, the greatest personal struggles become the greatest gifts to the world. Those people who have the courage to follow their dreams, to harness their vision, to be true to their destiny and make their fate a reality bring the greatest blessing to the world.

Every one of us has a calling, a lodestar that gourds us on, that inspires us and gives us meaning and purpose. This does not mean we need to be famous or conquer the world or climb Mt Everest, but it does mean we need to be true to ourselves, to follow our heart with conviction and listen to that still small voice within. It does mean we need to be true to the law of our being. It does mean we need to honour our inner spiritual self especially when those about us tell us it cannot be or that we are crazy or mad or dreaming.

Yes, we are dreaming, and it is our dreams that give us our purpose. It is our dreams that direct us and guide us. It is in the language of dreams that our soul talks to us. It is what excites us and what we are most passionate about. When our souls are stirred with passion, with vigour, with excitement, with determination and commitment: that is our purpose.

Throughout history all the ancient races and cultures understood the power of dreams as the language of life directing our destiny and guiding our path to personal fulfillment. It is only since the negative ego usurped control via the logical rational mind that dreams have become suspect and discarded.

When you examine your life from this perspective, being true to yourself, you will find those recurring times when you were closest to your path, when things flowed, when the Tao of the universe flowed through you strengthening you, making you more noble. It is these times you cherish and remember with pride and glory. You are fulfilling your life purpose precisely when you are in the zone of flow.

And you will also know those times when you betrayed yourself, when you abandoned who you are and gave into the world, into your doubts and fears, when you forsook your path and got distracted by some aberration. We have all got lost. We have all wandered in the spiritual wilderness. We have all been afraid, becoming less than we are.

The quest is to become more of who you are. The gaol is to be true to yourself. Your purpose is to express your unique individual brand of divinity that you and you alone can be. Your purpose is to embrace your greatness. No one else can be you! No one else can fulfil your life purpose; no one else can even know what it is.

This is precisely where classic traditional religion fails. It tries to impose from without a teaching, a moral, a way, a path to follow but no following of any other path or person can bring you to yourself. Following others is the easier path but it leads to emptiness. Following your own inner voice and heart is that much harder but also that much more rewarding. Your soul knows your purpose. Your soul wrote the script of this lifetime. Your soul set up the learning, the lessons, the obstacles and the challenges. Your soul also gave you everything you need to overcome those obstacles, everything you need to master those lessons, everything you need to succeed.

The essence of your purpose is written in the story of your life. You need to learn to read that story by mastering the language of life and that language is buried in your heart. By listening to the inner law of our being, by being true to our self, by following our fate and realising our dreams we become one with the universal flow achieving harmony between our personal Tao and the Tao of the Universe. This is flow.

The problem is that in this fast-paced world with all its external stimuli, our attention is always focused out there in the world. There is so little time for solitude and reflection. We need to make time for ourselves; we need to develop a relationship with our inner self and our lives. Our sense of separation and isolation begins with our self. We have become disconnected from our own inner being. Many of us do not even know who we truly are. This is the greatest tragedy in life. Not the loneliness that comes from isolation from others but the loneliness that comes from isolation from the self.

While social and mass media have high jacked our attention and we crave to fit in with the social norm we have abandoned our uniqueness, we have forsaken our true identity and our originality. We are becoming clones of media prompted norms. The social narrative herds us along the path of conformity.

There is no time for solitude and if there is we run and hide. We do not want to face ourselves for we are afraid of what we may find. It is the rare individual who truly likes what they see and has the courage to face their reality and change it. We cannot discover our purpose out there in the world; it must be found within, in the inner depths of our being.

Once again, we find this divergence between the normal ritual of traditional religion where one goes to worship with the many and another is the arbiter of one's goodness. In the new spirituality, religion is an entirely personal matter. It is one's personal relationship with life, with creation and the creator, with the self that matters and is the arbiter of one's spiritual journey. The only measure of one's spiritual progress is one's inner state of peace and oneness with oneself.

We need to heal the division within before we can find peace and harmony without. The outer is only a reflection of the inner. Inner division and schism become outer conflict and angst in the world. Inner peace manifests as flow and ease of being in life. In many ways, the new religion is one of health and healing. This is why so much of the New Age revolves around concepts of healing, health, well-being, mindfulness and so on. We need to BeCome One with ourselves first.

As the baby-boomers age, there is an obsession in the western world to discover the fountain of youth, the elixir of life. Many studies have been done of the oldest peoples on the planet, the so-called Blue Zones, to discover the secret of aging gracefully, the recipe for longevity and the basic conclusion is that there is no secret formula or recipe but that it is in one's attitude to life and the necessary attitude is one of quiescence and acceptance. The people who live to over 100 are at peace both with themselves and their tribes. They live in harmony; they exude inner peace and happiness. They are content and one with themselves and their lives. They do not exist in separation or disconnection. It seems the more one we become, the longer we live.

The other interesting ingredient is that these people have an incredibly clear sense of their personal purpose on the planet, and it always revolves around giving to others, contributing to their community, playing a meaningful role in their tribe and family. It is never grandiose and never vain. It is not based in their ego and definitely not related to social media but a small and meaningful social tribe or community. It seems the smaller and more intimate our circle, the more meaningful our lives become and the more fulfilled we are as people.

One is reminded of the story of two people walking along the seashore that is littered with literally thousands of jelly fish washed up on the sand. One of the two is methodically picking up one jelly fish after another and throwing them back in the sea. The other asks what is the point as there are so many, to which the first one replies: it sure made a difference to that one!

We can only change the world one jelly fish at a time. We can only do what we can do – this is our unique contribution, our personal gift, our life purpose – to make a small difference for the good to those around us. Our purpose does not need to be grandiose or up there in lights. We do not need to be famous or change the world: we just need to be ourselves and fulfil our destiny. But we do need to change our own personal world.

In the end, your purpose is to fulfil your destiny and you can only do that by following your fate, by riding your wave, by pursuing your path like a horse that does not look sideways but goes straight ahead, by attuning your personal Tao to the universal currents of life: by becoming a cosmic surfer. By mastering flow.

Your life is a gift, and it is given freely – there are no strings attached as most traditional religions would have us believe: that we are not worthy, that we need to suffer and do penance, that we need to earn or pay for the gift in some way by being a good Christian, Muslim, Buddhist, Hindu or Jew. The conditions may change from one sect to another, but the basic message remains the same: you are beholden to God and thus in His service and need to suffer to pay for life. It is interesting that in all these religions God is a male!

What a gift! Is this not the essence of martyrdom? I love you so much: look at what I have done for you; look at my sacrifice; now you need to suffer for me. But what if this traditional religious perspective is simply not true? What if the gift of life is a pure and free gift from God and all we need to do is to accept and enjoy? Not in some hedonistic and self-destructive indulgence but in a measured and sincere form of deep and meaningful appreciation. This is the real meaning of the word religion: to hold a reverence for life, to be religious in our attitude and appreciation; to sincerely enjoy life with deep gratitude.

The negative ego is always caught in not enough. The present is never enough so we cannot fully be here appreciating the immensity of the gift or the grandeur of the journey. We are lost in either the past or the future forfeiting the immediacy of the present. We are not really enjoying, appreciating the gift. If our quest is this acceptance, then there is the discipline of mindfulness. This is not a spiritual discipline that springs from lack and a need to suffer, but rather a discipline that springs from an earnest and true desire to be fully here now and totally cognisant, aware, awake and engaged in every moment of your being. This is the gift. The true gift is jubilant joy!

Think of the difference between two people on some health regime. The first truly loves to be healthy, to get up in the morning and exercise, eat well, stay fit and live a full and healthy life. They do the regime because they love it and love being healthy. The second is doing the regime because they must – they either need to lose weight or suffer ill-health. But they do not enjoy the exercise and would truly rather sleep in and eat. They do the regime under sufferance, obligation and to achieve some end of a desired weight or be rid of their physical symptoms.

The difference is in the motivation. Their Why. We either do because we truly want to, and the act is the true expression of our being, or we do in order to get. This is the difference between the ego and the Tao. The ego always acts in order to obtain something: there is always an ulterior motive, a reason, an objective. The Tao of your being acts from spontaneous self-expression. It does because it is. There is no ulterior motive. The really great artist paints because that is what their soul needs to do. The really great singer sings to express their inner voice. The true leader leads because that is their true nature.

You can only fully enjoy and appreciate the gift of your life when you are truly living it. This means first and foremost being true to yourself, expressing your inner divinity, doing what comes naturally, honouring your own feelings and emotions, knowing who you are, riding the wave of your personal Tao. In the zone of flow.

If you become distracted by your ego, you are no longer on the wave: you have fallen off your board; the law of your being is no longer carrying you along on its momentum. You are no longer one with the universe and need to generate your own energy. This is precisely why living from your ego is such an exhausting practice. We are no longer supported by the wave of our own being nor the greater cosmic currents of the universe.

So, although we say this is your life and that your life purpose is revealed within the story of your life, you still need to do the due diligence of ensuring your own authenticity and identifying those times in your life when you were being true to yourself and honouring who you are as opposed to those times when you allowed your ego to distract you. Hence, we need to begin by identifying our ego.

When we honestly look back upon those times when the energy just flowed, and everything was in harmony, we can be sure those were the times we were attuned to the law of our being: being true to our self. On the other hand, those times filled with conflict, resistance, misunderstanding, difficulty and effort were the times we allowed our ego to usurp control. The work consists in correctly identifying these two opposing forces – the yin and yang of our lives – and understanding and reconciling their potential difference. We need both! The goal is not to eliminate the ego but to embrace its role within our collective being.

By facing our distractions: our fears, doubts, uncertainties, lacks, posturing and conceit, we can zone in on those forces that separate us from oneness. We then know our life purpose for that purpose is to become one with all there is by eliminating the forces that pull as off balance. One of the most essential concepts to grasp is what is called being central and correct. In our surfing parlance, this simply means having all the opposing forces in balance: the wind, the water, the wave, the board and our own weight and position. We are squarely on the wave being carried forward.

So too, in our lives there are always a myriad of opposing forces operating: our own motivation, other people's influence, social norms and conventions, the necessity to earn money, eat and live, looking after our family, social obligations and so on. We can either allow these forces to swamp us like a turbulent storm or we can harmonise their forces into a synergistic whole that makes sense and affords us grace.

Being central and correct means just that: we have balanced the conflicting forces in such a way that we are being true to ourselves, honouring our being, flowing with our fate and fulfilling our destiny but also doing our duty in life. We are on our path. We are not being pulled off that path by either an inner distraction or the interruption of another's energy and will.

In the modern world with its prevalence of mass media, social media, advertising and the need to conform, this is probably the biggest trap. There are simply too many voices; too much noise. If we return to the Blue Zones on the planet of optimum health and longevity, one outstanding characteristic shared by these people is a disconnection from mainstream reality. They are all self-contained communities isolated from the daily broadcasts of mass communication that now circle the planet on the world-wide web.

To be central and correct you must be authentic; you and you alone must be the author of your story. You cannot discover your life purpose if someone else is writing your script! Think about it. If you are living a false life, meaning one dictated by another or some external injunction, you cannot be true to the law of your being. This is where the original separation and isolation begins. We set up an inner resistance; we become disconnected from our truth.

On some deep inner level, we all know what is right for us; we all know who we are. The choice is: we either honour that truth and listen to our own inner voice at all costs or we give into the noise of social conditioning. No matter how well-intentioned that outer voice is, it is not our own. It does not know what is right for us. My mother always wanted me to be a doctor, but it just was not me. We may be caught in a destructive relationship that has overstayed its welcome and become toxic and it is time to leave. We may meet the love of our life but be too afraid to leave. The cost – both financial and emotional may be too high. We may be in a job that is no longer serving our career, but we are too comfortable to move on.

Fear is an insidious force that can run and ruin our lives!

We all know the scenarios and we have all faced them. The difference is in how we respond. And once again, both polar extremes of the permissible zone of variance are wrong and lead to miscalculation and misfortune. Being true to ourselves is not to be confused with adolescent selfishness that justifies hurting others in the name of my own liberation. Obeying the law of your own being does not give you the spiritual right to impose your will on others. As in all things it is a delicate balancing act – that is why it is called being central and correct.

To carelessly unleash destructive forces in your life will most definitely not lead to a harmonious conclusion. But neither should one meekly give into the destructive forces inflicted upon one by another. We need to be able to stand our ground. We need courage and conviction. We need strength of character. We need to stand squarely within our own truth planted firmly on our wave. Those people who are truly successful have the strength of their own convictions and the courage to be true to themselves and not be swayed or distracted by other external influences.

The real question is: who is writing your story? Is your life your own? Do you know your own plot and thesis? Do you know your moral, your direction, your destination and your destiny? Do you know where you are going? Too many people do not want to make these decisions. Far better to listen to the noise of social conditioning and live my life in compliance with the norms and mores of my society. Far better to fit in, be normal, not stick out, not bring attention to myself by being authentic.

Any time you are authentic you will be different because you will be unique. You will be expressing your unique, authentic, divine individuality. How can you not be noticeable? The most respected and admired quality on the planet is individual authenticity. This is true and natural leadership. People just naturally gravitate to the person who is in touch with and expresses their own inner law. It is what everyone craves. In a world of mediocre mass conformity, we seek the unique.

Unique people have interesting stories. Their lives are rich and varied adventures. Their law leads them on exciting journeys. The meek obediently follow the cyren of social conditioning and then wonder why their lives lack lustre. Your life is like a raw jewel, and you are the master jeweller who must work and polish that gem to its final glory. It is a similar concept to the statue. We begin as a block of stone or an uncut diamond, and we need to chisel the block of our lives into a work of art, to uncover the pearl of wisdom that is our unique being, to hone our skills, our expression, our being so that it shines like the morning star acting as a lodestar to inspire others to also find their greatness.

It is not that some of us are greater than others. It is not that some of us are more gifted or fortunate. It is not that some are born with a silver spoon in their mouth or are given more wealth, talent or fortune. It is merely that some of us mine the depths of our being for that kernel of truth, that some of us recognise and meet the latent greatness of our being and are prepared to work it, to hone it, to distil it, to polish it, to bring it forth in all its glory and perfection. It never just happens! It requires work, discipline, perseverance and consistency.

The world is littered with stories of people who supposedly achieved great success over night but when we examine more closely, we see, the heartache, the failures, the challenges, the obstacles overcome to achieve that final victory. It is just that the personal story is private, and the final accolade of success is public.

Your greatest gift is your life. Your only gift is your life. Without that gift, you would not be incarnate on the planet whatever your personal belief is of an afterlife or multiple lifetimes or whatever. We all scientifically, rationally know one thing: we are born and we die. These two events are the doorways into and out of life on this planet. They are the entry and exit of being physical. Many people try to answer the question of Why by exploring other lifetimes, having psychic readings, tuning into past and future lives.

This is all an unnecessary distraction and just as irrelevant as the noise of the world. Your soul purpose and your sole purpose is contained within this lifetime. By being brutally honest with yourself, by investigating the known of your reality in the here and now, your life story reveals the truth of your being. The language of life is written in the present tense of this lifetime. The key is contained within the projection upon the screen of your life.

Traditional religions preach that the path to enlightenment, to self-realisation, to nirvana, to heaven necessitates a rejection of the world, a retreat from the distraction of daily reality and a denial of the present for some future salvation. This is epitomised in interviews with Muslim extremists who firmly believe that by killing others in a holy war they will be rewarded by Allah in some mythical heaven of girls and gold. What an absolutely childish and infantile view of life. That one's own salvation can be obtained at the expense of another's life and that any God would call for and condone the senseless killing of another for one's own selfish greed and lust.

If the purpose and goal of life is oneness with all of creation and the absolute realisation that all of life is sacred and that we are all one, there can be no justification of killing or injuring or rape or plunder. It is man's ego that creates senseless and selfish destruction; it is the divine Tao that creates oneness. This oneness must be based on a sincere and genuine appreciation not only of the sanctity of the gift of my own life but also the sanctity of the gift of every other life. To take life carelessly is to cross the boundary.

To be central and correct, all forces operating in our life must be in harmonious balance. This is the wisdom of the Taoist sage. This principle is taught in most disciplines of eastern martial arts where the master aligns the forces of the universe with his or her own force to become impenetrable. Moreover, most great performers, athletes, artists and artisans achieve this state of oneness when the flow takes over and they become one with their work. Most of us have achieved this state, even if only fleetingly, at some time or other in our lives. The goal is to travel through life consistently on this wave; to be central and correct most of the time; to live our lives authentically; to be true to the inner law of our being; to express our personal Tao in harmony with the universal currents of life.

To live within the zone of flow not just in rare moments of peak performance but as a daily reality.

The story must become pure. If we listen to a great symphony or piece of music; if we gaze upon a great work of art or beautiful sunset; if we read a great novel, there is always a simplicity and purity of plot and structure. It is never complicated nor convoluted. Truly great artists express in the harmony of simplicity. Our personal story needs to follow this design principle. Is our life not only unique but is it consistent? Does it possess a singularity of being; a purity of purpose? Does it make sense to our rational scientific mind? Will it bear the scrutiny of the light of reason?

In other words, can you verbally articulate what it is that your life is all about – not only in terms of your outer achievements and accomplishments but more importantly, in terms of your inner challenges, your private battles, your personal quests. What is your Mt Everest? What is your basic fear? What is your personal distraction? What are your weak points? What separates you from Oneness with All That Is?

This is not being negative, myopic, melodramatic or self-obsessed. This is the dialectic, the yin and yang of your life; this is the plot of your story. Every great story has the protagonists of good and evil usually personified by the two main characters of the plot and the drama revolves around their struggle for supremacy. Literature mimics life. We live in a binary universe. Planet Earth is a School with a capital S. We get so caught up in academic learning, in career credentials that we forget the real school, the essential teaching is the lesson of life.

You need to know your lesson; you need to know what faculty you are enrolled in; you need to understand the challenges you face. You need to know the protagonists in your screen play: your strengths and your weaknesses; your spiritual quest and your nemesis. You need to know your story. Your life is your university. Your story is your curriculum and like any school if you do not learn your lessons, if you do not pass you get to repeat the class, the lesson until you do! That is why many of us end up in timeless loops of repeated experiences with senseless feelings of déjà vu. I have been here before.

To move on we must master the lesson!

Chapter 11

The Curriculum of Life

The absolute quintessence of life is its uniqueness. As the creator exploded in the big bang of creation, divinity burst upon the material plane in an infinite explosion of sparks of consciousness. Each and every one of those sparks is totally unique. Every single moment in time will never be repeated. Every moment, every cell, every molecule and every atom. Every microscopic subatomic particle. Like every spark that flames up from a burning fire, every spark of consciousness is unique unto itself. No two are alike.

Humanity likes to preserve this distinction for itself, objectifying nature and perceiving only trees or plants or animals or stars or planets or whatever and fails to grasp that every part of creation is the creator made manifest. We like to think that all leaves upon a tree are the same or that all ants in a colony are alike or that animals do not possess individual consciousness.

It is in this way that traditional religion has failed us. We would like our own lives to be sacred but fail to invest that sanctity into all of life and every living being. We do not even perceive matter as being animate. We do not bestow consciousness on anything but ourselves. Gradually, this philosophy of life has left us emotionally and spiritually bankrupt, for how can any philosophy of life fail to account for life itself as if humanity is somehow separate from creation?

But is this not the root cause of our feelings of separation, isolation, alienation and loneliness? For if we, meaning humanity, are separate from the field of creation, we have already lost our sense of belonging, we have lost our place in the Infinity of Being. We are by our own definition separate from and apart from rather than being a part of. As already mentioned, it is this erroneous definition of ourselves that has led to our current crisis where we have become an endangered species and a cancerous growth upon the planet.

We think of global warming as the effects we have had on the planet and the fact that we may be causing the demise of our host, planet earth. We fail to appreciate that in placing ourselves apart from the field of creation we have created our own obsolescence. It is not so much that the planet is in danger but that we are in danger of becoming extinct. The planet will survive quite nicely without us and life on planet earth will be much better, harmonious and healthy without our pollution, destruction and insensitivity. It is not so much a matter of global warming but one of global warning. The planet – our host – is warning us that we have reached our permissible zone of variance. To continue is both foolish and fatal.

The fact is we are giving the planet no choice. It has a very clear and stark choice: allow humanity to continue to jeopardise the whole living fabric of life in this delicate and precious ecosystem or curtail humanity's harmful effects upon the earth and the only way to do this is to cull our numbers. Maybe, in this dire predicament we may come to cherish the sacredness and sanctity of individual expressions of the oneness of life.

All of life is on this glorious journey of evolution towards progressive perfection. Every cell, every organism, every sub-atomic particle and every star. From the most microscopic to the greatest galaxy; from the most inanimate to the most exquisite expression of life. Like an individual sperm thrusting towards the womb to create new life, every particle of consciousness is swimming towards its destination back to godhead.

So many species demonstrate this honing instinct in returning to their birthplace, sometimes decades later: turtles return to the very same beach up to 40 years later; salmon swim upstream to their spawning ground and so on. Nature seems to know instinctively where it is headed and how to get there. Every particle of life is on its own journey back to the original point from which it sprang – the initial explosion of consciousness.

What is important to grasp is that every single journey is unique; no two sparks follow the same path. Each is on its own trajectory back to the oneness of universal consciousness. Each one of us is unique and so too is our own individual path. Once again, this is where traditional religion fails the individual: it posits one path for all its adherents. It offers a cookie cutter recipe, a formula for goodness that supposedly, if we follow, we will gain admission to the gates of heaven in an afterlife. It does not stress nor condone individual interpretation of one's own law. It does not allow customisation of the commandments. The recipe is not flexible.

We need to follow the prescription. Yet, if we look at the practitioners of any established religion, we very quickly see the failure of this system. We have catholic priests raping altar boys on the steps of the alter after Mass; we have Muslim fanatics senselessly killing scores of innocent people in the name of Allah; we have meaningless rituals in all faiths that do not seem to bestow goodness or kindness. Followers of religious tradition do not seem to live the truth of their leader.

Your path is your own. Krishnamurti once said: truth is a pathless land meaning that there is no predetermined path – you must find your own truth. As long as we try to follow some religious formula, we will not find the truth of our own being and thus our life purpose. We need to design our own curriculum. Your soul knows its way back home just the same as any animal instinctively knows its way back to its birthing ground.

Your soul has designed this lifetime carefully constructing it to teach the necessary lesson to perfect your being. The curriculum is designed around qualities of being – what do I need to learn to become more of myself, to express my true self more fully, to be one with all that is? What are the obstacles and impediments to my fullness? Where am I separated from the totality of being? Do I express myself openly and honestly? Do I lack self-confidence? Do I love myself? Do I unconditionally accept myself as I am? Am I afraid to speak my truth? Do I allow other people to pull me off my path? Do I want another to make decisions for me so that I do not have to take personal responsibility for my actions? Am I kind, courteous, considerate? Am I compassionate? Do I love others? Can I receive love? Am I able to love and be loved?

Do I honour myself?

These are the questions we must ask ourselves to discover our destiny. You can never say I am done; you can always BE MORE loving, kind, honest and so on. You can always become more of who you are. Ideals are there to guide and inspire us, but we can never achieve the ideal. Evolution is ongoing; life is eternal. We are on a journey of progressive perfection to return to the godhead from which we came. I can always become a better person. I can always express my inner authenticity more fully, compassionately and wisely.

But I need to discover exactly, precisely, what I am working on in this lifetime. I cannot work on all aspects of myself all at once just as any great artist can only work on any one masterpiece at any point in time. If planet earth is a university and your life is your curriculum, you need to know what that journey is. By examining your story, by looking at the detail of your life, you will come to understand its essence. You will uncover the theme, the plot, the moral of the story and that discovery leads to your purpose.

You will also understand why so many events have happened in your lifetime. You will no longer feel the victim or that life is unfair or question why certain things have happened to you as if you had no say in them. You will understand why you chose that path, why you needed those events. You will also discover that the negative pain and suffering was invariably caused by your own resistance to the flow, your own stubborn refusal to follow your destiny even when you knew instinctively what was right for you.

How many times when calamity happens do we intuitively know exactly when we took that wrong turn, made that erroneous decision, listened to that significant other, who although well-meaning, led us down the garden path and off our own? How many times do we hear the injunctions of our inner law and conscience telling us what we need to do but fail to follow that prompting? How often do we allow the negative ego to gain dominance and usurp control of our ship? How often are we motivated by greed, fear, envy, desire, jealousy or any other negative emotion? What is your particular nemesis? We all have one!

Your path, your purpose is to know yourself; to understand what your life is all about, to know your story. This is not the dinner party version where you rehearse the sanitised story of either how great you are or how much other people have done you wrong. The negative ego only has two versions: the better than and the less than. We are not interested in either of those versions: they are both wrong and lead away from the truth. They are fabrications designed to conceal the truth of who you are. They revolve around justification, rationalisation and denial. They are the Hollywood version in which you play the role of either hero or victim. And possibly both.

Can we just be? Can we just accept our story without the emotional embellishments? Can we just simply face the truth with the courage to be brutally honest with ourselves and tell it like it is? This is entirely private. We do not need to share this inner truth with anyone else, but we do need to tell ourselves the truth! It is our life; it is our story. It belongs to you and is your most precious possession. In fact, it is all you have – your life. When all else is gone, you will still be with yourself, your soul and its journey home. This is what you face at the moment of death; this is your transition and exit from life on planet Earth when you ask yourself whether your life was well lived.

By identifying the major trends and those delicate points of pain when we went wrong and lost our path, we discover both our strengths and our weaknesses: the yin and yang of our lives. From this dialectic, we come to understand the continuum we are on and the potential difference that generates the energy of our wave.

For example, I may be dealing with anger or rather the correct expression of anger. I may attract people into my life with anger management issues who are explosive and temperamental. But I am meek and mild and very self-controlled, so it is hard to understand why I am attracting these angry people into my life. But the lesson is that I am not expressing my own anger correctly and in a healthy way. If someone crosses my personal boundary and interferes in my personal space, then appropriate anger is the correct response to safeguard that personal boundary. Angry people feel it is OK to inflict their negative energy on others.

But healthy anger lasts about 13 seconds and is gone. We have dealt with the intrusion and kept our space sacred. We have not allowed another to walk all over us. It is gone, and we move on. Anger is an emotional collision where another interferes in our energy field.

There is nothing wrong with protecting your space – asserting healthy boundaries. To not do so is weakness.

Life does not always reflect like a normal mirror. We have all seen those convex and concave mirrors in fun-theme parks that distort the image to make it humorous or shocking. Life reflects the lesson in many guises, and it is not necessarily one to one. Even a normal mirror will reflect at 180 degrees so that the image is backwards. We need to get adept at correcting and interpreting these distortions and refractions so that we can get the real meaning of the lesson.

Traditional religions teach us to be self-effacing, self-deprecating. This is not honouring the sanctity of the self. To honour oneself is not to be in ego; it is to fully appreciate, in humility, the divinity of one's being. To honour the self is probably one of the hardest lessons on the planet today because the continuum of honour has been so badly distorted at either end. On the one hand, we have the complete narcissist who thinks they are lovely and on the other the person who is constantly putting themselves down. Neither is honouring who they truly are.

To honour the self is to accept yourself exactly as you are and to embrace your emotional nature; not to make yourself wrong when you feel, as long as those feelings are true and appropriately expressed.

If one looks carefully, it becomes apparent what is the major focus of a lifetime. Just as any great play or novel has one overriding plot with subplots that echo the theme, so too, our lives have one major focus that is repeated on higher and lower octaves to create the symphony and tapestry of our lives. Think of a beautiful Persian rug or wonderful tapestry. If we look at it from the front, we see the picture, but if we turn it around and examine it from the back, we discern the patterns of the weave that have created the picture. One can listen to a beautiful piece of music and simply enjoy the melody or read the score and discern the themes and chords that go to compose the whole. We can gaze upon an exquisite building or examine the architectural and structural drawings that have brought it into being.

Similarly, we can just take our life at face value in terms of the outer daily story, or we can dig deeper into the strands, patterns, themes and chords that make up the structure and give rise to meaning and understanding. A child has a naturally curious mind and wants to know how things work. Unfortunately, as we get older, we lose this innate natural curiosity; we become cynical and jaded or maybe we do not want to look! But if we re-find this natural curiosity and turn it upon our lives, we will very quickly discover the themes, the plots, the chords, the octaves and the patterns that give it structure. We will come to appreciate the rich tapestry that is our life with its opportunities, challenges, strengths and weaknesses. We will discover the amazing beauty and complexity of our own being and life will never be the same again.

For once you discover the meaning and purpose of your life, the apparent and seeming chaos resolves itself into the most exquisite and beautiful design. All of nature makes sense. The universe is an ordered cosmos not chaos. Life exists in perfect harmony and balance. We see this order everywhere except in the human world. Your life is an ordered and organised whole. It has meaning and purpose. You are on a grand and glorious journey. It all makes wonderful sense and like all great works of art, it is pleasing. The mathematics of the universe keeps order. Our lives are unfolding with mathematical precision. We merely need to ride the wave of our destiny and be central and correct. To learn to flow.

Your curriculum is composed of those things that pull you off balance. To ride the wave, we must be central and correct. To be central and correct there can be no forces operating that pull us off the wave, that make us lose our balance. Remember, once we lose balance and fall off the wave, we forfeit its momentum and need to go catch another wave. This is either done consciously where we decide to exit a strategy, or a chapter and we do so gracefully and graciously. This is not falling off the wave or being dumped. We are talking about those things: people, significant others, events, emotions, desires, weaknesses, temptations and so on that sabotage our reality, that trip us up and let us down. Those things that apparently seem to come out of nowhere and collide with our path.

However, upon closer and wiser inspection we discern the pattern, we see the recurring theme. We identify the extreme node points of our continuum and acknowledge that we did indeed go beyond the permissible zone of variance, crossing the border or boundary of our lane, our highway, our path entering into the danger zone of probable collision. Was it thrill seeking? Did we think we could cheat and get away with it? Did we take our eye off the ball and lose control of the steering wheel? Did we willingly hand over control to another? Did we allow them to usurp our reality? Did we listen to another's advice against our own inner knowing and proceed down a path we knew was not correct for us?

There are many variables that can pull us off our balance and we need to get good at identifying which ones are our predilection, which ones are our pattern so that we can avoid those pitfalls in our future. This is the path of learning to become a perfected being. A perfected being is not necessarily a saint or a yogi or a monastic guru but rather one who is attuned to their inner being giving full and correct expression to the inner law of their being. They are on their path, content with themselves and at one with the world. They have a gentle resignation to life in general and with regard to the detail. They have learnt to harmonise their fate, their personal Tao and the universal currents of life. They are one with themselves and the fabric of life. There are no forces operating to pull them off balance and hence there is no karma. I call this state *The Simplicity of Being*.

But even this exalted state is not the end of the journey. Perfection is progressive. Learning is eternal. The gift of life is that it never ends. It will not be taken away and neither will we live out our days in heaven, hell or purgatory. We will continue to grow and evolve and participate in the wondrous evolutionary journey of life back to godhead. Life is God seeking to know itself.

But right now, we are just humble human beings on planet earth and the mere fact we are here means there are lessons to learn and master. The choice is: do we do this willingly, intelligently and with enthusiasm or do we resist, making the learning that much harder? Having enrolled in university do we spend our days in the local pub having fun or do we attend our lectures and take our study seriously?

If the definition of insanity is doing the same thing but expecting a different result, then the definition of stupidity must be knowing that we need to learn something but delaying or postponing that learning. Far wiser to get on with it and master the lesson promptly.

If we accept that we are enrolled in the Earth School, is it not the mark of true intelligence to identify the lesson, apply oneself to the learning, master the lesson and graduate as efficiently as possible? Why prolong the learning? Why indulge the negative ego? Why go about blindly crashing into all sort of misfortune when one can tread the path of life, swiftly, valiantly and simply? Why create suffering when it can be a totally enjoyable experience? Why not embrace the evolutionary journey of life seeking the fullest expression of who we are?

To be in the moment is to be fully present. There can be no distraction. To fully enjoy life, we need to live in the present, we need to be here now not regretting the past or worrying about the future. These are personal disciplines. To obtain mastery is to become the self; to be able to live in the moment; to be present in every moment of one's being; to enjoy life.

The end result of a truly religious life is not the rejection of life here on planet earth but to be able to appreciate the divine in every moment: to see the exquisite splendour of life on earth; to know truly that this is the Garden of Eden, and it is only us who have been wondering in the wilderness too blind to see the beauty before us.

To read Krishnamurti's meditations is to glimpse the conscious awareness of one who has reached that state of oneness. There is no longing for another life only the total acceptance and oneness of being in harmony with the beauty of what is. There is no separation, no interruption. The petty self ceases to exist as a separate unit of consciousness and becomes merged with the greater field of awareness. One just is! The experience and the experiencer are one. This does not mean the journey ends, or we transmute or ascend to heaven in some glorious rapture, it means we move into and out from this oneness at our discretion as we fulfil our destiny. This is the essence of flow.

But it does mean the angst of separation ceases. We still have lives to live; duties to perform. We still have a role to play on the Earth plane and we can become an instrument for good. We can assist the process of evolution rather than being at odds with the flow of life. We move from being part of the problem to being part of the solution.

Chapter 12

The forces of instability

Most of the forces of instability are within! Unlike surfing the ocean, where one needs to deal with many extraneous forces like wind, waves, rips, other surfers etc., the cosmic surfer mainly needs to negotiate the inner voices of one's own negativity and personal demons: fear, anger, self-doubt, jealousy, pride, vanity, arrogance and all the other attributes of the negative ego. It is these inner voices that create the disturbance in one's vortex.

Life on planet earth is all about being incarnate in a physical body. Any form of physical movement, sport, athletics or activity involves mastery of one's musculature. One only needs to observe the clumsy movement or lack of physical coordination of the toddler or person suffering stroke or other forms of motor disease to realise how important this discipline is and how much able-bodied people take this motor control and coordination for granted.

If we further witness great acts of dance, athletics or sport mastery we become aware of how much one can actually take body discipline to its heights of performance. One can only watch a great athlete or gymnast in awe and wonder. To reach this level of mastery takes relentless years of training and practice.

But life on Earth is not just physical; it is also a spiritual experience. The planet is a school, and we are here to learn and attain spiritual mastery. This also requires perseverance, diligence and training – the same 10,000 hours to become a master at any activity. The adept cosmic surfer must not only master the forces of the Universal Tao but also and more particularly the inner forces of one's personal Tao. We all have our inner demons. We are all on our own personal spiritual journey. We are all learning our lessons to BeCome

One. These forces represent those aspects of ourselves that keep us from unity, that keep us separated from the flow of life and keep us within our own egoic shell.

We all know our own weaknesses. We all know our own temptations and distractions. We all know when we are not being true to ourselves, not listening to our own inner voice, not obeying the dictates of our inner law. We all experience moments of anguish, self-pity, doubt. We all have our personal vanities, arrogance, anger and better than. We all hide behind walls of separation that protect us from the world; we all build egoic shells to shelter our fragile egos.

The outer world is merely a reflection and projection of what is going on within our consciousness and our psyche. To flow freely with the currents of life there can be no impurity, no impediment and no interference. This unadulterated state is the most difficult to attain as it requires the relinquishing of thought.

Thinking is an essential part of being human and has its essential place in our psychic makeup. But as in all things, this thinking can be positive or negative, healthy or unhealthy. Remember, this is the plane of duality, and all things exist within their own continuum of yin and yang. Mastery exists in achieving the middle road of balance by harmonising these opposing forces and staying in the centre. Anything that goes to extremes has lost its way and become aberrant.

Over the last several thousand years, the human mind has been usurped by the negative ego which now has control of the thinking apparatus and the mind thinks constantly. The on button is permanently jammed on and most of us do not have the ability to switch our minds off. The mind was not designed to think constantly and most of our thoughts are negative. We ruminate rather than think creatively.

The mind is designed to operate best in silence with the occasional creative thought which designs the future and solves problems: this is the creative force of the universe, the innovative thrust of evolution which is constantly pushing life to higher and better forms. We operate best when we are at peace. To operate at peak performance or be in the zone of flow one's mind must be still and focused. When nervous or anxious, the mind is restless, agitated and destructive. Mental self-control is the sine qua non of personal excellence and being in flow.

It is not that thinking per se is wrong but that it has become unhealthy in the modern human. As we have given control over to the negative ego, rational linear thinking has taken over from the more holistic, intuitive, spatial process of thought. Just as language is nonsense without punctuation, so too, continuous thinking without the pauses of silence becomes destructive and meaningless. The Taoist mind exists within the eternal sea of Oneness and Now. Creative thought then emerges from this silence as necessary, but the base point is rest and stillness.

The egoic mind's base point is restless agitation driven by the inner forces of comparison with others and dwelling in either the past or the future but never the present. We cannot be central and correct while our minds are elsewhere! The restless thinking mind needs to be brought under disciplined control if we are to achieve self-mastery. The egoic mind only exists within the two states of better than or less than combined with preoccupation with the past and the future.

To be still means to be at peace with oneself exactly as one is and to be here now. These are the two prerequisites of success and the hall mark of any great person. To accept oneself fully as one is, is not to be confused with complacency, arrogance or smugness but to end the eternal, internal dialogue of striving and comparison. It is only by acknowledging the present, exactly as it is, that one can creatively design and move into a better future.

We need to begin with what is!

As in all continuums, true inner peace and quiet means keeping still when it is time to keep still and moving forward when it is time to move. Once again, we see the importance of timing and the ability to know, intuitively the demands of the time. More than any other skill, this is the essence or key to mastery of successfully surfing the Tao and the discipline of flow.

It is not about lack of motivation or laziness or some form of mythical pre-determinism where one expects an external deity to do the work for you; neither is it about the negative ego's vainglorious attempt to do it all by itself. It is a cosmic partnership; it is an act of co-creativity where one harmonises the forces of the Universal Tao with one's own personal Tao. This is an intelligent reckoning that one does exist within a broader field of possibility and that within that unlimited field one creates the probability of one's own future by carefully recognising the inherent possibilities on one's path and turning them into a probable future.

Although we exist within an infinite sea of potential, none of us can actually realise this infinity. We need limitation. We need to accept and acknowledge the limitations of our own life and our own spiritual being just as we need to accept that we exist within the confines of a physical body. Life on planet earth is all about limitation and successfully negotiating these limits to achieve success – this is the point about permissible zones of variance. We cannot achieve all things. We must choose a path and stick to it. The successful person knows their path and gets on with it. They do not become distracted. They do not indulge in wishful thinking. They do not ceaselessly compare themselves with others – whether more or less fortunate.

As Don Yuan teaches Carlos Castaneda: choose a path with a heart!

There is a great line in Desiderata that expresses this truth eloquently:

'If you compare yourself with others, you may become vain and bitter; for always there will be greater and lesser persons than yourself. Enjoy your achievements as well as your plans.'

We need to graciously accept our limitations and our path – it is only by devotion to this path that we achieve both inner peace and outer success in the world. To do this the mind must be at rest. Once we tame the restless mind, we achieve an inner stillness and operate from a deep sense of calm whereby we are no longer caught up in the continual conflict and striving of the negative ego but are in harmony with the deeper levels of reality – the great laws of the universe.

Think about any great athlete competing in an elite event: the true winner focuses entirely on their own race, their own performance without comparing themselves with other competitors in the race. They merely do their personal best and focus on the outcome.

If we allow the negative forces of fear, doubt, anger, arrogance, conceit, jealously, vanity, greed or any other negative egoic emotion to penetrate our being and rule, this influence will operate as a psychic force pushing us off-balance. We will eventually lose our balance and forfeit the chi of the wave. It is essential to understand, acknowledge and come to terms with our own inner forces of instability for this is what the Earth School is all about.

As mentioned, we only need to honestly examine our own life story to discover the purpose of our life which is always the quest to deal with these negative influences so we can BeCome One. These forces work to create division within the self. We split ourselves into two – we are divided within and set up conflicting meta-waves that cancel each other out and destroy our ability to manifest a successful and harmonious life.

The study is all about understanding the self! There is no arcane book; there is no external catechism. Your life is your book. Your life is your story. Your life is your quest. Your life is your opportunity to achieve perfection not in some academic completed form but in the ongoing quest for progressive perfection where we are continually becoming more of who we are at our source.

Every day we need to become more of who we are; more able to be ourselves, more able to express ourselves truthfully and faithfully in all situations, no matter what is going on about us; more able to be true to the inner law of our being. This is riding the chi of your own wave, your own personal Tao. The purpose of life is to express our own divinity; to become more of who we truly are, to be congruent and one with ourselves: to BeCome One!

Anything that divides us weakens us. Any inner force that is not congruent with who we are will only cause negative waves in the ether of our manifestation bringing some form of disharmony and destruction into our daily reality. This does not mean there are no challenges; nor does it mean life is over. Quite to the contrary, the gift of life is eternity. This is the core difference between traditional religious dogma and this more positive philosophy of life. Life on Earth is not some penance, suffering or means to some other end in an afterlife.

The gift of life is just that – it is eternal. Although physical life on planet earth is limited to one lifetime at a time and although we cannot definitively say what happens after the death of the body, one must accept the eternity of life. It is not my intention to be drawn into discussions about reincarnation or any other form of life beyond death more than to say one must travel into the depths of one's being in meditation where eternity exists, and the question becomes irrelevant.

To the Taoist such concerns are unnecessary. One accepts the limitation and transitoriness of life on Earth, but this does not mean one is robbed of one's inner freedom. One accepts the condition of a limited time upon the planet and works diligently to make the most of this lifetime. One does not berate the fact of the approach of death nor waste the preciousness of life by giving into melancholy. One accepts one's time on Earth, cultivates oneself and thus harmonises one's life, one's fate and one's Tao.

Life continues on eternal. The inner soul – our inner being goes on. Once again, it requires a strict decision – are we going to focus on the eternal present and exist within that power of now or are we going to lament the future with foreboding and doom. Any deeply religious person who has encountered the depth of their soul knows they will go on. The physical form of the body becomes irrelevant as one knows it is only an outer vehicle to allow access to this physical plane of reality. As such, one understands to look after the vehicle with care and intelligence just as hopefully one looks after all of one's physical vehicles, none of which last forever.

What does endure is our path, our personal Tao, our spiritual journey to Oneness. This is precisely why this is such a profound and necessary distinction between this and traditional religion. As long as we make life on Earth a means to an end, as long as we view an individual human lifetime as some form of penance or punishment for either something we did in a past life or something our forebears (Adam and Eve) did eons ago, we denigrate the inherent dignity and sanctity of life. We effectively rob ourselves of the true beauty, majesty, magnificence and grandeur of life.

Life is a gift. Our job is to recognize, acknowledge, enjoy and accept that gift by living life fully: every day, every moment of our Being. We simply cannot do this while we view life as some form of test, trial, punishment or suffering.

Moreover, the real gift is not limited to this lifetime. The gift is not that you have been given one precious lifetime on this planet and that is it. It is not that life is limited to this physical definition or boundary. It is not a means to an end, and neither is it a one-off. Life is eternal. The gift of life is eternity. That is why we better get used to it and learn to enjoy it – it goes on forever. What a shame to suffer in hell or purgatory endlessly. Far better to enjoy the journey and make it an interesting journey of endless discovery and delight!

So, the purpose of life is to BeCome One for it is only in this state of Oneness that we can ride the cosmic waves successfully, joyously and harmoniously. To flow. That life is challenging; that the Earth is a school and that we need to learn our lessons does not imply any form of not being good enough. The basic position of the negative ego is not good enough and that we need to do something in order to become good enough. We are fundamentally lacking and lesser than. We are flawed at our core. This belief is the opposite of flow.

These attitudes are wrong and are the basic cause of pain and suffering. To be central and correct one must be in the right place – this means having the correct attitude as required by the conditions of the time. The only constant in the universe is change. Life moves on. Eternity does not mean some static form or condition. Eternity means constant change from one moment to the next.

Just as the surfer must be continually adjusting posture, weight and position to adapt to the changing forces of wave and water, so too, the Taoist must be continually adjusting to the ever-changing conditions in one's daily reality. No position remains the same. Life is continual adjustment and evolution. We need to be continually adjusting our position, which is our stance, our attitude our place. And as the outer circumstances change, we need to monitor carefully our inner attitude towards those outer changes.

Do we begrudge, resent, resist? Do we get stuck in a comfort zone and become unwilling to change, to adapt? Do we give into temptations of life being unfair? Do we take our eye off the ball and fall asleep expecting life to remain the same? Do we become complacent? Do we become arrogant, conceited, proud? Do we assume an air of entitlement?

Thus, one's attitude is crucial. One's attitude is the medium of harmonisation between the Universal Tao and one's personal Tao. As one becomes more adept at both tuning into the reality of the circumstances before one and accepting these conditions with good grace, one becomes better at adopting the right attitude. Resistance is pointless. One must accept the conditionality of life. Human beings spend far too much time, energy and effort fighting the external reality of their lives wishing they were different, lamenting their misfortune, unfavourably comparing themselves with others or blaming some external entity for their circumstance.

All these attitudes are wrong and counterproductive. One is creating division between what is going on and oneself rather than embracing a harmonious acceptance, for it is only this uncompromising truthfulness and recognition of what is that gives us the power to change it. We need to be totally honest with ourselves about what is and have the courage to face things exactly as they are, without any sort of self-deception, illusion or blame, that allows us to discover the path to success.

There is a spiritual truth that we are never faced with any challenge that we cannot overcome; there is always an answer, and that solution is the path of personal growth. The essence of Taoism is that opposition is a prerequisite for union and that adversity is an opportunity for personal growth and self-development. We need to embrace the time of adversity for what it is – a challenge and opportunity for personal betterment.

A time of difficulty is a time to pause and to reflect and not a time to plunder ahead forcing the issue or to blame another. We need to seek the cause within as a personal error in attitude. Somewhere, we have lost our way; fallen off our cosmic surfboard and lost the chi, the momentum of the wave. This opportunity for introspection is exactly what the self needs to learn its next lesson. Thus, the obstruction becomes an opportunity for inner enrichment and education. This is the modus operandi of the Earth School.

We are human beings, alive on planet Earth and enrolled in this University of Life. Far better to get with the program, understand the curriculum and enjoy the learning rather than resist the lessons and delay the journey of self-discovery. Life cannot be cheated. One will face the same situation, albeit in another guise, until one successfully masters the lesson. The only choice we really have is to learn quickly, efficiently and easily or to make life hard for ourselves via inner resistance to what is.

It is not that life is hard per se but rather we make it hard by having the wrong attitude and resisting the path. We are not punished for our sins but by them! The I Ching, or Book of Changes, which is the basic Taoist manual of life, is all about adopting the right attitude in any situation. Once one adopts that right attitude, the resistance and suffering fall away and one commences the process of successfully negotiating with life and creating the path to overcome the difficulty or time of obstruction.

The I Ching often talks about the misfortune arising from an attitude not permanently in harmony with the demands of the time. We have discussed the importance and the concept of time at length previously. Time is both the medium and the message. We exist within the continuum of space and time which together create the situation or circumstance that we find ourselves in. So, it is not that time has power over us or that we are beholden to time. Rather time is the passage of life. Everything constantly changes. What is right today may not be right tomorrow and vice versa.

Taoism is all about meeting one's fate and one's destiny with an attitude of acceptance and voluntary compliance: this implies docility and humility. Life is conditional, and we need to graciously accept that conditionality. We accept that we cannot fly or live under water. We accept that we cannot live without air, water or food. We accept, that within this economic system, we need money to survive and so on. There are certain laws of life, descriptive laws, that we need to accept as defining the process of life. Taoism is ultimately pragmatic in that it does not postulate what one should do because of some moral code but what works in harmony with the universal laws of life.

Life is a constant process of change: circumstances and situations are always changing, and wisdom lies in being able to adapt to those changes and negotiate successfully with what is going on. Too many people live in denial or self-delusion refusing to acknowledge or accept the circumstances they find themselves in.

It is not that time has some power over us but rather that time conveys the message of our story. We need to be cognizant of that message – exactly where we are at and what is required of us in any given situation. We need to adapt our position, our stance our place and our attitude. The essence of all martial art training is finding this correct stance – adjusting one's position to the prevailing external forces so that one stays in the centre of balance and is not thrown off-balance by one's opponent. Similarly, Taoism teaches us to remain central and correct by conserving for oneself the strength and power inherent in that central position. We are constantly adjusting our attitude so that it is in harmony with the demands of the time.

The more we can empty our minds in meditation, the more humble and receptive we can be to become aware of those prevailing forces, the more likely we are to succeed in finding that correct attitude. This is not to be confused with pre-determinism. It is not that one remains passive but rather that one awaits the right time for action. Rest and action are viewed as another of these yin/yang polar extremes on the continuum of movement. There is a time to wait and a time to act. When that time arrives one must act decisively, lest one misses the crucial opportunity.

The martial arts master stands firm within their own strength and centre, but when necessary, moves with speed, agility and decisiveness. The spiritual warrior does the same!

There is no fixed point. There is no attitude that is always correct. The correct attitude is determined by the time, by the situation one finds oneself in, by the circumstances of one's life. All things come to those who can wait.

The ultimate determinant is whether one is influenced from within or without. The right attitude comes from tuning into and obeying the dictates of one's own inner being rather than being dictated to by external influences, people or events. One must remain true to oneself. One must reside within one's own strength and self-confidence. Weakness expresses itself in restless agitation and anxiety – one is unable to wait and acts prematurely trying to obtain by force something for which the time is not yet ripe. On the other hand, wisdom lies in the calm strength of patience.

The concept here is that the time will fulfill itself but that one needs to be able to wait. Think of a ripening fruit on the vine – one can prematurely pick the unripe fruit, but it will not be eatable. One needs to wait until the fruit is ripe. So too, life matures; life moves inexorably towards its fulfillment, but we need to be able to sync, to harmonise, to adjust our stance to this flow which is the movement of time. On the other hand, if one waits too long and misses the right time to pick the fruit it will spoil or more probably be eaten by the birds. One has forfeited one's opportunity for right action.

It all depends upon our inner preparedness – our inner freedom, and this inner peace can only come from the practice of meditation. Having an inner point of peace; a quiet, wordless, self-contained joy where one transcends the external vicissitudes of fate, where one resides in the eternal knowing of one's own being. One does not need to achieve anything external to validate one's self. One is! One is secure within the journey knowing one is in harmony with one's fate, fulfilling one's destiny. There is nothing to prove because there is nothing lacking. One is full – content with life, content with oneself, content with what is!

Chapter 13

The dialectic of force and power

One of the hardest continuums to master is that of power and force. Many years ago, I coined the word 'powah' as distinct to the word power for the word power has too many unfavourable connotations attached to it as power over another: images of domination, aggression and arrogance. I use the word powah to signify personal powah – an inner attribute of strength and self-centeredness that has nothing to do with power over another.

The whole point of being central and correct is that in that position lies a powah and a strength that one wants to cultivate and harness for oneself. Think of the pivotal point on the surfboard. If we hold to that central position, we harness the flow or current of the wave and ride it successfully. If we forfeit that position, we will fall off the board. If we hold to the central position in life, we harness the inherent powah of our destiny to live our lives successfully. If we lose that central position, we lose our momentum.

This truth is the secret of all martial art training and the essence of flow.

Just as there are the node points of rest and action on the continuum of movement, there are also the node points of power and force. Power is an integral aspect of creation. The creative or yang element is all about power: the power to create, the power to bring the un-manifest into reality, the power to bring the potential into the actual. The yang force has great power! But this attribute is not to be confused with mere force.

Great power springs from inner worth and does not degenerate into mere force. Force is when the petty ego attempts to force a situation that is not yet ready. The weakness of restless impatience will often try to force things prematurely that we want to happen, precisely because we do not possess the strength to wait. We lack the self-confidence and the faith in our own destiny and thus try to use our personal will to force the situation before the time is ripe. Often this will end in failure and humiliation precisely because circumstances were not configured correctly for success.

We cannot get ahead of the wave if we wish to ride it!

Thus, there is an intricate relationship between these concepts of time, movement and power which go to the heart of Taoism. If one wishes to align one's fate putting one's destiny on a firm footing and being central and correct, one needs to master this triad. This is the attunement process and basis of *Tao Tuning*.

One's life is a journey of unfoldment to become more of who we are. The eternal now is in constant motion – life moves on just like the waves of the ocean. The goal is to ride these waves, to stay abreast of the movement of the wave, to align one's fate, destiny and daily reality.

Think of a musician in an orchestra. One must play one's own instrument, but one must play in harmony with the other musicians. There is a common score that everyone is reading and playing from. The conductor meets out the rhythm keeping everyone in tune and in sync. There is no point in playing your instrument quicker or slower than the other musicians – you will only succeed in being out of step and causing noise rather than music. Eventually, you will be ejected from the orchestra.

No one is a one-man band. No one is an island. We all live within the confines and limitations of the universal orchestra of life. The story of our life is the scoresheet that we must play to and keep in tune and in time with. There is no point in playing the right notes but in the wrong beat or time. We need to keep in time with the rhythm of our life's score. This is precisely where many people become unstuck. They are on the right path, doing the right thing with all the best of intentions but are out of time with the inner law of their being and thus their efforts fail.

As in all things, there is this delicate dialectic between being in control of our own musical instrument and taking responsibility for our own output, our own creativity but at the same time recognising that we are a part of something larger than ourselves – the celestial choir of creation. We cannot just do our own thing. We cannot just play at our own tempo – we must take our cues from the conductor of life which is our fate or destiny.

There is a rhythm, a tempo that makes the score both melodic and pleasing. Just as language depends upon punctuation for its beauty and meaning, there are pauses in life, there is a natural rhythm. For everything there is a season. The fruit ripens of itself in its own time. To pick and eat the fruit prematurely will not be satisfying and will only result in illness. The rain will come in its own time – we need to be able to wait.

The ego with its restless agitation has not the strength, patience or wisdom to wait but seeks vaingloriously to force its way to the goal. That is why so many people find life both hard and exhausting – they are forever trying to force the fulfillment of things that are just not ready. One needs to remain receptive to the impulses flowing from the universal current of life. If one pushes ahead of fate, relying on one's own force to achieve something for which the time is not yet ripe, one will lose one's way and forfeit the momentum and power of the wave.

This is a position of supreme arrogance and self-importance where one intrinsically believes oneself to be more powerful than the universe and where one refuses to listen to the inner law of one's being which intuitively knows it is time to wait.

It all depends upon whether one is listening to one's Tao or one's ego. One's Tao is the inner law of one's being that is inherently in harmony with the demands of the time. One's ego is anxious, restless and clumsy and wants it all at once, now! The Tao is yielding and devoted; the ego is hard and arrogant. The Tao is patient and strong – waiting for the right time to ride upon the wave of one's destiny and thus not having to expend any unnecessary personal energy: just get on the wave. The ego has not the patience to wait but seeks to force the situation, moving ahead of the flow of one's destiny and thus having to use lots of personal energy and power to force events. This is both frustrating and exhausting.

There is a subtle connection between rightness and greatness. Great power can only exist in rightness. Without this quality, there can be no greatness. Force simply does not work and certainly does not last. Universal power is eternal. To become great, one must cultivate rightness. To be right one must cultivate stillness.

The ego always wants more to fill the void of its own lack. The ego believes if it only achieves that next step, that next conquest, that next victory it will be exonerated, vindicated or justified. The lack will be filled; the inner pain will cease. The ego does in order to get; it always has an ulterior motive. The Tao does to simply express its divinity. The ego is only interested in the destination; the end justifies the means; the journey is only a means to the end. The Tao is content and wants to enjoy the journey; the journey is the purpose; the journey is both the end and the means.

Life is the journey; life is the gift; the gift is eternity! We were not given life in order to get somewhere but to become more of who we are. To be here, now. To express our inner divinity. To manifest the inner law and light of our being; to enjoy the journey.

There is no need for force for there is nothing that one has to achieve in order to; there is no destination that one has to arrive at to prove one's greatness. There is no point in time or space where it is going to be alright if we do not make it right within, first. The rightness must spring from within. There is no external situation or circumstance, there is no other person that can make it right for you. You must make it right for yourself by BeComing One with yourself. In this unity, there is a fullness and a contentment – a self-contained joy that seeks nothing from without but rests content with everything. This is the still point of the heart; the essence of pure creativity that any great artist has experienced and from which all successful endeavour springs. This is the zone of flow.

If one experiences a lack within, one will attempt to fill this lack with diversion, temptation, distraction, amusement and indulgence. One will try to bend life to one's own will; one will remain the victim of one's desires forever attempting to fill the void within. The more one gratifies these desires the more the ego craves further indulgence, and one needs to pull opportunity to the self. This becomes a vicious downward spiral that is destructive, debilitating and exhausting. Many people on this self-destructive path end up spent with no energy, power or chi. If one tries to use force, one will consume oneself like a meteor and burn up the precious vital forces that restore life: one's chi.

Modern western living is all about living one's life with force; being on the treadmill of keeping up appearances, being constantly influenced by advertising, media and other external influences. Having to have it all; never achieving inner peace or stillness. Never having time for solitude to tune into the inner voice of one's being; not knowing oneself. Living in haste, noise and exhaustion. There is always something going on: work, people, television, mobile phones, the internet, social media. One is caught up in the continual whirlwind of incessant activity going nowhere fast.

Because of the notion of original sin and the erroneous belief that we are here to earn our salvation, we have bankrupted the sanctity and meaning of life. We are all rushing, seeking to restore that sanctity and meaning but looking outside of ourselves when the whole time the answer lies within. There is no external objective that if achieved will restore that dignity. There is no destination, whether in this lifetime or another that will compensate for the purity of the journey.

We simply need to stop, go within in peace and stillness and reconnect with our inner divine nature: the law of our being. This restores the dignity, purpose and meaning of life. This fills the void and overcomes the lack. In meditation, we simply are. There is no need to do, nothing to have, so there is no need to expend force to achieve anything artificially or prematurely. We are content to flow with life, confident within the surety of our own being. We know life will unfold. We know we will succeed, that the time will fulfill itself.

We are quietly confident, optimistic and positive. We get on our board which is having the right attitude. We ensure we are central and correct which is maintaining balance. We align our fate and our destiny and become one with eternal law. We ride the wave of our personal Tao, enjoying the journey of our story and feeling immense gratitude for the sacred gift that life is.

We always end up where we begin – this is the meaning of the importance of being in the right place or having the correct attitude. If we begin with discontent or emptiness and do to fill that void, we will end up with further frustration and failure. On the other hand, if we commence with innocence and a pure heart, doing for the enjoyment of the act, we will succeed. If we seek love or companionship because we are lonely and miserable and want someone else to fill our cup, the relationship will not work, and we will end with only more loneliness and despair. If we seek wealth because we feel poor and want that wealth to make us feel better, we will only end up with less. Over 80% of people who win the lottery end up with less money after 2 years than they had before they won.

Attitude determines all. We call it a vibe! Businesses with the wrong attitude fail. People in relationships with the wrong attitude experience conflict and bitterness. One of the most productive disciplines we can cultivate is to regularly check and cleanse our attitude to life in general and to specific issues and areas in our lives. This is an inherent part of the process of meditation. I have always found when encountering any difficulty or challenge in my life, that if I stop, go within and examine my attitude to that situation, I can usually change the experience of that situation by firstly changing my inner attitude.

It is interesting that although I have done nothing external, firstly my inner experience changes to one of acceptance and quiescence and then the external reality changes. A spiritual law is at work here: what we resist, persists; precisely because we are energising the situation via our own power and force. Quiescence is defined as the state or quality of being in repose or at rest: being content with life.

As previously mentioned, this is not to be confused with being complacent or merely passive in one's life but rather existing within that central position of stability, serenity, peace and stillness. Too often in life, when encountering a time of difficulty or challenge, we energise or make the situation worse by fighting it. Once we surrender to our destiny and accept our fate, we can then work out how best to deal with it. But it is only by first stopping and going within that we can arrive at that still point, at that point of acceptance, so that we can work inwardly to realise how best to negotiate or work our way out of the difficulty.

If one gets bogged the worst thing one can do is to put one's foot on the accelerator and try to force the situation – one will only get further caught. Sometimes, we need to stop, get out of the car, examine the situation and determine the best way forward. Taoism is all about finding the path of least resistance. This does not mean we give up or become diverted from our goal. On the contrary, what it does mean is that we are so sure of our goal and so sure of ourselves, that we can actually do something that leads away from the goal, knowing that our inner strength and inner purpose will prevail in the end.

In other words, we do not force the situation but rather acknowledge the difficulty as a time of self-development and learning. Quiescence is neither blind acceptance nor passive resignation. It is a superior understanding that difficulties throw us back upon ourselves and that we need to change direction. This means change our attitude! We need to look within and examine our attitude. Through this process of introspection and contemplation, we adjust our position to one of waiting for the right moment for action. That moment will come only after we do the inner work.

We need to distinguish between meditation and contemplation as these are two distinct but necessary practices or disciplines in the Taoist's arsenal. Meditation is stillness; achieving that quiet mind where the 'yamma-yamma' of the left brain ceases and we stop thinking. But after we achieve stillness of whatever duration, we then need to go into positive introspection where we do actually reflect and examine our lives in a healthy and holistic way. This is an altogether different way of thinking that is not subjective nor limited, where we see everything from our own narrow, egotistic point of view. We begin to reflect and think slowly, constructively and objectively.

This means we become concerned about the impact of our lives on others, on the world around us. In this way, we become accountable. It is essential that our lives are productive of good; that we are an influence for good. In contemplation, we put aside the personality of the ego and come from our Tao. This is a completely different way of being and thinking that is objective, deliberate and intuitive – it comes from the right side of the brain. We seek to understand and be in harmony with the great laws of life, to operate from that state of oneness, to put ourselves in harmony with not only our own personal law but also Universal Law. It comes from the depth of our being, but we need to plumb those depths before we can achieve this state of clarity!

Whoever operates from the depths of their being is in harmony with the universe. One puts aside the restlessness of the ego and arrives at stillness. Once again, we come to one of the essential continuums of life: movement and stillness. But this time not of external movement but the inner movement of the mind. And once again we encounter a fundamental distinction between Taoism and other forms of Eastern religion.

Buddhism and other Eastern practices strive for the complete cessation of thought through intense and prolonged periods of meditation in a monastic retreat from life. Life is a distraction from this inner quest for nirvana to be rejected and withdrawn from. Taoism, on the other hand, views rest and movement or stillness and thinking, as two polar extremes on the continuum of thought. The goal is not to eliminate all thought but to cultivate positive and holistic thought through mastering the discipline of meditation and contemplation. This is the modern mindfulness movement.

As in all things, there is a time for quiet reflection, introspection, inner peace and stillness but there is also a time for movement. The trick is to get these two into balance and harmony with the demands of the time so that there is an inner light that develops and guides one in one's life. Indeed, Taoism sees forcing stillness as unhealthy and leading to physical injury. Too many people embrace the discipline of meditation and forget the art. The art is moderation. Stillness must develop naturally from a state of inner composure and acceptance. This is the importance of quiescence as the correct attitude to life. Things must develop naturally over time. True meditation cannot be forced but must come gradually by cultivating the correct attitude to life and achieving stillness and composure from one's acceptance and compliance.

It is all about dealing with one's ego not just the mind. The mind thinks constantly, and these thoughts are dictated by the ego. As one gets control over the ego with its restlessness, the mind naturally becomes quiet. One arrives at inner stillness and a state of calm. In this calmness one no longer sees the struggle and tumult of life but rather a coherent whole. One is at peace; one is in harmony with the laws of the universe and acts accordingly. From this position one no longer fights life; one no longer struggles to impose one's personal subjective, limited, egotistic point of view by force. One just is in this *Simplicity of Being*.

We BeCome One with who we are. We are not trying to achieve anything artificially. We no longer use force. We no longer make mistakes. In Taoist terms, we become central and correct; in harmony with our own Tao and that of the Universe. The ego always wants its own way and will do whatever it takes to force it. This is going against the flow. This is the path of highest resistance where we are at odds with life and life becomes a struggle.

In the *Simplicity of Being* we accept ourselves unconditionally – there is nothing to prove, no void to fill, no lack to compensate. The outer world is of little concern apart from our having a beneficial influence upon it. In other words, the outer world is no longer a cue for our behaviour or action. We become self-determining, acting from the core of our being, guided by our own inner light and law, in harmony with Universal Law.

The mind is no longer constantly being activated by external stimuli that distract and tempt it. The mind no longer thinks constantly going around in subjective and limited circles like a dog chewing its tail. The mind achieves that stillness necessary for coming to terms with the essential meaning and purpose of our lives: it starts to make sense. We know who we are, why we are here, what our lives are all about. We begin to examine our lives from the perspective of what we are achieving, what good we are creating, what beneficial influence we are having on the world.

This is an entirely different perspective than that of the negative ego which is purely concerned with what is in it for it: what it can get, what it can attract, what it can conquer. What it can take rather than what it can give. We begin to examine the effects we are having on the world rather than being obsessed about the effect the world is having on us. We move from idle brooding and subjective egotism where it is all about us to constructive creation of a better world where we play our part in the cosmic orchestra. It is interesting, but from this perspective we actually need nothing – all our desires are fulfilled, and we lead incredibly satisfying lives for there is no lack to fill, no void to compensate.

So, it is not about forcing the mind to stop thinking. This is definitely not meditation – this is still the restless ego trying to force a result. Silence must come of its own accord, and it must come naturally and gradually. Yes, we need to do the work. We need to get our lives in order. We need to study, to reflect, to understand. Above all, we need to change our attitude to life so that we arrive at tranquillity. We need to come upon that state of rest which is all encompassing, where we have overcome the restlessness of the ego, not by dominating it or forcing it into submission but rather by working with it and assigning it to its rightful place as described in *Personal Sovereignty*. When the ego is embraced and cultivated it turns from a negative, destructive, myopic force in our lives to a positive and cooperative companion and servant. We need a positive ego to live our lives successfully on planet Earth! There is nothing wrong with the ego: ego is not a dirty word.

There is nothing wrong with thinking. Positive, creative thought is synonymous with being human: it is our essential nature. To deny thought is to deny your humanity and your divinity. The only definition of God that makes sense is a self-sustaining generative thought that has created and sustains the universe. The physical universe is thought made manifest. To deny thought is to deny our very existence. We need to embrace thought and learn how to master the thinking process so that it becomes positive, creative and holistic.

This is the art of Taoist yoga. We do need to liberate ourselves from the pernicious hold and dominance of the negative ego. We do need to cultivate and practice stillness. We do need to discipline our minds and our hearts. We do need to become quiet. We do need to achieve an inner peace and calm that only comes after we get our lives in order. Order and beauty are prerequisites to quiescence. Again, the dialectic. We work on our outer life to do our duty; to become square. We work on our inner life to become straight; to become central and correct. We need to do these things first.

We need to work on our character so that it is firm, upright, strong. Strong character means strong principles and firm boundaries. Strong character means we are self-determining, resolute and true to ourselves. We need to work on the inner and the outer at the same time as both are two sides of the one coin which is our life.

Remember, this is all about understanding our story – who we are, why we are here and discerning the meaning and purpose of our lives. Our life is both the message and the messenger. We need to develop a spiritually and emotionally mature relationship with our lives and with ourselves to become whole.

It is all about healing the pain of separation and BeComing One. It is only in that unity and wholeness that we can achieve peace and arrive at stillness. If we remain divided, at odds with ourselves, we are divorced from the essential unity of our being and cannot communicate clearly with our inner law: the message will be garbled by the division, and we will be misled into inappropriate action. Intuition is always correct. If in hindsight we are in error, it was not intuition but our ego. We need to get clear, and that clarity is essential for our lives to be on track, for us to be central and correct.

Neurology has now established the immense complexity of the brain and we have come a long way in understanding how it works and the various centres that control different functions of our being. The most important of these is the division of the brain into the left and right hemispheres which is another of these yin/yang dialectic polar extremes. The left brain connects with the right side of the body and is associated with linear logic and language. It is the seat of the rational thinking brain of the ego which is the custodian of physical preservation of life on planet Earth. The right brain is connected to the left side of the body and is associated with spatial, holistic and feelings. It is the seat of intuitive awareness.

The East has understood for millennia the importance of training the brain to think creatively with both martial arts and spiritual enlightenment being dependent upon disciplining the wandering mind. Today, we are becoming more aware of this importance via the practice of meditation and the mindfulness movement. What is important here is to understand the difference between the two modus operandi of the two hemispheres. The left brain thinks constantly and needs to be tamed if we are to be able to hear the quiet, still voice of the intuition which does not think constantly but drops pearls of wisdom into the silence.

However, our minds must be alert and still to recognise and hear these thoughts. It is essential to understand that both hemispheres operate through thought. However, there is a subtle difference between the two languages and the two processes. As we become more adept at distinguishing between the two our lives become immeasurably richer and more peaceful.

We enter that zone of silence where we are able to flow. The body-mind continuum operates more successfully and efficiently. As stressed previously, the goal is not to subdue or eliminate all thought through force. The goal is rather for the mind to become quiet, naturally and gradually so that one enters that state of tranquil calm where one's life is in order and one's mind is at rest. We still think but that thinking is creative and positive. There is a stillness within, and thoughts emerge from that stillness rather than the mind being jammed on at full blast, thinking constantly, going around and around in circles, being negative and myopic.

Visualise a still and tranquil pond. If we drop a pebble into that calm water, we can trace the concentric circles out from the point of impact upon the clear surface. If, on the other hand, the water is choppy and turbulent from wind or some other interference, it is very difficult to distinguish the circles. The mind needs to be like a tranquil and clear lake if we are to discern the patterns of our life's journey. If we live in chaos: excited, restless, anxious and worried, we will never hear the voice of our intuition, we will never achieve stillness, calm or inner peace. We will always be on the go, thinking continuously, agitated and angry.

This is probably the essence of the new spirituality. There are no gurus, masters, intermediaries, saviours, avatars, priests or messiahs who will save us. There is no bible, catechism or set of rules that we can learn by rote to tell us how to live our lives. There is no external source or party to follow to salvation. These are all outmoded and outlived notions of an infantile humanity.

There is only the self and the inner law of our being. We need to follow this path and this path alone. This is the path of our soul, of our essence, of our life. But we must attune to that path and that requires intense focus and concentration which must be done each day at the beginning of the day. We spoke earlier about the day as being the unit of measure, the one step we take each day. And the key to the day is early dawn when the day begins, and we emerge from sleep. It is essential to preserve composure and get control of the mind in that early dawn.

This is when the mind returns to waking consciousness; when we return to our daily life upon the planet. This is when each day begins, and we resume the journey of our earth-life. Each day is like another page in the story. It is in this precious moment that we either assert our conscious control and bring the mind to order or it takes off on its flights of fantasy and is swept along by the bustle of life. I have always found this moment to be the most sacred and the most important.

If we drowse and hover in that twilight zone between sleep and waking, we lose momentum and forfeit the favourableness of the day. We end up in what I call the *psychic soup* of dreams and images of the astral plane. If we discipline the mind and enter the stillness of meditation before the mind has a chance to resume its thinking, we set the day upon its right path. It is in that precious moment that the seed of the day is planted. The longer one can hold stillness the better one's day flows. It is absolutely essential to cultivate concentration in those first waking moments if one wants to experience peak performance moments of flow and creativity during the ensuing day.

It is a pivotal choice! Have you ever noticed that if you give into that temptation to indulge in sleeping in, in drowsing and dreaming you end up lethargic, wasted and tired before the day has even begun? The earlier you rise; the more disciplined your mind in those first few moments, the more successful your day will be and the more energy you will have. Focus and concentration are essential at dawn. It is imperative that one attains this inner composure before the daily bustle of life takes over and sweeps us on its path of haste and activity. There will always be things to do. There will always be challenges. There will always be chores, deeds, projects that you wish to achieve. And this is how it should be. Remember we want to achieve a balance between rest and activity; we want to be successful in action; we want to flow freely and not be beset by obstructions.

We want to live our daily lives in the zone of flow. Cheerful joy rather than worrisome effort.

To harness that flow you must be still at dawn! I have found this the cardinal rule of success. But you must discover it for yourself. You must find your own rhythm. You must create your own daily regime. All I would encourage or suggest is to assert clarity of consciousness as soon as you awake going into a meditative stillness rather than allowing the mind to wander in a slumber or think agitatedly about what needs doing.

To still the pond of consciousness at dawn allows the impressions and messages of the intuition to be gleaned clearly. It is interesting that without thinking about it you will receive solutions to problems, directions for the day's path, messages of importance and things you need to do today. Have you ever tried to remember something or find something you have lost, and it is only when you stop trying to remember that the answer just comes into your mind? So too, if the mind is empty, it can receive the messages that are important for that day. If you learn to follow that prompting and achieve each day what is essential, your life will be on track; you will be on your path; you will become central and correct. You will be in the flow.

One can only walk one step at a time. The longest journey begins with a single step. Quite often in life, taking that first step is both the hardest and the most significant, for once you have made that first commitment the rest seems easier; we have broken the resistance of inertia. We have overcome entropy. We can only live our lives one day at a time and each day is both significant and sacred. To optimise every single day is the surest path to a happy and fulfilling life. To not allow the mind to wander, to worry, to interfere, to become anxious and restless is the key to inner peace and joy.

Chapter 14

The Attunement Process

Tao Tuning is an inner process of spiritual attunement very similar to fine tuning your television or tuning into a radio channel. We have all experienced the annoyance and lack of clarity caused by static or interference if we do not have a clear channel.

It is very much the same in life: we are either clear about our direction and where we are going in life or we are hazy, confused and distracted. The more certain we are about our destiny, the stronger our focus and determination, the less likely we are to become distracted by other people or influences. We are also more likely to achieve our objectives if we are clearly focused on where we are going. Clarity is a prerequisite to lasting success. Moreover, we are calmer, more content and tranquil when we are securely on our path. Confusion and chaos breed anxiety, apprehension and uncertainty.

So, the attunement process is essential. Some of us just do this naturally, achieving a state of inner calm and tranquility easily and without bother. Others suffer from anxiety and inner doubt worrying about every move and becoming paralyzed by fear: the paralysis of analysis. The art of *Tao Tuning* is to arrive at that state whereby we are so in tune with our path, our destiny, our inner law and the greater laws of the universe, that we just naturally know and do the right thing. We do not need conscious effort, we do not need to worry and interfere, we instinctively and intuitively know what is right for us without the crippling force of self-doubt and unnecessary scruples.

We simply flow with the inner law of our being that guides us in all our decisions.

We now need to put all these various components together to achieve this synergistic flow. Think of dancing or playing a musical instrument or learning any complex brain/body task. At first, one is awkward and clumsy – gaining mastery seems impossible: there are so many steps. But as we become more fluid, as we put the process together and understand its rhythm, we become more proficient. Eventually, we hand the process over to our autonomic nervous system that does a much better job at performing these complex processes and we arrive at effortless flow. It is all about practice and self-discipline.

Tao Tuning is both an art and a science. It requires understanding, patience and practice. We need to understand the component steps. We need to adopt the correct attitude: be in the right place. We need to be on our wave. We need to be listening to the inner law of our being which means we need to have quietened the noise of the restless ego. We need to be strong, resolute and firm. We need to know precisely where we are going. And finally, but probably most importantly we need to be patient!

To put all this together we need to return to the beginning: to our original question of the meaning of life – why we are here. Any philosophy of life must help us to answer this question – must create order and make sense of the world. It must assist in the development of a more intelligent and pragmatic world view. It is our hypothesis that the current religions do not do this, that they actually mislead us into an erroneous and destructive world view that is limited and past its use by date. The old religions no longer serve humanity, and the current perilous state of the planet can be directly attributed to these outmoded concepts that have not kept pace with humanity's evolution.

The world we live in today is diametrically opposed and completely different to that of yesteryear: the tremendous advances in technology - smart phones, the world-wide web, social media, disruptive technology, self-driving cars, air travel and so on have delivered us into a completely different world. Yet our predominant metaphysical world view has not changed!

We thus live in a fundamentally disassociated and divided psychological state that is breeding anxiety, confusion and mayhem. We desperately need a new philosophy of life that is in keeping with this new world that we live in and we have argued that the ancient concepts of Taoism provide a more accurate philosophy or world view than traditional western religion. To be clear, we are not advocating a complete acceptance of Taoism but merely postulating that it presents a better starting point than any other philosophy to create this much needed new spirituality.

Taoism is not the answer, but it does provide a firm footing or foundation upon which we can build a new world view or philosophy of life that is more mature, intelligent and relevant to today. There I still much work to be done.

Fritjof Capra in his masterful work, *The Tao of Physics*, makes this same point of the correlation and convergence between the discoveries of modern science, particularly quantum physics and the teachings of Taoism. Capra explains that the word physics comes from the Greek word, *physis*, meaning the observation of or seeing the essential nature of all things. Thus, physics is the study of the nature of reality.

In ancient Greece, there was no division between science, religion and philosophy. Their concern was to understand reality and to form an accurate world view. They understood that these three studies were merely three different ways of viewing the nature of reality and that one needed to put the three perspectives together to form that accurate picture. In other words, there was no division between the rational, linear, logical perception and the mystical, religious appreciation: both were two sides of the one coin forming the philosophy of life.

Moreover, Heraclitus believed in a world of perpetual becoming, where everything was in a state of constant change and flow and this flow arose from the dynamic and cyclic interplay of opposites that merely represented the polar extremes of an essential unity. He called this unity the *Logos* and it transcended all the pairs of opposites. His world view was therefore very similar to that of the Taoists and other ancient mystics.

This view was very prevalent in both the east and the west in ancient times before the emergence of the mechanistic world view of separation and division which particularly occurred in the west, based on the work of Rene Descartes, Isaac Newton and Francis Bacon. Rene Descartes' dictum - '*I think therefore I am*' – led to an over-identification with the egoic mind and to a view of the separation between mind and body. This created the modern western concept of the supremacy of the mind and its attempted dominance of the body and matter. We view ourselves as separated egos living within our own egoic shell and distinct from both our bodies and the external material world. This is the psychological basis of this process of division which so plagues the modern human as he or she firmly believes that matter is dead and inanimate and thus to be dominated and exploited.

This inner psychological sense of separation is reinforced by the Aristotelian model of the world which viewed reality as being constructed of indivisible building blocks of matter, atoms, and has been the basis of the western world view for over two thousand years. Newton then took this concept further postulating a mechanical universe made up of separate parts interacting according to Newtonian physics of cause and effect.

The end result of both of these developments – the inner psychological division of Descartes and the outer division of Aristotle and Newton – has led to a very fragmented world view based on the rational linear thinking of the left brain and negating the holistic, organic view of the intuitive right brain. This division is also characterised by the associated division between science and religion that sees science, on the one hand, becoming overly fixated in the rational process and religion degenerating, on the other, into myth, parable and fantasy.

An accurate and meaningful world view or philosophy of life must be based on both a robust rational and scientific understanding and an organic, holistic appreciation of the nature of reality. One without the other will lead us into an inaccurate and therefore misleading world view: we will either be too cynical and insular or too fundamentalist and evangelical. Both are symptoms of excessive separation and division. Both are collisions with the permissible zone of variance at the extreme.

We need to appreciate that the scientific process is based upon analysis, division, measurement and separation. We dissect, analyse and measure to understand. We examine interrelationships and interconnections. But this scientific process can never really lead us to the truth and is only an approximation pointing to the nature of reality, just as words and language are not to be confused with the actual object. Any world view can only be a theoretical representation of reality - it is an intellectual map of the terrain upon which we live. But as in any map, we need to be cautious we do not confuse the map for the terrain which it represents.

Just as technology has taken over the outer western world, the scientific map has taken over our inner psychological world view to be one of separation and division leading to the divorce from and the domination of nature. We now live in a very fragmented universe. Bacon taught that humanity needed to control and dominate nature and that nature was subservient to humanity. The rationalists under Descartes, Newton and Bacon declared war on nature.

Interestingly, just on one hundred years ago, the first quantum physicists: Niels Bohr, Werner Eisenberg, Erwin Schrodinger, Max Planck, Wolfgang Pauli and of course Albert Einstein, had their Newtonian world view shattered by their observations and discoveries of the behaviour of sub-atomic particles. One by one the basic laws and beliefs of the Newtonian mechanical model were brought into question to the extent that these erudite scientists had to eventually discard the accepted classical world view.

The fundamental principles of classical physics simply no longer applied in the microscopic world of sub-atomic particles. Firstly, there were no basic building blocks or indivisible particles. The more they researched the more particles were discovered. Secondly, these particles were not inanimate billiard balls acting on each other as in some cosmic machine but exhibited the characteristics of both waves and particles. The wave-like nature of the universe, which is the Taoist world view, has now been empirically proven by nuclear physics. Third, these particles are not indivisible solid billiard balls but are composed mainly of empty space. Fourth, these particles do not exist in a specific place but only exhibit tendencies to exist at a given place at a given point in time and atomic events only have tendencies to occur. The classical world view of solidity and certainty dissolves into wave-like patterns of probabilities and tendencies.

Probably the most disconcerting result of quantum theory is the outcome that there is no absolute space or absolute time. Einstein's relativity theory demonstrates that space and time are relative to each other and are connected to form a fourth dimension called space-time which, as already mentioned, constitutes another of these yin/yang continuums within which we operate.

Moreover, space and time are both curved by gravity and not linear so there is no universal flow of time as depicted in the Newtonian view of the cosmic machine of cause and effect. Events can exist in different sequences depending on the position of the observer. The outcome of relativity theory is the plasticity and interconnectivity of space, time and matter so that none exist independently or absolutely in their own right.

The other most dramatic outcome is that one cannot absolutely separate the observer from the observed. As the traditional concepts of absolute time, absolute space and the division between mind and nature collapse, we find a world view that is fundamentally at odds with that of the western world. Humankind no longer stands outside of nature but becomes an integral part of an all-inclusive, deeply connected whole which is the fundamental world view of ancient mysticism most particularly Taoism. We are One. All life is One. There is no division or separation on that level which is both the microscopic and the macroscopic.

The overriding feature of this world view is the wave-like nature of reality as opposed to discrete and distinct particles or building blocks. We have moved from the rational, linear, logical, sequential world of cause and effect existing in an absolute world of time and space to a holistic, interconnected, interrelated world where everything stands in relativity to each other and there are only probabilities and densities of energy patterns and the likelihood of events as determined by the wave aspect of sub-atomic particles.

We end up in a relative world of duality rather than the monistic world we believe we live in. It is essential to grasp the significance of the importance of the outcomes of quantum physics and relativity theory for if physics is the basis of our understanding of 'physis' or the nature of reality, it becomes necessary for us to rewrite the consensus reality of our accepted world view which we simply have not done even though these experiments were conducted one hundred years ago.

We no longer live in the beginning of the 20th century or the 17th or indeed the world of the ancient Greeks, yet we still cling onto a philosophy of life or world view dictated by the outmoded and now disproved theories of Aristotelian logic, Newtonian physics and Cartesian partition. The singular feature of quantum theory that distinguishes it from classical physics is the wave nature of electrons and other sub-atomic particles as opposed to the solid indivisible building blocks of reality. As I have repeatedly mentioned, waves are the building blocks of reality, not matter. Indeed, quantum theory proves there is no such thing as matter only relative densities of energy that appear as matter to our minds. Human consciousness creates matter in the human brain! It is a trick of perception.

The other disturbing and distinguishing feature is the dual nature of these sub-atomic particles appearing as both waves and particles at one and the same time depending upon how we look at them. This is the dualistic world of yin and yang as described by most ancient world views where the opposites are viewed as two poles of the one continuum. Western humanity has spent the last two thousand years trying to construct an absolute picture of reality based on rational, logical, linear, definable, divisible unambiguous connections of cause and effect only to find that the end result of this scientific method is the absolute denial of this erroneous picture.

Yet, we still stubbornly hold onto this outmoded and inaccurate picture in our consensus reality. Why? Why has our accepted world view not kept pace with our scientific progress and technological discoveries? Why are we still dominated by concepts put forward hundreds and thousands of years ago? Why do we so tenaciously cling to these outmoded and erroneous beliefs?

It is our addiction to the egoic world of separation and fragmentation where we live within the egoic shell of our rational minds, falsely believing that humanity is distinct from and separated from nature. Our picture of the world comes via our sensory perception which we then translate into our intellectual concepts. From percept to concept. We simply cannot view reality from the non-sensory, immediate and direct perception of the intuition which sees things holistically as an interconnected whole. This is the world of the mystics of all persuasions – both east and west and the world of the nuclear physicist.

It is essential to understand that both methods – the rational scientific and the holistic intuitive rely upon direct observation of reality to arrive at understanding. The difference is that one is linear, sequential and based upon division and separation: the world of objectification, of language, of measurement, of words and the other is based upon an immediate, direct and thus subjective or personal experience of reality. Indeed, both of these philosophies agree on one thing – that one cannot put this direct experience into words and the more one tries to do so, the more one loses its essence.

Western humanity has lost this ability to enter into direct and immediate contact with reality precisely because he/she is locked within the egoic shell of separation. The overriding distinguishing feature of this intuitive perception is the appreciation of the Oneness of creation! Nuclear physics has proven that we cannot separate the observer from the observed and that, ultimately, the universe is an extremely complex interconnected and dynamic whole that can only be understood from the perspective of continuous flow and change and where we simply cannot measure or observe any part without understanding its connection to the whole.

Just as we all now live within the interconnectivity of the world-wide web, so too, the nature of reality is an interconnected whole of cosmic processes and patterns of probability: the cosmic dance of life! There are no discrete absolutes. There are no indivisible pieces. There is no fundamental structure. Moreover, all observation is intimately linked to that process of observation – there is no objective, outside, clinical and therefore accurate scientific method! All we can do is arrive at approximations of patterns, probabilities of occurrences.

The mystic does not seek to divorce himself or herself from reality. To the contrary, the goal is to BeCome One with that reality in deep and direct meditation, where all separation ceases and the observer and the observed are fused in another of these yin/yang continuums called the Infinity of Being. We are a part of and one with the universe. There is no egoic shell of separation. The thinking rational mind ceases to exist and there is only the immediate here and now. No other. No past and no future. Time and space collapse into the Unified Field.

The ultimate goal of meditation and all mysticism is this union with the beloved, the Logos, the universe, the creator, God, or the Tao. Call it what you will it does not matter. At that point there are no words, for the left brain of logic and language ceases to exist. One enters the holistic world of the intuition of immediate perception and integrated understanding. One has only to read the works of Krishnamurti and other mystics to glean the rapture of this reality.

Taoism, along with many other ancient world views, eloquently describes this new world of quantum physics where there is no absolute reality but rather the dialectic dance of dualism. This represents a quantum shift in thinking: a new paradigm where the relationship between the part and the whole fundamentally changes to one of process rather than structure. The I Ching or Book of Changes, which is the fundamental text of Taoism and is over 5,000 years old, still represents the most accurate depiction of this process and is totally congruent with the most modern of scientific discoveries.

Quantum physics tells us that we live within a world of process, of probability patterns, of waves of energy. We live within a sea of consciousness. We have been looking in the wrong direction seeking the certainty of a structure that simply does not exist. It is time to turn around and accept the error of our past thinking and adopt a new world view based in this new understanding. Not one based in mythology or mysticism, but one based in the actuality of the scientific method.

The beauty of this world view is that it totally validates the zone of flow and peak experience.

Part III

Paradigm Shift

Chapter 15

The I Ching or Book of Changes

The western world view is dominated by the left brain of rational logic and sequential cause and effect. This is the triad of Aristotelian logic, Newtonian physics and Cartesian division. '*I think therefore I am*' is in itself a logical argument of cause and effect. However, the premise upon which all of this thinking is based is the notion of absolute time and that time flows in an orderly sequence from past to present to future in a linear way and that cause and effect are grounded in this linear sequence with cause preceding effect in this linear flow of time. This is called the principle of causality.

The eastern world view does not adhere to this strict linear sequence but is more holistic and synergistic. In other words, cause and effect do not have this traditional immediate relationship. The best example of this is acupuncture where the body is not viewed as a number of disassociated parts but rather as a comprehensive flow of chi or energy and thus interconnected at all levels. The basis of the scientific western world view is that we need to be able to pinpoint the connection between cause and effect and describe the mechanics of that causality in Newtonian terms.

This is the basic error and trap and cause of the misunderstanding.

The Taoist views the universe as a dynamic and interrelated whole where the parts and the whole are all connected across time and space and there is not this linear equation between cause and effect. The limited human mind may not always be able to see or understand all the variables acting to cause an outcome. Interestingly, one of the most recent theories of quantum physics, S-matrix theory, arrives at very similar conclusions to the premise of the I Ching where all things are dynamically interrelated synchronistically rather than causally. This means there is not the classic definition of cause and effect through space and in time and that we, as the observer, may not always be able to directly point at all the causes operating. Rather than being linear in space and time it is more of a web with many strings attached to the outcome.

The I Ching is concerned with the patterns and process of change based on the eternal interplay of the forces of yin and yang and seeks to give us an understanding of this dance which is the beginning of wisdom. This wisdom is not knowledge but is rather an intuitive and holistic understanding of the way of the universe, the Tao. The Tao flows ceaselessly in recurring patterns and wisdom consists in understanding these patterns as stages in that flow and perceiving at which stage of the cycle one is at. By mastering the ebb and flow of the chi, the sage is better able to ride the waves of these cycles as described earlier and hence flow.

What is important to understand here is that, like in quantum theory, the events in our lives only have probabilities or tendencies to occur and are not absolutes as in western pre-determinism. The importance of a world view is that it is the brain's attempt to create order. All living beings crave stability and order – they need to find their place in the world. But it is essential that this world view is an accurate and correct representation of how life works and not just an artificial construct that is man-made and erroneous.

For example, once upon a time the world view was that the world was flat, that the earth was the centre of the universe and that the sun revolved around the earth. We now know that this world view was totally and completely incorrect. Similarly, the currently accepted consensus world view has been shaken to its core by the recent discoveries of quantum physics and we now know we do not live in a solid world of linear cause and effect as described by classical physics. But we have not transcribed that understanding into our view of how life works in daily reality. We still cling to outmoded concepts because they give us a false sense of comfort and security. Humanity has always had an irrational fear of the unknown and would rather cling to an erroneous known.

We seek the security and stability provided by the atomistic, linear, logical, causal universe where every cause is directly related to its effect in a linear and thus easily understandable fashion. But what if, as quantum physics demonstrates, this linearity is incorrect? What if life is far more complex so that life is a set of probability equations where there are many variables determining outcomes and one of the most significant variables, if not the most important, is your attitude?

According to quantum physics, there are no solid indivisible particles but rather clusters or patterns of probability that are intricately interconnected to all other things in a cosmic web. Quantum physics highlights a world not of discrete objects or particles but rather of a web of interrelated relationships and waves. Moreover, the observer is an integral part of this web with outcomes being dependent upon the inner psychological state of the observer.

The western world view wants an objective reality that stands apart from the human being: where we can arrive at some distinct, verifiable and objective conclusion that is divorced from the individual. Quantum physics demonstrates that this simply cannot be. The observer exists firmly within the web and constitutes a major part of it. So too, we crave a philosophy of life that stands apart from us, that is fixed and immovable, that is set in stone like the 10 Commandments. We want a truth or a set of rules, a prescription or recipe to follow that will guarantee our spiritual salvation. Just tell me what to do so I don't have to think for myself and make decisions!

Hence the western preference for prescriptive rules. The Taoist world view is diametrically opposite to that of the west seeing all things in constant change and interplay and does not seek any form of concrete absolute. The Taoist sees security as coming from understanding how the universe works and learning to live in harmony with nature and the cosmic flow of the universe. Thus, this is not a world view limited to life on planet Earth but rather a cosmic or universal view as to how life works throughout the cosmos.

The Taoist seeks to develop wisdom via understanding this dynamic interplay of patterns and probabilities just as the quantum physicist is no longer seeking to determine exactly where a particle is but rather the probability of its tendency to exist. As one becomes more adept at determining these patterns of life, one becomes better equipped to stay within the permissible zone of variance and stay on one's path.

The Book of Changes seeks to teach us the way of the universe. Although viewed as an oracle to be consulted as a book of divination, it is not to be confused with fortune telling or prophesising the future. Just as there are only tendencies to exist in particle theory, there are only tendencies for outcomes to occur – it all depends upon our attitude.

One consults the oracle just as one consults a map on a journey: to better understand where one is at and what is the best possible path to take to arrive at one's preferred destination. But the map is not to be confused with the territory and the map certainly cannot guarantee the future journey. There are far too many variables and contingencies that one may meet with along the way. Nevertheless, when embarking on a journey in an unknown terrain, a map is an essential tool to assist in a successful outcome.

The I Ching merely describes the territory or terrain one finds oneself in. It makes clear the variables and the contingencies; as already explained it describes the demands of the time. But Taoism is clear that the overriding determinant of success is the inner attitude of the person consulting the oracle. Taoism firmly adheres to the premise that we do indeed create our own reality and that it is the inner psychological and psychic variables that determine our future more than any external variable.

The result is that the responsibility for creating our path lands firmly at our own feet. One does not consult The I Ching to know the future but rather to understand the matrix of the present so that one can decide for oneself the best route forward. The present is a matrix or gestalt - not in strict linear causality but rather in a synchronous web of interconnectivity, similar to particle theory.

Moreover, one cannot arrive at this standpoint via logic or reasoning. This is not an intellectual exercise. Rather one must enter the immediacy of the present, becoming one with the web and thus develop an intuitive understanding of all the variables operating on the situation. This is the attunement process. By going within in deep meditation, one becomes a part of that gestalt and arrives at a higher intuitive perspective where the polarity of the earth plane ceases and we are freed from the duality of yin and yang. As we transcend this state of opposition, we arrive at Einstein's Unified Field not in some scientific abstract way but in our inner psychic awareness.

In that state one just knows the path forward: the best course of action to take. What is important to understand is that this higher perspective cannot be found via following any external set of rules, injunctions or commandments. It cannot be learnt academically. There is no recipe to follow. The western world view is one of prescription: of an external force or influence telling us what to do. The Taoist world view is rather a listening to the inner law of one's being: the attunement process of honouring the self, of allowing one's inner innate wisdom to guide one. One must be still. One must become innocent and spontaneous, trusting in one's own inner nature.

The emphasis moves from a security that is based on solidity and linear causality to a security that comes from living one's life in harmony with nature, being in the flow and understanding the patterns of change. Whereas the western world view is all about formulae, recipe and rules, the Taoist world view is all about spontaneity, naturalness and innocence. One is based in logic and reason; the other in the wisdom of the Now! One must learn to trust oneself.

Ultimately, one either lives in a world of separation, division and linear causality where one stands apart from the world and views it as an outside objective observer or one understands that the self is an integral part of the web and has one's being firmly rooted in the Infinity of Being. The discoveries of the last 100 years have dispelled the illusion of the former and validated the view of the ancient mystics. The problem of course, is that the predominant world view of the masses has not caught up with these radical scientific discoveries probably because they would have too shattering an effect on classical western society and our sense of identity.

We need the illusion of separation and division to live our daily lives upon planet earth. This is precisely why this view is such an integral part of the egoic process: the ego's function is to navigate terrestrial life and keep us physically safe. But a world view is concerned with much more than physical security and safety – it is the way we view life and how we live our lives as a species. It is precisely because this current western world view is so erroneous that we face immanent extinction as a species!

It is the thesis of this book that modern western humanity has failed to adapt to the lessons of quantum physics and that our current world view or philosophy of life is outmoded, childish and immature. It is also leading us down the path to global destruction and species annihilation.

We need as a matter of urgency to adopt the lessons learnt from quantum physics and get on with adjusting our world view to one that is more accurate and in keeping with the time. One of the main teachings of the I Ching is to be in harmony with the demands of the time – not to be stuck in the past but to recognize exactly where one is at on one's cosmic journey. What are the variables and the configuration of the matrix that one finds oneself in right now, not yesterday?

If one can accurately do this, success and good fortune is assured. But if one cannot adjust to the present, one's future path will be fraught with difficulty. Humanity is stubbornly refusing to adjust its world view to the description of reality that our own science is showing us. We are not being asked to accept the teachings of some ancient mystical text, but we are being confronted by the outcomes of our own rational scientific process.

Quantum physics destroys the illusion of an objective outside world divorced and distinct from the observer. We are all participants – this is a participatory universe. and we need to take responsibility for the impact of our behaviour on the world around us. This is the shattering truth confronting us!

This means we need to enter the dance of life on planet Earth and take up our rightful position as custodians of the planet. It means we need to formulate a world view based on unity where all things are living and a part of the sacred web of life. Western society wants to see itself as distinct from and apart from nature so that it can dominate and exploit the natural resources of the planet without compunction. To accept the indivisibility of life, to accept the unity of all things would necessitate a totally different perspective where humanity could no longer sit in its exalted position of false and erroneous superiority and blithely rape Gaia.

The western world view still believes in an absolute time and an absolute space even though it is more than 100 years since Einstein's relativity theory demonstrated that neither space nor time exist independently of each other but rather form a yin/yang continuum called space-time. Moreover, neither of these are linear but curved and relative to each other via the speed of light. This is why it is called relativity theory.

In more recent times the outcome of this view has been taken even further by Geoffrey Chew in his 'bootstrap philosophy'. The classical world view of linear space and time sees God creating the world at a distinct point in time and that world consists of solid particles and entities that interact with each other according to certain preset principles and laws laid down by God in the original process of the creation of a mechanistic universe. God created a machine and set it in motion. Thus, there is very little room to move or for flexibility. There is rather the false comfort and security of a mechanical world that runs according to linear causality.

Newton argued that it was only a matter of time before science 'learnt' all the laws of this mechanical universe and could thus rule the world.

The bootstrap world view says that it is impossible to break the world up into discrete building blocks that operate according to mechanical rules; that we simply cannot understand the world via our process of division and separation but that we need to accept the totality of creation as an indivisible whole. In other words, we cannot isolate one set of variables from the rest to understand its nature; that everything is interrelated and to understand any part, taken out of the whole, is only an approximation and distorts the truth. The more we separate and divide the further we move from the truth.

In other words, we exist within a relative universe of interrelated interconnectivity where everything is somehow connected and impacts upon the rest: the Butterfly Theory. Moreover, there are no mechanical rules ordained and imposed by an external god or deity but rather a set of fundamental laws that are intrinsic to and a part of nature. These are not externally imposed prescriptive rules but intrinsic rules or laws that express and explain what does actually happen in an orderly and harmonious universe: the cosmos.

The western world view believes we need divine law to tame the beast within and keep us from anarchy which would be our natural tendency. The Taoist world view and that now being expressed by the bootstrap view is of an inherently harmonious whole where all parts just naturally exist in cosmic order because they obey the inherent wisdom, natural order and law that is within their own being.

In this way, we begin to understand that human theories are just that – products of our own rational mind and not really adhering to the natural world. They are a part of the rational thinking mind and the language we use to describe reality, but they are not really a part of that reality just as the word is not to be confused with the object and the map is not the territory.

Moreover, we cannot create an accurate world view from just the rational logical brain for the universe is far too complex and beyond rationality. We need to embrace the holistic intuitive mode of consciousness to understand the nature of reality. The rational mind can never accurately describe the world because the nature of reality is not purely logical. The truth of the universe can only be approached via deep meditation where we merge our individual consciousness with that of the wider world and become one with that reality.

This is non-linear and non-logical, not in the sense of being illogical but rather beyond reason. This is that direct experience of reality that is the mystical experience and transcends the thinking logical brain. Indeed, it is only when we quieten the thinking mind that we can approach the true nature of reality.

Because western humanity denies the intelligence of the whole and views itself as the only intelligent being, it is extremely hard for it to adopt the correct attitude that the I Ching stresses is necessary for coming to terms with the matrix of the present. We are no longer being guided by the spontaneous and natural wisdom of our inner being. We have lost our way; abandoned our Tao. We are not in the flow.

It is important to understand the way the mind works and why we form a world view. It is said the single most important step in the evolution of the human being was the development of language. It was once believed that humans were the only species to communicate verbally but we now know that many species do in fact communicate verbally, but none seem to have developed the rich complexity of language that humans have, and none have developed the written word.

Quantum physics has dispelled the notion of indivisible particles and solidity. We now know that matter is no more than extreme densities of energy and that inside the subatomic world is mainly space. So, we do actually live in a swirling world of energy that appears solid to us as matter. Indeed, we need the appearance of this solidity to exist on the physical plane and the ego, as the earth resident expert and aspect responsible for our physical survival, needs to differentiate these energy patterns as distinct objects. This is the neurological process of objectification whereby we identify and name individual discrete localisations of energy as solid objects.

However, we need also to be mindful that the word is not the object and that the object does not really exist as solid matter. The word points to the object; language facilitates communication about reality, the world out there, but language and words are not to be confused with that external reality. They are merely a representation, a pointer. They are not the thing being pointed to! Words are a tool, an instrument of the rational mind.

Moreover, there are numerous languages on planet earth with many different races developing completely separate languages and alphabets. One cannot compare, say, the English language to that of Mandarin for structure, language and spelling. So, there is nothing unique or sacrosanct about any language per se. All language is purely a tool humanity uses to facilitate observation, communication and relationships.

There are also many customs, cultures, mores and patterns of behaviour just as there are many diverse belief systems, religions and philosophies. One could even say that more division, separation, hostility and war are created by our separate belief systems than anything else. Moreover, if we look back historically, we can see an even greater variety of customs, cultures and beliefs.

These systems are purely representations of the world around us and no one race has a monopoly on this representation or can lay claim to a more valid belief system even though each culture believes their particular interpretation is correct. Invariably, what happens historically, is that the dominant economic power of the day gets to impose its world view, its philosophy, its interpretation of the way the world works on the people within its empire. Empires do not just dominate people militarily and economically, but more importantly culturally and spiritually.

Every empire has imposed its world view on the peoples and countries that it has dominated. Today, we live in a predominantly western world view precisely because the planet has been dominated by first the Dutch, then the British and now the United States of America. This domination is not always overt but can be quite covert and insidious. One can look to the dominant currency of the age to determine who is the ruling power of the time. We are currently witnessing the decline of the greenback as the medium of exchange as American economic dominance is replaced by that of China or quite possibly India.

The predominant western world view that we are talking about represents an extremely limited and narrow window on reality. It is just that the predominant economic powers of the last 2,000 years: the Greek, Roman, European, British and now American empires have all come from that perspective and imposed their view on the world.

When we contrast the western world view with that of Taoism, it is essential to realise that Taoism is not the only world view that holds this alternative perspective. Indeed, there are many ancient cultures and many current religious perspectives, that align more with this point of view. If we look statistically at the pure number of human beings that have adhered to either, the western perspective is definitely in the minority. It is just that the west is the dominant economic power and has been for the last 2,000 years.

The Roman empire used the Judeo-Christian philosophy to assert its dominance, thus becoming the Holy Roman Empire, which then became the western world view.

The Taoist world view does not stand alone, and we are only using it because it represents the most articulate and the closest to recent scientific discoveries. We commenced this discussion by making the assertion that humanity needed a new spirituality and a new philosophy of life that worked, that was practical, that was grounded in reality and that could be verified by the rational scientific method. But we need to be wary of presenting any particular point of view as the answer. This would be as foolhardy and dangerous as the situation we find ourselves in right now.

There is nothing sacrosanct about any particular perspective and humanity needs to develop and adjust its picture and understanding of the nature of reality as it evolves and as it matures. To become fixated and stuck in any perspective is the inherent danger of the human mind precisely because we become comfortable and secure in the known and fear the unknown.

It is my hypothesis that humanity is stuck in the past with a world view that has not kept pace with recent scientific developments and that the existing world view no longer serves us. To replace one fixed perspective with another is not the goal but to generate a fluidity, a flexibility and a receptivity that fosters growth, learning and evolution. The rapid rate of scientific discovery and technological change guarantees that our understanding of the nature of reality will be radically different in 100, 50 and even 20 years' time. We need to ensure our philosophical construct changes and evolves accordingly!

When the first atomic physicists made their initial discoveries just over 100 years ago, it shook their world view to its core. Many realised the implications of these discoveries and the erroneous picture we held of the world especially that of Newtonian physics. As these discoveries have progressed over the last 100 years, they have only reinforced the dramatic change in understanding and thus perspective required to come to terms with this new reality. The bootstrap theory is just one of a long line of theoretical discussions resulting from the paradoxical nature of reality that is being uncovered as we explore deeper into the world of subatomic particles and nuclear physics.

In the end, there needs to be a convergence of mind and matter or science and religion. As already mentioned, in ancient Greece where our western world view started, there was no separation between philosophy, science and religion. These three were merely three sides of the one prism that the ancient Greeks used to look into the 'physis' or nature of reality. Western culture then went on this 2,000-year journey or detour where the linear, rational mind took precedence over both the material and the spiritual.

Matter was viewed as inanimate, dead and thus nature was to be dominated and exploited via the scientific rational process of division and separation precisely because mind was viewed as separate from and superior to the body. Bacon argued that humanity had a moral obligation to subdue nature and thus nature became the enemy.

Moreover, the spiritual world was denied its appropriate place in the true scheme of things: the intuitive, holistic sense of unity, the mystical perception and understanding of the inherent harmony and oneness of creation gave way to the superstitious and mythical world of religion where parables and bibles were accepted at face value and as articles of faith without being subject to scientific scrutiny or rational discourse.

We have thus ended up in a very precarious situation dominated by a limited rational interpretation of reality that has discounted both the empirical results of modern science and the ancient intuitive appreciation of oneness. As we enter the 21st century and emotional maturity as a species, it is essential we develop a more holistic and thus healthy understanding of the world within which we live, or we may not live within it for much longer!

All maps are just that – they are mere depictions or representations of the terrain upon which we tread. If a map is faulty, it is worse than useless as it will most definitely lead one astray by giving false and misleading information. Our scientific understanding of the nature of reality has dramatically changed in recent times and it is imperative our intellectual appreciation or philosophical outlook changes accordingly.

There have been many peoples, many cultures, many perspectives and windows on reality that differ fundamentally and intrinsically from that of the modern, classic, western world view. Many of these have lasted a lot longer and created more harmonious, happier and healthier lives for their adherents. Our perspective has created unprecedented economic wealth, prosperity and technological development but has left us spiritually bankrupt, emotionally unwell and strategically vulnerable.

As a species, our current path is unsustainable and unviable. Our world view is dangerous for the planet, ourselves and all that dwell upon it. Like lemmings heading for the precipice, we need to stop, turn around and examine our Why! That why is intricately connected to our world view, our raison d'etre, our philosophy of life and the way we see ourselves as the dominant and separated species on the planet. A more holistic comprehension of reality, where we are intimately connected to all things in a deep interrelated web, as is being shown to us by modern science, is essential if we are to survive.

Chapter 16

Models, maps and territories

We began this discussion by making the assertion that humanity needed a new religion or philosophy of life that was more appropriate to the 21st Century and that this philosophy needed to be based in reality and subject to the examination of the rigors of science – that we could no longer just accept religious beliefs as articles of faith without analysis or reason. It is also essential that a world view is an accurate representation of the nature of reality and that it is flexible enough to be updated as humanity and our understanding of life evolves.

A world view is a map or manual of how life works. Any map is only as useful as it is accurate; if not it is worse than useless because it provides wrong information and leads us astray. Both the scientific method and the mystical experience rely upon direct observation of the world albeit the former utilises the rational brain and the latter the intuition. Both are valid and complementary functions of the intellect.

We need to understand the key findings of nuclear physics and incorporate them into our world view. There are three major outcomes that are at odds with the traditionally accepted view of the nature of reality. The western model is based upon the concept of the atom as the building block of the universe. This led to the search for that indivisible and separate unit of the smallest particle of matter. This Aristotelian view also held that matter was inanimate and dead and were merely passive particles that were acted upon according to fixed and immutable laws set down by God at the time of creation.

Indeed, it was this very search for these indivisible particles which ultimately lead to the science of nuclear physics some 2,000 years later which concluded that there were, in fact, no fixed, indivisible and solid billiard balls or building blocks. The sub-atomic world is not filled with indivisible particles that exist as separate and distinct entities but rather a complex and integral pattern of networks, interrelationships and probabilities.

Particles come into existence and dissolve again in a continual flow of energy. Solid matter does not exist at all in its own right, but the appearance of solidity is a part of our intellectual construct and perception. Matter does not exist at all. It is an illusion. The appearance of solidity is a function of this ceaseless oscillation and dynamic movement at very high speeds of these energy waves just as a very fast spinning fan 'appears' as a solid wall.

The significant conclusion is that these particles do not exist as separate units but form part of a cosmic web of interrelationships: separation is not a characteristic of nature. Everything is part of a larger cosmic whole and cannot be broken down into discrete entities that exist on their own. The concept of separation and fragmentation, which is the fundamental corner stone of the western world view, is simply wrong. The universe is an integrated whole moving continuously in organic and harmonious patterns.

The second significant outcome is the dual nature of these subatomic particles: being at one and the same time particles and waves. Rather than being the solid building blocks of matter, atoms are composed almost entirely of empty space within which these sub-atomic particles operate as both waves and particles. Moreover, these particles do not exist absolutely at any fixed point at any given moment in time but only exhibit tendencies to exist. In this sub-atomic world, there are no certainties only probabilities.

It is the wave like nature of these particles that represents the greatest breakthrough in the true nature of reality. Rather than living in a solid world of separate and distinct objects, we live in an ocean of swirling energy patterns that only demonstrate probabilities to exist. The solid world of classical physics dissolves into probability patterns of interconnectivity. Once again, the conclusion is that we do not inhabit a solid world at all! Rather reality is just a sea of energy that cannot be divided or separated into discrete building blocks of matter.

For example, we all know that we can dive into water whereas a being that had never experienced the fluidity of water would believe it to be a solid mass. The supposed matter of the universe is no different than the plasticity and fluidity of water except that our neurological processes view it as solid.

We have previously stated the importance of waves as the real nature of the world in which we live. Rather than inhabiting a world of solid particles, modern science proves we live in a cosmic ocean of interrelated probability waves. This has far reaching implications for our classical world view.

The third significant outcome is that there is no objective world out there that can be observed in isolation from the observer. The world can only be understood in relation to its interaction with the observer. The true nature of reality is a harmonious whole within which all parts are related to each other. Humanity is an integral part of the equation. The notion of separateness is erroneous! The classical mechanistic model of the universe has been replaced by a more fluid, organic, interconnected and dynamic whole which cannot be defined objectively without reference to human consciousness.

The universe is not a machine with moving parts that operate according to Newtonian laws. The universe is an interconnected and dynamic whole that operates in perfect harmony according to an intrinsic and divine intelligence. We separate to observe, to analyse and to understand. But every time we dissect, we lose a little truth. The more we break up into fragments, the more we move away from the true nature of reality. Ultimately there is no such thing as objective science.

We live in a world of relativity and the observer is the predominant variable! Knowledge cannot be viewed as independent of the process of human observation. How we do the observation, how we do the intersection and dissection will determine the outcome. We simply cannot take ourselves out of the equation. We simply cannot speak about an external, clinically verifiable objective reality.

The classical world view of Aristotelian logic, Newtonian physics and Cartesian division presents a picture of the nature of reality that is fundamentally wrong and erroneous. We do not live in a machine composed of indivisible building blocks or parts that interact in rigid and predefined ways and that is inanimate, dead and separate from us. There is no separate and objective reality.

We live within a sea or cosmic ocean composed of energy patterns or processes that is holistic, interconnected and relative. The overriding characteristic of the mechanistic model is separation, division and fragmentation into parts. The overriding characteristic of the new model is a harmonious unity and oneness that cannot be broken up into parts. The old model is one of functional structure and mechanics; the new model is one of organic process and patterns.

The classical model seeks to give humanity a sense of comfort and surety by dissecting, analysing, defining and ultimately dominating the world in which we live. It is based on the premise of separation and fragmentation – a separate and scary world out there that we need to dominate and overcome lest it overcomes and dominates us. Conflict is an inherent characteristic of this view thus the geopolitics of the modern age is built on conflict and war.

The mystical model delivers security by embracing and becoming one with the All That Is, through flowing with one's destiny and achieving harmony between one's individual Tao and that of the universe. It is based on the premise of inclusivity and oneness and the understanding that there is no division, that the world is one and that the sense of separation is a functional illusion. Harmony is an inherent characteristic of this alternate view. Disharmony is the crux of the western paradigm.

As we separate the world into its myriad parts in the pursuit of objective science, we lose the true nature of reality. We come to live in a fragmented and dysfunctional universe. We see ourselves as divorced from the world in which we live. We view ourselves as separate from everything and everybody else. We become isolated, fearful and neurotic ready to both defend and attack. The world is inherently dangerous.

We see ourselves as living in this mechanistic universe that is regulated by rigid, religious, prescriptive laws that we must obey, or we will suffer. We have created a separate god and a separate devil. Just as we view the world as made up of indivisible building blocks or billiard balls that are acted upon by outside forces, we see ourselves as discrete and separated units of being that are acted upon by these outside forces of good and evil. It is still a mechanistic paradigm of powerlessness and passivity based on Cartesian division; that the world exists out there as something separate to us. We have reduced the universe to an absurd billiard table where god and satan hold the cues and we are mere balls within the machine.

In fact, it is this sense of separation, powerlessness and fear that creates the desire to dominate. We needed to dominate and control nature because we saw it as dangerous, as something scary and to be feared. The pursuit of knowledge ceased to be an attempt to understand the nature of reality but an attempt to subjugate and dominate. Since the 17th century, science and technology have been at odds with nature and have created the pollution, environmental destruction and human malaise to the extent that we are now on a collision course with nature rather than an attunement to being one with life.

Although this divisive and reductionist scientific process has brought us immense technological development and material wealth, it is questionable whether it has made us happier and healthier as human beings and it most certainly has not delivered us from anxiety. The current epidemic of mental illness, anxiety and stress are merely symptoms of this malaise. Our technological development has not really delivered us to a safer and saner world. If anything, we have fulfilled our own prophecy of the world being a scary place but not one created by nature but rather by humanity.

The number one function of a world view or philosophy of life is to deliver the wisdom and understanding of the nature of reality and how life works so that we can live our lives more joyously and in harmony with the inherent laws of the universe. As we come to appreciate and live in harmony with the natural flow or order of the universe, we live in the current of the Tao; we are at one with the supreme cosmic forces. It is this and this alone that can deliver true peace, comfort and freedom from anxiety. The more at odds we are with the natural order of things the more we are filled with anxiety, unrest and inner turbulence.

As opposed to this classical reductionist perspective, the mystical one is concerned with the direct perception of the totality of existence, the oneness of creation. Whereas the classicist wants to separate him or herself from the world and view it objectively from a distance, the mystic wants to embrace the world and enter a divine rapture or appreciation of its oneness. The classicist lives in a perpetual world of separation whereas the sage seeks the transcendence of this separation directly merging individual consciousness with that of the beloved.

There is no sense of separation, hostility or fear. Rather there is an acceptance of the divine benevolence of the universe; an understanding that we are all connected and form part of the one divine cosmic dance as alluded to by nuclear physics and as demonstrated by sub-atomic particles. These particles have their nature grounded in this cosmic soup. They appear and dissolve into and out of beingness; they do not hold onto a separated sense of identity as we do. They exist within probabilities as we do; it is just that we do not allow ourselves that freedom!

We cling to the certainty of separation as the only means we know to retain our identity of self. We cannot accept a paradigm where we dissolve into and emerge from oneness. Where, in fact, our identity is not defined by our separateness but rather by our unity with the whole. The classical world view from the ancient Greeks down has been based upon the premise that to understand something we need to break it up into its constituent parts: the reductionist theory. We have been splitting up reality into smaller and smaller pieces, dissecting, separating, seeking these essential building blocks with their attendant laws of interaction to define ourselves and the world within which we live.

The basic problem with this methodology is that it ignores the essential relationship between part and whole and the intrinsic nature of unity or harmony which is the overriding characteristic of life. We fail to see the forest for the trees, and we mistake the map for the territory. Nuclear physics taught us that we cannot divide reality without losing some of its essential nature and that we could not take the observer out of the equation. We simply cannot define parts absolutely and objectively without reference to the whole.

This is the importance of Geoffrey Chew's bootstrap theory in that it fundamentally questions this relationship between part and whole. This means we cannot define any part without reference to the whole for everything forms a part of this dynamic web of interrelatedness and everything affects everything else. These is no sense to artificially breaking up complex matrices into component parts as the more we do the more truth we lose. This view resembles that of the mystics in their appreciation of the essential oneness of creation and that the goal is to enter that state of oneness rather than the isolated state of fragmentation.

It is a fundamental characteristic of human consciousness that the mind seeks to create order by understanding how things work. Humanity has always sought to explore the nature of reality and the dynamic workings of the world: this is why an appropriate world view is so vital for our composure and surety as beings. The classical view believes in this mechanistic model which basically says that God created the world (whether in 7 days or not) much like mankind makes machines. This means there are component parts which are the indivisible particles that interact according to predetermined laws also made by God.

These laws are prescriptive in that they are defined by an external entity (God, the creator) and imposed upon creation. The western concept is thus of an eternal law maker or divine law of nature that controls and regulates life. Scientists like Newton and Descartes believed that God created these solid billiard balls or indivisible constituents and put them together according to principles or laws that were also fixed throughout time. God then put these particles in motion, and this is the way the universe works much like a man-made machine.

The important result or implication of this view is that the universe becomes static, rigid, completely causal and deterministic. Causes have effects and if one knows all the variables one can calculate the outcome. The whole point of Newtonian equations is to determine these fixed laws and thus understand the dynamics of the universe. It also implies that human beings stand outside this machine separated from it and thus able to objectively observe and quantify the mechanics. This knowledge could then give humanity the certainty and surety needed to overcome the anxiety that comes from the fear of the unknown.

It is essential to grasp that the whole of classical science and the western world view is based upon this division between the world and humanity and our ability to objectively observe the workings of the world without being an integral part of that dynamic or observation.

However, we now know that this process of objective observation is impossible, that somehow the observer and the observed form another of these yin/yang continuums where the inner psychological state of the observer does in fact influence the outcome of the observation. In other words, there is no fixed, rigid and static world out there that does not change but is in a continual state of flux. We cannot talk about the world without understanding that we are not an abstract and distinct observer but a participant and key variable in this matrix of change.

If we now translate these outcomes of nuclear physics to our personal lives, it becomes even more interesting. The western world view also holds that human beings are distinct and separate units of life and that our lives are similar to the atomistic structure of the universe. In other words, we are subject to the prescriptive laws of nature and acted upon by external influences in much the same way that Newtonian physics believed particles were acted upon by immutable forces of nature. Whether it is Lutheran pre-determinism, the wheel of karma, the Biblical eye for an eye, or the Christian Commandments, somehow, we are subject to the law of cause and effect that is external, immutable and beyond our control. To some extent we are passive particles in the game of life.

The mystical view is that we are an integral part of the process of life; that we are a part of one undivided whole; that we live in a sea of universal consciousness and that we do in fact create our own reality by our inner states of being. There is no rigid division between observer and observed. Rather we are key participants in the game determining and creating our future by our thoughts, feelings, desires, attitudes, expectations, choices, decisions and so on. We create it all; not some external and absolute entity or deity.

Moreover, the only fundamental truth of life is the process of change. Life is always evolving, always changing in an eternal state of flux and flow. We either resist that change seeking false security in an artificial construct of solidity or we go with the flow. Quantum theory has shown us that particles are not isolated and solid particles of matter but probability patterns and waves of change. So too, our destinies are not set in stone, but are fluid probability patterns that adjust, change, weave and flow as we evolve.

The classical world view is fundamentally static – seeking a fixed point of reality that provides certainty and surety. The nuclear world view is one of constant motion where particles become processes. Our lives are a process of unfoldment changing at every moment of time. We are on a spiritual journey to become more of who we are; to uncover and discover more of our true essence.

Einstein's Unified Field states that things do not exist independently from the field or background within which they dwell, that we cannot separate the particle from the process and that we cannot dissect reality into constituent parts. The only reality is the underlying field or web of consciousness.

Throughout history humanity has sought the laws that regulate life. Classical science sees these laws as externally imposed prescriptive laws defined by God. Bootstrap theory sees these laws as being an intrinsic part of the process of nature where life is regulated by a self-consistency that is a characteristic of the fundamental harmony and unity of the whole. Taoism and other mystical views see the laws of life as being descriptive laws that describe what does happen rather than being laws telling us what should happen.

Laws are not laid down by an external divine law giver but represent an inherent part of the natural process. For the Taoist sage, the highest good is to live one's life in harmony with these natural laws of the universe. Wisdom consists in learning and understanding these laws which one can only do by direct experience: by living one's life and by observing not the world in some isolated mechanical sense but rather one's interaction with it. In other words, understanding that one is a participant, acknowledging that one's inner states of being do have an impact upon the whole and that the most significant variables in the matrix are not outside forces over which we have no or little control but rather inner psychic states of being which we are 100%, totally responsible for.

We move from particle passivity to process proactivity. We are the creators of our own reality. This is not a mechanistic model where we are mere billiard balls being acted upon by an uncaring and dangerous world out there. Rather we live in a world of natural order and harmony; a world that works from the most microscopic sub-atomic level to that of the far reaches of outer space. There is an inherent intelligence that exists within all things and regulates the workings of the universe. This intelligence is the Tao and is the one law behind all being.

Moreover, this model presupposes what I call the divine benevolence of the universe. Newton's mechanical and rigid laws of motion are replaced by a caring and benevolent consciousness that permeates creation and is the basis of the self-regulating mechanism. The universe is not some gigantic machine as Newton described. There is a divine intelligence, a universal consciousness, a will and a volition that operates for the highest good of all of creation.

The world is not some scary place that we need to subjugate and dominate. We are not separate from the field in which we dwell. We are an integral part of this divine consciousness and the only definition of God that makes sense is the harmonious unity of the whole. We cannot take the Creator out of Creation just as we cannot take the observer out of the observed. There is no separation; no division; no dissection!

There is only the unified field of divine consciousness! This field is in constant motion and unfoldment becoming more of who it is. The world is god seeking to explore itself. The universe is constantly expanding. We live in an indivisible universe where everything is interrelated and connected via the web of life. Moreover, the Cartesian split between mind and matter where matter or nature is viewed as dead and inanimate and separate from human consciousness is a totally false view which has led humanity down its self-destructive path.

The important point to realise is that this holistic view of reality is no longer confined to the mystics or mythology. Cutting edge, modern day rational science proves the unity of all things. The more we discover, the more obvious it becomes that we do not live in a machine of component dead parts but rather in an organic living interconnected web that is harmonious and unified. The universe is more akin to a hologram where every part is a microcosm of the whole. The holographic principle of creation.

Nowhere is the result of this erroneous view more apparent than humanity's relationship with its home – planet earth. The Cartesian division between mind and matter has resulted in the ecological disaster we now find ourselves in where human activity is fast rendering the planet uninhabitable. The Anthropocene Age is characterised by the fact that human activity is now having an impact on the planet's environment and this impact is not good: it is a direct result of the western world view that nature is to be dominated and controlled. We are living in the planet's most destructive extinction event since the demise of the dinosaurs with approximately 100 species becoming extinct every day. Will humanity go the way of the dinosaurs? It is estimated that up to 50% of all species will soon become extinct because of our activity.

This extinction is the result of the rampant greed exhibited in the toxic combination of capitalism and colonialism where the results of science are used predominantly for purposes at odds with nature. It is interesting that pollution, global warming, deforestation and so on are all attacks on the collective common: those global treasures we all share for free and have not been registered in the GDP or any other measure of wealth. Fresh air, drinkable water, natural habitats, the wilderness are all natural resources not only taken for granted but also seen to be plundered and raped by humans as their right in this contagious world view.

As underdeveloped countries emerge into the capitalist system, they join the queue of pollution forsaking their age-old interconnectedness and oneness with their environment. Old growth rainforests that have taken millennia to grow are being destroyed at the rate of 375 square kilometres per day! We have already destroyed 80% of the world's forests for farming and agriculture. We are using 50% more natural resources than the Earth can provide. We are generating enough waste to fill a line of garbage trucks 5,000 kilometres long every day. All of this is the natural and inevitable consequence of an erroneous world view that pits man against nature; that fosters the separation and alienation of part and whole. It is also symbolic that this mass destruction and pollution is the direct result of a mechanistic age and a mechanistic mind set.

There needs to be a fundamental and radical change in our world view and in our view of the world within which we live. This is now dire and urgent. We need a new set of values and perspective where we understand the oneness of the universe and learn to live and work in harmony with nature rather than being at war with it.

This is the mystical world view where we follow and learn from nature rather than dominate and control it. For eons, humanity understood its rightful place in the garden. The idea that nature was to be attended to, served, worked with, looked after, respected and followed was an integral part of the human psyche and paradigm until the dominance of the classical world view. All ancient communities lived in harmony with nature and understood their place within the whole.

The Taoist view maintains this humility and receptivity – that one needs to learn to live one's life in harmony with the natural order and flow of the universe. The reason why this perspective is so important in the art of *Tao Tuning* is that, as already mentioned, the primary variable in our matrix of creation is our inner attitude toward the world. If we approach life with an arrogance, a dominance, a lack of respect and a negative ego of supremacy, we will simply not be able to take our lead from nature.

The most essential prerequisite to creating a positive reality, to harmonising one's personal Tao with that of the universal Tao is to embrace the whole; to totally realise and appreciate the intrinsic harmony, oneness and interconnectedness of life. If we do not come from this fundamental premise, we simply cannot manifest a positive future. We cannot experience the supreme happiness and contentment of being in the flow.

Humanity is faced with not only ecological disaster but also its own extinction because it must change its attitude towards life, the universe and the planet upon which we live. There simply is no choice. Whether we get that now, hopefully before it is too late, or later when we have passed the point of no return and we turn the planet into a dead planet as per our predominant world view is the only choice.

The point is we do create our own reality both individually and collectively. Humanity has accepted this Newtonian and Cartesian mechanistic model of separation where the world out there, nature, is viewed as inanimate matter with no consciousness, no feelings and no intelligence. It is inevitable, therefore, that this is exactly what we will create: a planet devoid of life, an ecosystem robbed of its biodiversity and beauty but also its ability to sustain life – ours!

What is even more fascinating and tragic is that we seem to be suffering from some form of collective amnesia or paralysis whereby we are rendered incapable of ceasing our senseless destruction and mending our ways. Our psychic disassociation and disconnection from nature, our inability to appreciate the intricate web of life on planet Earth, of which we are only one small part, stems from this erroneous world view. Like the lobster in the slowly boiling water, we have become so comfortable in our cocooned material world that we choose not to see the inevitable.

Over half of humanity now lives the urban lifestyle of separation and isolation from nature. We have become disconnected from our source. We have lost our ability to be one with nature, to flow with the universal current of the Tao.

The end result of the classical western world view is the total domination and control of nature: humanity is now witnessing the end days of this 500-year-old experiment and error. The end result of the mystical and nuclear world view is the ability to live one's life in supreme harmony with nature taking one's cues from the flow of the current. The basic difference between these opposing world views is the denial or acceptance of the consciousness that permeates all things not just humanity.

Chapter 17

Holograms & probability

The western world view is that humans alone are consciously aware and intelligent. The mystical and nuclear world view is that divine consciousness exists within every particle, every wave, every cell and every being. The world is intelligent! There is an implicit order in creation as dictated by these descriptive laws that are inherent in every part as well as the whole. I call this the holographic principle of the universe where the whole is contained within any part and vice versa.

In other words, *Tao Tuning* is that ability to have an intelligent and meaningful conversation with that whole. In the end, it does not matter how one divides or separates that consciousness. Indeed, in holographic and bootstrap theory terms, it is meaningless to do the division. We do not need to have concepts of God or a deity or guides or guardian angels because these are merely mental attempts to personify or describe that which is beyond words. These are all aspects of the mind map not the terrain within which we live.

We do not need to localise, objectify, personalise or mythologise. But we do need to humbly accept that there is a divine intelligence that does regulate and order the universe. We also need to accept three fundamental characteristics of this divine intelligence: it is objective and impartial in that it operates according to the descriptive laws of nature; it is vastly superior to limited human intelligence and thus is beyond our comprehension and third it is benevolent in that it operates for the highest good of all concerned.

These three concepts represent a radical departure from the classical western world view and are a prerequisite to being able to flow with the Tao. Both the I Ching and modern science describe a universe of nonlocal connections where causality is not necessarily apparent or direct, where change is the essential characteristic and where there is an implicate order to this process of change that we can understand and master.

In this new world view, consciousness becomes an integral aspect of creation and the division between mind and matter ceases to exist. Mind and matter become two complementary poles of the one yin/yang continuum of divine consciousness. They are not separate; they are not divided, and they certainly are not at war with each other as in the classical Cartesian and Baconian split.

David Bohm, one of the most celebrated nuclear physicists of the 20th century, has combined the essence of relativity theory with quantum physics and bootstrap theory to argue that there is an implicate or enfolded order within creation that goes beyond space and time to its essential oneness. The I Ching is based upon this implicate order demonstrating the sequence or phases of the process of change that exist regardless of person, place or time.

Just as the surfer learns to master the forces of water, wind and wave, the cosmic surfer learns to ride the currents of the Tao by mastering the variables of the manifestation matrix. Unlike classical theory, which is predominantly deterministic, the holographic world is a matrix of mind and matter which are interdependent and correlate to form our future. We create our lives via our inner states of being: thoughts, feelings, beliefs, attitudes, choices and decisions.

We now know that matter is merely a localised form of energy as per Einstein's equation: $E = mc^2$. We also know that supposed indivisible solid particles are composed almost entirely of empty space and that these particles are waves of probability. In the same way, the matter or events of our lives are simply out-pictures of our mental activity which demonstrate probabilities to occur rather than rigid certainty.

We do not live in a divided and deterministic universe but in a conscious field of probability. The art of *Tao Tuning* is to master the manifestation matrix that creates our lives: to learn to ride the wave of our own personal Tao and to ensure it is in harmony with the holographic principle of the universe. In other words, to ensure we are at one with cosmic law; that we are in harmony with this implicate order of nature.

Humanity has tried to go its own way; to impose its supremacy over nature; to swim upstream and go against the flow. We are now witnessing the dire consequences of this arrogance and folly. It simply will not and cannot work. The universe is an implicate whole of harmony and order. Any aspect or part of that whole that is not in harmony with that order must be eliminated to safeguard the integrity and health of the whole. These aberrant parts will merely eliminate themselves just as humanity is doing right now.

We are out of order. We are not in harmony with the rhythm of nature. We are not listening or attuned to the inner law of our being. We have already become an extinct species. It is just that the process of extinction may take 100 years; but it is inevitable.

We need to turn around. We need to start attuning to not only our own Tao but also the universal currents which regulate the flow of life. If we adhere to the principle of the divine benevolence of the universe and that divine consciousness is the fundamental characteristic and nature of creation with an implicit and implicate order, we must come to the conclusion that we do know intuitively and spontaneously what to do, what is right and noble.

However, to be able to do this we need to learn to think differently: to retrain our thinking brain so that mind and matter do form a harmonious whole rather than thinking fragmentally. In each person's life there are two complementary flows: the inner flow of consciousness or thought and the outer flow of life or events. The goal of *Tao Tuning* is to bring these two separate flows into a harmony of movement so that the two waves are in phase, in sync and productive of peace, harmony and prosperity. This is the divine benevolence of the universe; this is being in the zone of flow.

In our discussion of wave theory, we spoke about complex waves being the sum of the component waves and these were either in phase or out of phase. If the flow of energy or the wave generated by one's conscious mind is in phase, in sync with one's outer life then one experiences a harmonious destiny, travelling the path of life without mishap. On the other hand, if there are discordant waves being generated, one will experience choppy seas and rough water – life will not be as pleasant nor as productive.

In order to become an adept cosmic surfer and master practitioner of *TaoTuning*, one needs to retrain the brain and learn to think differently. We hear a lot today about brain gym, memory exercises and other ways to improve cognitive function. The brain is no longer viewed as a given and fixed entity; neuroplasticity has demonstrated that, like any other muscle or organ in the body, the brain responds to mental exercise. We can retrain our brains! We can learn to use them more constructively and positively. The human brain, like everything else, is fluid rather than fixed and is infinite rather than finite.

Intelligence is not a limited or finite given at birth. Intelligence needs to be worked and developed. The single major outcome from nuclear physics and the study of the sub-atomic world is that the universe is not a machine created by some deity in the distant past operating on pre-determined and fixed mechanical rules of linear cause and effect. Rather the universe is more akin to a living being with its own attendant implicit and implicate order. In other words, it is self-regulating.

The basic difference between a machine and biology is that man-made machines (up until recently) have no innate intelligence and thus cannot regenerate parts or organise themselves holistically and spontaneously. The overriding characteristic of living beings is their innate ability to self-regulate, heal and direct their own development from within. This is true from the minutest cell to the largest galaxy.

The classical western view of the world is a given and fixed machine composed of basic entities or particles that interact according to fixed principles set down by God in the initial work of creation. The modern view that derives from quantum physics and relativity theory is that the world is not an assemblage of pieces or parts but an interconnected web of probable events. The world does not work according to the prescriptive laws set down by God, like the 10 Commandments, but according to the descriptive laws that are inherent in nature and an integral part of that implicate order.

Nature demonstrates this holistic, self-regulating consistency and order that a mechanistic universe does not. When a machine breaks down, it does not fix itself. When a living organic body is injured, it has the ability to heal itself. The outcome of modern science is therefore a return to the ancient and mystical view of the universe which has at its core a divine intelligence that regulates, orders and directs life. Whether we call this divine intelligence, cosmic order, nature, God or the Tao is irrelevant. As Lao Tzu says the name that can be named is not the constant name.

We can call it what we like, as long as we realise the map is not the territory and the word is not the object. We need to retrain our brain to cease the process of objectification: dividing, separating, naming and putting labels on things so that we can 'know' them. We live in a constantly evolving, changing web of interrelationships and events where everything is in a constant state of flux and dependent upon the observer; there is no fixed reality out there we can know. We need to get used to the discomfort of not knowing but of flowing. This is a totally different way to live one's life precisely because one is no longer looking for the fixed points.

We need to free our minds from this incessant and neurotic need to know, to explain, to label, to think and use words, to create objects. Both Eastern mysticism and bootstrap theory agree that the universe is an organic, integral whole with no one part being different from or superior to any other part. It is purely the human mind that does the breaking up, the dividing, the separating and labelling but this division is not a part of nature.

If the world is not a machine created by God but demonstrates self-consistency and natural order, then it is conscious and intelligent. Consciousness is an intrinsic quality of the whole. There is nothing in creation that does not possess this divine intelligence. The universe is alive and exhibits an exquisite and divine sense of beauty and order that can only come from consciousness.

If we return to the basic concept of the classical western view, it is based on the Cartesian principle of duality: the division of the world into mind and matter where matter had no life, no intelligence and no consciousness. Indeed, Descartes' dictum: '*Cogito ergo sum*' is in fact the wrong way around. Descartes' logic was that I think therefore I exist – thinking coming first. The correct logic is: 'I am – therefore, I think. Consciousness comes first, and consciousness is not dependent upon thought. I exist whether I am thinking or not.

Consciousness exists with and without thought. I am conscious therefore I exist. Thinking is not necessary to existence! Thinking is only one aspect of consciousness and a very limited part at that. I can be, I can exist without thinking but I cannot think without being. All squares are rectangles but not all rectangles are squares. Being is the fundamental state of consciousness not thinking.

Because of this Cartesian split humanity has come to over-identify itself with its thinking brain. Egoic thought has taken over the world. It is as if we are afraid to stop thinking because, and according to Descartes, if we do, we will cease to exist. Eckhart Tolle has written eloquently about this, likening the ego to a basket within which we place all that we identify ourselves with: our possessions, material and non-material. Tolle emphasises we are not the thoughts in our head.

More than anyone else, Jiddu Krishnamurti taught the destructive power of egoic thinking and the senseless chatter that goes on continuously in our heads. As mentioned, we need to retrain our brains. All forms of Eastern meditation strive to silence the thinking mind, but for too long they have been associated with religious dogma rather than being seen for what it is – the correct use of mind and thought. The practice of meditation is not religious but neurological.

The thinking egoic mind exists in an isolated state viewing itself as distinct, different and separate from the rest of the universe. We exist within our own shell. It is this division which creates sorrow, ignorance and suffering in Buddhist terms.

Meditation does not need to be associated with any religious dogma or practice. Just as one can and should practise yoga for physical health, one should also practise meditation for mental and emotional well-being and health without any religious connotations or overtones. Just as we cannot reduce the universe to fundamental constituent parts that are the indivisible building blocks of reality, similarly, we cannot reduce ourselves to separated egoic beings.

Our tendency to divide the perceived world into separate objects and to experience ourselves as separate human beings or isolated egos is the illusion of maya. We have become trapped by the structure of our own thought and lost our true perspective and perception of oneness.

The reason why this analysis and understanding of nuclear physics is so vitally important for *TaoTuning*, is that in the Taoist view, the universe is alive and conscious and thus can be communicated with in an intelligent way. Moreover, we do not and indeed should not localise or personify this intelligence. We do not need to define guardian angels or spirit guides or Gods or gurus. It really does not matter what you call it, and it does not need to be divided up into objectified terms. The process of objectification is a function of linear rational thought which is the defining characteristic of homo sapiens but not a characteristic of the rest of the living universe.

It is just the divine intelligence of the universe, and this intelligence is within every particle and cell from the most microscopic to the largest interstellar cluster. This intelligence is the regulating order of the universe and does operate according to universal law. It is just that these laws are descriptive and an implicit part of the whole rather than being imposed from without. This is the implicate order of David Bohm from which the explicate order of the phenomenal world manifests or in the words of the I Ching: the way of the universe, the Tao, is a law running through end and beginning, bringing about all phenomena in time.

The I Ching argues that this intelligence or wave, the Tao, operates in probability patterns very similar to the probability patterns of subatomic particles or events. We can learn to work with these patterns; we can learn to communicate with life by acknowledging the divine intelligence of creation. The I Ching lays bare these patterns via the component trigrams which represent all probable life situations. What is significant to appreciate is that these trigrams are based in nature. Nature becomes the teacher; we learn from the situation we find ourselves in and the configuration of circumstances operating at that point in the time/space continuum.

The I Ching is called the Book of Changes. The Taoist universe is in a constant state of flux or change but this change is not haphazard or chaotic. It follows the laws of nature, the cycles of the seasons, the rhythm of the cosmic dance. The Taoist sage arrives at wisdom by closely observing nature, not as an outside impartial observer but as an intimate participant very much like the nuclear physicist. And like bootstrap theory with its s-matrix, the Taoist understands the nature of reality is a matrix within which we are a very important variable.

And although understanding the I Ching is a lifetime study, it is not to be taken literally. Taoists realise that words are only pointers. The I Ching is written in a completely different language but not a language of the left brain. This is why we need to retrain our minds how to think intuitively. We need to dispense with the linear logic of the ego and move into the spatial awareness of the intuition where all things are connected and where causality is non-linear. This is what Bohm calls non-local connections, where everything in the universe is connected in an unbroken wholeness and everything affects everything else.

This is the holographic principle of the universe where each part contains the whole and vice versa. Interestingly, Bohm also uses the hologram as an analogy for this implicate order of creation. He coined the term holomovement to describe this dual aspect of the structure of movement being both a unified whole and a dynamic process of change and unfoldment.

We can also use this term of *holomovement* to understand the patterns of change described by the I Ching. As there is no distinction between a human being and other life forms, the probability patterns occurring in our lives are the same as the cosmic patterns occurring in nature. Humanity is viewed as an integral part of nature and not separate to or distinct from it. Thus, by closely observing and monitoring the patterns in our lives we can foresee the future just as a meteorologist can foretell the weather by observing and monitoring emerging weather cells, fronts and high and low-pressure systems. There are patterns in nature, and we can and do learn those patterns. Similarly, there are patterns in the life of a human, and we can learn those patterns.

One does not consult the I Ching to '*fortune tell*' or predict the future but to gain an understanding of the variables in one's current matrix: in other words, what are the component forces operating in one's present situation and what is the best course of action just as an ocean surfer might consider the prevailing weather patterns, tide, swell and so on before going for a surf.

We spoke about this process earlier. The classical western view is dependent upon linear causality: x causes y in a linear and connected fashion. The Taoist view operates synchronistically where there are myriad forces operating at any given point in time and space and the universe is to be viewed not as a linear machine but rather as a gestalt of awareness. Once again, as in nuclear physics, there is no certainty, there are no definites; there are only the probability waves of events occurring. The gestalt is a matrix of probable futures. We need to decide and choose the optimum path dependent upon our expertise and wisdom.

Everyone will play their cards differently!

The essential point to grasp is that the universe is not so much a mechanical structure made of fixed parts but rather a structured process of change that is orderly and follows definable patterns. These patterns are evident everywhere in nature and we only need to open our intuitive eyes and look: William Blake's doors of perception. '*If the doors of perception were cleansed everything would appear to man as it is, Infinite. For man has closed himself up, till he sees all things through narrow chinks of his cavern.*'

This is the fundamental retraining of the brain necessary to learn the language of the I Ching and to exist within the zone of flow. The probability patterns speak to the holistic intuitive mind rather than the logical brain of reason. This is not because it is not rational, but it refers to the implicate order of Bohm that lies in deeper dimensions of the universe and is thus hidden in that we cannot perceive it with the limited rational mind. In implicate order, everything is connected to everything else, and causality is non-linear. Moreover, there is no distinction between mind and matter with these two merely being another of those yin/yang polarities that we need to master.

As we become more adept at discerning the underlying cosmic patterns, we learn to negotiate the process of change better: we become more proficient cosmic surfers. We align our personal Tao with that of universal law and experience a more favourable reality. The paradoxical nature of reality as testified by the sub-atomic world shows that even though these so-called particles are moving at tremendous speeds there is a fundamental solidity and stability within the atomic structure. The probabilities are not random!

So too, even though we live in a probability field there is a solidity and stability to our lives. Life is not random or chaotic – there is an implicit order that we need to learn to work with not because of the wheel of karma or the law of retribution but because we need to learn to live our lives in harmony with the natural implicate order of the universe, the infinite Tao to prosper.

We began this discussion with the assertion that humanity needed a new religion, a new philosophy of life and a new world view: a complete change in the meta-paradigm of our reality. And that this new spirituality needed to be based in an emotional and intellectual maturity not a mystical illusion. We also said that that this spirituality needed to be able to withstand the scrutiny of the rational scientific method, that we should not just accept biblical stories as an act of blind faith but discover the truth by strict observation.

The reason nuclear physics is so relevant to this discussion is that it has scientifically given us a completely different perspective and picture of reality. Just as we cannot directly see subatomic particles without the aid of extremely complex and sophisticated scientific equipment and years of training, we cannot view the correct nature of reality without intense concentration and mental training.

In the subatomic world, predictions cannot be made with 100% certainty, only with degrees of probability. In the life of a human, one cannot foresee the future with absolute certainty, but one can view the probable futures of one's life and make more intelligent and wiser choices and decisions. Nuclear physics has taught us the paradoxical and ambivalent nature of reality: the dual character of wave and particle, energy and matter. So too, our lives exist within the binary duality of the yin/yang continuum, and we need to adapt our perception and understanding of life to this discovery.

Tenaciously holding onto outworn concepts for the sake of certainty and security is only leading us down the garden path to the certainty of extinction because we are just not dealing with reality as it is. We are vaingloriously trying to get the universe to do what we want rather than learning to adapt intelligently to what is. When any living species or system refuses to acknowledge the reality of its environment, it causes its own demise just as we are rapidly causing our own extinction as a species.

In this context, it is significant to remember that homo sapiens is the only remaining species of the genus homo of which many other separate species such as Neanderthals and others are now extinct. Homo sapiens is the seventh homo. So, it is not inconceivable that this current form of the genus homo may also become extinct. We also need to be cognizant of the fact that our extinction does not necessarily mean the end of life on Earth.

Evolution is a fundamental characteristic of life. One could even say that life and evolution are two sides of the one coin or that life and evolution form another of these binary poles of yin and yang and we need to learn to ride that continuum. Darwinian science has demonstrated that life does indeed ride that continuum via the process of adaptation: that life continuously adapts to the changing circumstances of its environment and that those individuals or species that adapt the best survive and prosper, while those that do not fall by the wayside. In this regard, universal law is impartial, objective and absolute – it shows no favour and is merciless: adapt or die!

Humanity is currently caught in a 5,000-year-old time loop and is refusing to either acknowledge or more importantly adapt to the reality it finds itself in. Even in the last 50 years, the world has changed dramatically, and the speed of that change continues to accelerate. It is the thesis of this text that our inner world view is not keeping pace with these external changes and is no longer in harmony with our current scientific understanding of how the world works. Thus, our 'physis' is no longer a true and accurate representation of reality.

The reason an accurate world view is so important is not even so much that it is about the world around us, as it defines who we are and our relationship with that world. Humanity has erroneously defined itself both collectively as a species and singularly as an individual. We have become disconnected from the root of our being, from our source and from the universe that sustains us and in which we have our being. As a species, we have become a cancer upon the planet precisely because we are no longer in harmony with the greater natural laws that govern existence. As individuals, we have become separated, alienated and disconnected from each other and the unity of creation.

Because of the classical split between mind and matter or humans and nature, humanity defines itself as distinct from and apart from the field of nature – it does not view itself as a part of or a variable within the matrix. We view ourselves as separate from the world. Because we have created a personal God or Divine Principle of whatever name as something external, standing above and beyond the world and directing it, we no longer view that divinity as being a natural and integral part of creation.

For over 2,500 years, western classic thought and philosophy have moved down this binary path separating human from the rest of creation. We have also identified ourselves by our characteristic of rational, linear thought: the Cartesian world of I think therefore I am, to the exclusion of all other characteristics. Indeed, traditional education, training and upbringing revolve around the 3R's of the rational mind: reading, writing and arithmetic.

Collectively as a species we define ourselves as thinking beings. Individually, we now live within a shell or bubble of egoic thought. Rational thought has been raised to the highest level, while all the other functions of the mind have been denied and negated. We are no longer human beings but have become human thinkings or human doings; the ability to just BE without egoic thinking, without the need to do or act is no longer available to most people. Most forms of intuition: meditation, daydreaming, psychic awareness, being mindful without thinking are not regarded as worthwhile pursuits.

We no longer exist within the continuum of being which is the intelligent universe, the divinity of creation, the Tao. We exist within our own minds trapped by the never ending '*yamma-yamma*' of the thinking brain. This is only a minute fraction of who we really are and is a fundamentally inaccurate definition of our identity as human beings. The rational, egoic, logical and linear left brain is only a very small part of who we are and to define ourselves by such a minor part does us a great disservice.

Just as we erroneously defined reality as being made up of indivisible and inanimate dead building blocks in a mechanistic world, we have similarly erroneously defined ourselves as discrete and separated units of thought rather than holistic beings. We now know that matter is part wave, part particle. We now know humans are part self but also a part of universal consciousness. We are an integral part of that cosmic unity. The individual is a holon.

We live within an ultra-holistic unity where everything is connected to everything else, and it is virtually impossible to really define any single component of reality in complete isolation, especially in isolation from the observer – being human! Moreover, subatomic particles relate and react across the normal boundaries of time and space being able to instantaneously communicate and respond to each other faster than the speed of light and thus not limited by distance.

In this new universe, everything exists inter-dimensionally – there is a deeper level to the universe that we just cannot perceive, and this hidden layer exists within its own order. David Bohm called this the Implicate Order which is the self-regulating and ordering principle of life. This principle is being guided and directed by an all-pervasive cosmic intelligence that is the source of the information ordering reality. This cosmic intelligence is not a completed state or structure as in a Western God or Deity but is a process of continuous unfolding, becoming and growing. Its essential characteristic is the eternal change of evolution.

I like to say that god is not a noun but a verb. God is not a person so much as the process of becoming. God is the evolutionary process of life in continual unfoldment. There is no such 'thing' as god, but there is nothing that is not god.

Our lives exist within this universal field of cosmic intelligence and there is an implicit order or meaning to the story of our lives – they make sense, have purpose, have an intrinsic plot or thesis and are not random or chaotic; we are not mechanical robots; we are not a bio-chemical accident. That plot, that story, that thesis is your personal Tao and that localised field of intelligent meaning is in constant and instantaneous communication with the vaster field of the Universal Tao. Information is constantly flowing from the one to the other and vice versa – this is the self-regulating aspect of the universe. This self-regulating phenomenon is consciousness.

Humanity has erroneously defined itself as a thinking machine and limited its awareness to the field of rational thought. But as already suggested we are much more than thought, especially rational thought. In the end, we are a localised field of consciousness in the much broader expanse of universal consciousness. It is this consciousness that is truly one and indivisible. Unlike thought, consciousness does not need to objectify or deal with individual particles or moments. Consciousness is our true nature which goes far beyond rational thinking.

The individual is in constant contact and communication with the whole and is a focus of that universal energy in much the same way that we can focus light into a laser beam and then direct that energy to do work. Individual human consciousness is the focus of cosmic consciousness, and we need to redefine ourselves as conscious beings rather than thinking beings. It is not *I think therefore I am* but rather simply *I am.* We are individualised units of consciousness not dissimilar to individual drops of water. But just as any individual drop has its being within the wider matrix of water, we too have our being within the wider matrix of cosmic consciousness.

Thus, we have a very simple but stark choice: we either shake off our erroneous and limited world view, philosophy and outmoded religious concepts and regain our rightful place within this field of intelligence and consciousness, being in constant communication with and receiving our information and instructions from this universal field, or we remain stuck within our prison of isolation, separation and ignorance. The ignorance is our fundamental belief in separation. The error is our classical view of indivisible particles, and that humanity exists upon but apart from the world within which it finds itself.

The belief of separation is not just about the atom or some other particle as the building block of creation. The real error is the perception of isolated, individual and separated units of life which we call human beings. We view ourselves as separate. Because we have defined ourselves as a thinking being and because thoughts are separate and isolated units of activity, we view ourselves as separate and distinct particles of being. We do not perceive the wave-like aspect of our nature which is collective consciousness. We fail to appreciate the interconnected and holistic principle of creation. Bohm calls this the cosmic mind.

Tao Tuning is that intelligent communication between the individual human consciousness and the cosmic mind. But this communication is non-linear, non-verbal and acausal, meaning it is not a normal rational language. We cannot force the universe to speak our language; we must quiet the thinking egoic mind, so that we can intuit or hear the sounds of silence. I call this the language of life.

The universe is regulated by the packets of information contained in the photons of light. These packets of photons contain all the data, all the information required to regulate the processes of life from the minutest sub-atomic world to the largest interstellar galaxies. These photons also regulate our individual beings: anatomically and psychically. Our bodies receive these instructions via the mitochondria. Mitochondria are the energy power houses of the cell producing 90% of the energy cells need to survive. Mitochondria also contain and disseminate the information required for cell self-regulation and organisation: they are the cosmic intelligence of the cells.

So too, our lives contain meaning and purpose, and these need constant fine tuning for our lives to remain on track and on purpose. The real art and function of meditation is not just to relax and still the thinking mind but to do so, so that one can receive the transmissions of universal intelligence from the cosmic mind. Human cells simply could not exist or function at their high level of complexity were it not for the function of mitochondria. Complex human lives simply cannot exist or function correctly without this constant inflow of information. To stay on track on any journey requires constant vigilance, monitoring and adjustment. To stay on track in our personal lives requires the same awareness and attention.

It is the height of arrogance and stupidity for humanity to believe it is running its own race, is separated from the ground in which it has its being and does not need to abide by natural law. The ego has become dysfunctional and has usurped control of our being. It has displaced consciousness as the control mechanism of our being. The human being, both collectively and individually, has become separated, alienated, isolated and neurotic. We are no longer a part of life but have divorced ourselves from the very process of life because of this 2,000-year detour which has led us to this dead end of immanent extinction.

We need urgently and desperately to reconnect with the flow and harmony of the universe. We need to get back on the wave of the Tao. We need to *BeCome One* and we can only do this by understanding the true nature of duality and that it is merely a lens by which we view the world. And although a necessary lens for life on planet earth, it does distort and fragment the image. This fragmentation is an inherent part of the human brain which functions via the process of objectification, identification and language. These are all separatist activities. They need to be balanced by the unifying function of consciousness.

I have always been amused by the evangelical tourist who never seems to just view and appreciate the beauties of nature without the ubiquitous camera or now smartphone: it is missing the forest for the trees. We simply cannot take in the magnificence of a sunset or the marvels of nature via a camera lens: we need to be there in the moment, in silence, in awe and wonder. Photos are great for memories, but they should not replace being in the moment of your journey.

Objectification is great for dealing with daily reality upon planet earth and for ensuring your physical biological survival, but it should not replace the experience of the whole.

Tao Tuning is a function of intuitive conscious awareness rather than logical rational thought. We cannot always see the cause as causality is not always linear. As Bohm demonstrates, quantum physics leads us to the conclusion of a deeper level of reality which remains hidden to the rational mind and where everything is connected to everything else. Unfortunately, we cannot view this level of reality without years of training.

The I Ching and *Tao Tuning* are vehicles to gain access to this hidden world just as we use electron microscopes to view the sub-atomic world and massive telescopes to view the far reaches of space. Surgeons can go deep within the body using microsurgery and miniaturised instruments. The Taoist surfer uses deep meditation to receive cosmic intelligence that is non-localised but holistic. We need to learn to operate within the gestalt of our being - the larger totality of ourselves. We need to redefine the human being as a spiritual being operating on many levels and in many dimensions: the rational, physical being merely one of many.

I am universal consciousness
having a human experience,
on planet Earth
in a divine and benevolent universe.

There are many forms of communication: linear, logical, language, emotional, intuitive, mathematical, musical, sign and they all have their nuances of meaning. *Tao Tuning* is a non-linear form of communication with the hidden deeper levels of reality. But simply because we cannot directly perceive all the causal variables in our reality matrix does not mean these variables are not affecting the journey of our lives.

There is a great line in the I Ching that describes this eloquently:

'if a man remains at the mercy of moods of hope or fear aroused by the outer world, he loses his inner consistency of character. Such inconsistency invariably leads to distressing experiences. These humiliations often come from an unseen quarter. Such experiences are not merely effects produced by the outside world, but logical consequences evoked by his own nature.'

There are a number of parallels here to quantum physics. First, the reference to an unseen quarter – Bohm's hidden or deeper universe. Second, the effect of the observer upon the plane of manifestation – we simply cannot take the human out of the equation: we are an integral part of the matrix. Third, that there is a logical connection that we just cannot see but it exists none-the-less. And fourth, the reference to non-linear logic: the causality is there, but it is within ourselves determined by our moods.

We do create our own reality and we do this via our thoughts, feelings, imagination, choices and decisions. We are in constant communication with the wider field of our being: we are not dumb automatons; we are not passive victims, and we are certainly not discrete particles. There is much more going on to being truly human: we are an extremely complex matrix of thoughts, feelings, hopes, desires, moods and a host of other things all going on all the time.

We need to start to take personal accountability and we need to get smarter at creating our own reality. The best way to do this is to learn the language of the universe. Life is constantly talking to us – guiding us, leading us, warning us, prompting us and showing us the best possible path to take. We do live in a benevolent universe that is run by a divine regulating principle and that principle is called the Tao.

As we reconnect with that wave, as we allow that wave to guide us and carry us on its back, we arrive at what I call '*effelcess*': easy and effortless success. We *BeCome One* with our inner law, our deeper being, our higher self and the law of the universe. Life becomes easy, enjoyable and meaningful. And fun! There are still challenges to be sure, but these challenges spur us on to greater levels of conscious fulfillment and expression. We become more of who we truly are; we express our inner divinity.

Our lives flow! We live within the zone of flow experiencing ever increasing moments of peak performance and enjoyment.

Chapter 18

The New Spirituality

Lazaris says that true spirituality is your own personal, living, breathing relationship with God, Goddess, All That Is. To be clear, we are not personifying nor objectifying God. God is not some mythical being in a remote heaven of whatever description. We are referring to this cosmic intelligence that pervades and regulates the entirety of all that is.

Nor are we asking anyone to accept on blind faith or mythical biblical narratives that are fundamentally childish and untrue. What we are asserting is that humanity's new spirituality, world view, philosophy of life and religion need to be grounded in the facts and findings of the objective observation of both the scientific method and the mystics. People who have travelled these two separate paths of discovery using either the rigors of science or the discipline of a devoted life. Both require diligence; both require commitment; both paths lead to the same truth. And it is this truth that we now need to rebuild our world view upon.

The outcome of the last 100+ years of scientific discovery has not led us to the fundamental building blocks of a mechanical universe that was created in a distant past by a remote deity. It has led us to the very different conclusion of a universe that is alive, that is self-regulating, that is pervaded and guided by a cosmic consciousness of a very superior intelligence – certainly one vastly superior to that of humankind.

And herein lies the real heart of the problem: can humanity humbly accept that it is not the smartest person in the room? Can humanity accept that matter is not dead and inanimate but rather that consciousness pervades every cell, every atom, every sub-atomic particle and that everything is connected to everything else; that we truly do live in a holographic universe? And more importantly, that all of life is sacred and to negate this reverence to any part of creation, ultimately brings our own self-destruction.

We cannot wantonly continue to believe in blissful ignorance that nature is here to be dominated and abused. We can no longer believe that matter is unfeeling, dead and at humanity's disposal. We live in a holographic universe that is alive and interconnected. The biosphere of the planet is demonstrating this to us in no uncertain terms: the more we rape the earth the more we tinker with the vital life support systems within which we live. We have become so obsessed with short term profit that we are robbing the future of its very existence. We will go down in history as the single most selfish generation that stole from its future generations.

This is the logical outcome of a myopic, negative ego that is isolated, alienated and separated from the very core of its existence. Humanity has lost its holistic perspective and thus its way. David Bohm stresses that it is the responsibility of every human being to contribute to the development of collective human consciousness – what he calls the noosphere. *'There's nothing else to do--there is no other way out. That is absolutely what has to be done and nothing else can work.'*

Now we need to emphasise, that this is not the preaching of a mystical or religious fanatic – this is the teaching of one of the leading quantum physicists of our age who worked at Berkeley, Princeton and Birkbeck and whose philosophy was the direct outcome of his experience as a nuclear physicist. Moreover, most quantum physicists as well as most astronauts have come to these same conclusions concerning the true nature of reality.

This reality is characterised by the qualities of order, intelligence, creativity and a sense of holiness or sacredness. The one overriding outcome that ultimately joins these modern scientists with the ancient mystics is the essential oneness, unity and sacredness of life; that there is a cosmic energy that holds everything together within itself and that this cosmic energy obeys and manifests through cosmic law. We have referred to this universal law as the Tao; Bohm calls it the holomovement which transcends both space and time in another dimension of wholeness or consciousness.

The other major similarity between nuclear science and ancient mysticism is that the universe is directed and regulated by an active and all-pervasive divine intelligence that is not static nor mechanistic but in constant flux and development, interconnected with every part of the whole. This intelligence provides the information, instruction, direction and data for life.

Moreover, this intelligence is distinct from thought and does not always operate via the rational thinking mind. Direct perception, moments of insight, flashes of understanding and intuition are all valuable non-linear functions of intelligence that preclude and exclude thought. The natural kingdom operates perfectly without rational thought!

As an individualised unit of consciousness within this vast field of superior cosmic intelligence and universal consciousness, it is beholden upon us to learn to communicate directly and intelligently with the divine source of our being. The two points of significance here are that it must be direct and intelligent, neither of which are delivered by the classical religious model.

In traditional religion, there is always an intermediary, a channel, an 'other' that we need to go through in order to communicate with God, whether that is a person – priest, rabbi, shaman etc. or a book or set of teachings. There is always a catechism, bible or set of commandments that one must follow to become holy, to be accepted.

Moreover, there always seems to be an establishment that takes control and that one must pay homage to that interferes in this direct relationship. It is always about prescriptive rules or commandments that tell us how to act and rob us of our own personal validity and sovereignty. This creates a psychological dependency upon that religion and its establishment.

Tao Tuning is your direct communication with that cosmic consciousness that regulates the world. It is your direct conduit to omniscient intelligence that knows what is best for you. But you must honour yourself; you must be true to your inner being; you must be able to acknowledge and adhere to the dictates of the law of your being – your own personal Tao. The only single way to truly communicate with the all-knowing principle of life is by going within.

Second, it must be intelligent based both in rational logic and intuitive awareness. We need both to complete the circle. The days of just blindly accepting half-truths or biblical stories because they form part of a religious doctrine are well and truly over. As I mentioned at the beginning, humanity now needs a new religion based in scientific fact and experiential reality.

It is no longer enough to pray; it is no longer appropriate to be the dumb supplicant who puts it all back on God and expects the universe or this cosmic consciousness to do all the work for us. Humanity has been given free will to exercise its freedom of choice, to join in the creative process, to become an integral and intelligent part of the evolutionary process of life. To be the co-creator and flow with the evolutionary wave of life.

As I have explained in *Personal Sovereignty*, evil is not an inherent characteristic of the natural world but exists within the ignorance and abuse of human freedom. Humanity has been given the gift of free will choice so that it can be a part of the creative process of life, but it also means it can abuse this gift for destructive purposes. The fundamental characteristic of the universe as discovered by both the ancient mystics and the 21st century scientist is the natural order and harmony of the whole. There is no disorder in the non-human world. Disorder is the dysfunction of human free will operating in the ignorance of separation and division. As long as humanity insists on this separatist path and has a closed mindset to the oneness and universality of life, it will remain outside of that wholeness and oneness.

This is the real meaning behind the parable of the Garden of Eden.

To have this intelligent conversation with cosmic consciousness we need to start at the beginning just as in learning any language one first needs to learn words, syntax, grammar and so forth. Listening to any young child learn the process of language is always entertaining.

However, in this instance we are not only learning to speak a new language we are actually learning to operate a completely different modality like learning sign language. Divine intelligence does not operate so much through linear thought as it does via the holistic process of intuition and insight. But the first step is to acknowledge the unity of human consciousness: that we are all one and that there is no division for so much of our ignorance is based in separatism and division. Once we acknowledge this oneness many of our supposed problems disappear.

The language of the universe is light. Light is the modality that carries the information, and the mind is the receiver of that divine intelligence, so to begin one must open one's mind and become receptive to the light, to the order, to the information that comes in as photons of data. But the human mind has become closed through the egoic bubble of separation. The classical view is one of discrete and separate human entities very similar to the indivisible building blocks of the mechanistic world view. The mind has become closed and dark. This darkness is ignorance and is a very real neurological disease that needs to be cured. The egoic shell is real.

That cure is the opening to your own divine intelligence which is the law of your being – your own personal Tao. Step one is to go within and honour who you are, fully knowing that all the information, all the wisdom, all the answers are within in the vehicle of our intuitive awareness not in the rational mind of the ego. The closed mind of the negative ego acts as a deflective shield to this intuitive insight or gestalt of knowing. The negative ego does not know the answers and cannot guide your being. It is incapable of attaining this level of wisdom.

How often, after working on a problem that one cannot solve. do we walk away only to have that 'aha' experience where the answer just drops into our consciousness when we are least thinking about it? We have all had these experiences of superior non-linear intelligence, yet we still do not trust this non-rational mind. Cosmic consciousness does not operate via linear thought but via the gestalt of pure awareness or insight – suddenly one just knows what to do or life delivers some clear path or guidance. Seemingly out of nowhere comes the answer.

We need to retrain our mind to the discipline of looking within to receive divine inspiration or insight as the modus operandi of being human. This in itself is a radical departure from the dominance of the classical view where logic reigns supreme and the rational egoic brain closes the mind to any other functionality for fear of being found out in its ineptitude. The ego simply cannot operate in this exalted and superior state as it has limited intelligence and functionality. The ego was not designed to make decisions.

Moreover, intuition and insight operate through paradox and dialectic unity meaning that we learn to ride the yin/yang continuums being able to hold, understand and transcend that apparent opposition arriving at the superior vantage point of oneness – understanding the complementarity of the opposites, transcending the apparent division and separation of individuality to arrive at the underlying oneness and unity of creation. This is not only a different way of thinking, it is a completely new and different way of being that few humans have attained.

Wisdom is often arrived at by being able to look at things from several vantage points and not being overly fixated on any one position. Ignorance is often associated with bigotry, blindness and a refusal to acknowledge another's point of view. The egoic mind loves to become entrenched and fight to the bitter end, to hold onto its particular perspective rather than seeing it as just one of many. Most human wars and conflict arise because of egoic entrenchment.

Creative intelligence is able to hold both opposites and transcend the polarity, coming up with a totally new and revolutionary outcome: this is the true creative thought – something brand new! God was not created in the image of man; mankind is learning to become divine, to participate in the creative intelligence of the universe, to emerge from the murky swamp of egoic ignorance and allow the light of pure consciousness to illuminate its mind to intuitive awareness.

When we do this, life takes on a totally new meaning – we enter that intelligent dialogue with cosmic consciousness, with the divine intelligence that regulates and directs reality, with the evolutionary and creative process of life and finally with our own life story. That story starts to make sense – we know why we are here, what makes us unique, what is our gift to the world and what we need to do. The journey moves into a completely different dimension. This is precisely what we are here to do – to live our lives gloriously, happily and majestically. To live with awe and wonder. To co-creatively participate with the creative forces of life. To live in harmony and oneness with the universal laws that regulate life. To be blessed! To *BeCome One*! To become the new human.

Most successful people do what they love and what they need to do – which is to live their lives purposefully. Most know their life's work and are passionate about fulfilling their dreams. It is interesting that the universe works through imagination, dreams and desires. This is what truly moves and motivates us. Yet, none of these are left brain rational thought processes. Nearly all major scientific, technological and social breakthroughs are the result of imagination and daydreams, but we are taught as children not to indulge in such fantasies!

Most truly successful people are not motivated by money or short-term gain but rather by creating something significant for the future and making the world a better place. It seems the overriding distinction is whether we do to profit ourselves through separatist selfish greed or whether we do to enrich the world. True fulfillment, happiness and joy can only come from the latter.

We can only know our path when we are in contact with the essence of our being obeying the inner law of that self. To stay on that path requires continual adjustment to the matrix of our lives. The only constant in the universe is change. The nature of the universe as revealed by quantum theory is eternal flux. We live in a sea of turbulence and change but that change is not chaotic and haphazard. There is an essential unity and order to that process of change. There are definite patterns, rhythms and seasons.

Learning to ride the waves of those changes is *TaoTuning*. We are now aware that the universe is built on waves of energy: everything breaks down to this level not indivisible particles of solidity. The wave-like nature of reality now needs to dictate our world view and understanding of the cosmos. In other words, we need to build a new cosmology that is more flexible, malleable and fluid than the one we now have which is based on the mechanistic model.

Human beings are not discrete and solid indivisible units of biology that end at our skin and our lives are not predetermined or set in stone. We are waves of energy with probability patterns; we exist within a manifestation matrix and the dominant variable in that equation is our inner attitude to life and what happens. How often do we need to witness this – it is not what happens out there but what happens within that determines our reality. Two people can experience the same upbringing, exactly the same set of circumstances, yet their inner attitudes are completely different and thus create completely different outcomes.

We are the creators of our own reality. We are the drivers of our own bus. We are the storyteller, the writer, producer, director of our play. It is our imagination, our dreams, our desires, thoughts, feelings and attitudes that create our future. This is the overriding and distinguishing difference between this new cosmology and traditional religion: the empowerment of the individual. Precisely because the universe is alive and unfolding, cosmic consciousness is never static. Everything changes every second and in that change, affects everything else. The world is one! The entire universe is a gestalt of Being on its own journey of unfoldment.

The real question is whether humanity en masse or even you, as an individual, can align your personal journey with that of the universe. This requires constant vigilance, alertness and awareness. It is not a set and forget. You cannot engage auto pilot or cruise control and then go to sleep. You cannot learn a set of rules or commandments and then blindly follow them for life. You cannot even say I know my life purpose and then rigidly cling to that knowing or direction.

Life is far more subtle than that; life is forever changing ever so intricately. We cannot wait to hit the wall of our permissible zone of variance. We cannot wait until life comes crashing through to tell us we are off our path or off balance. The ocean surfer certainly cannot go to sleep riding a 5-meter wave – that would be suicidal! Life requires intense intelligence. Life is the most intricate game we can play and requires full and utmost attention.

We must always be asking ourselves one question: what is going on? Is our awareness inside our heads in the washing machine of our rational thinking mind going around and around in meaningless circles, spinning endlessly in mindless madness? Stop and examine your thoughts. Your hopes and fears are the same as they were 10, 20, 30 or even 50 years ago. The thinking mind lives in closed circuits of old energy patterns. Although, the precise circumstance may be different, if you drill down to the core issue, it remains the same. And it will not change unless you change it.

Or is our awareness out there engaged in the eternal moment of our being? Rational thought exists in the continuity of the past. Cosmic consciousness exists in a never-ending series of moments. But these moments are not connected like linear thought. Each moment is new and thus exciting and precious. People who exist within the continuity of the past are always tired and lack vitality. People who engage with the moment are energised and revitalised by the excitement of the new. Consciousness does not exist within space and time. The space-time continuum exists within the higher dimension of consciousness or the holomovement.

Are we locked within the continuity of the past? Is time our master? Are we locked within the localisation of space? Are we isolated, separated and divided particles of biology or are we conscious beings of light? Are we limited by our fears or inspired by the magnificence of our being? This is a fairly simple choice, but probably the hardest discipline to master because the habit of rational thought has so dominated human existence for thousands of years. This habit controls humanity. To break free from its pernicious hold requires constant vigilance and commitment. But break free we must, or we will become extinct as a species.

Homo sapiens means the wise human. Is it wise to destroy the very foundations of your own life support system? In terms of *Tao Tuning*, humanity has reached the extreme point of its permissible zone of variance. It is now on a collision course with the Earth. We must immediately and urgently take remedial action and adjust our path to avoid that collision for there is no question as to who will come out of it worse off. Either way humanity loses.

The essence of this new cosmology is that man has been granted free will to become a sovereign being. The emergence from the Garden of Eden was not a punishment for Original Sin but an opportunity to graduate to a self-determining being, capable of controlling its own destiny. In evolutionary terms this is very recent development. If the planet is viewed in its 4,600-million-year journey, humanity is a blip of several minutes.

Will we go down in a blaze of ignominy, or will we correct our course in time? This is not a rhetorical or philosophical question but the very real genesis of this new cosmology. The old Bible begins with the Book of Genesis in which God created the world in 6 days and on the 7th day he rested. All done and dusted – nothing to do with us: a fait accompli. And therefore, no responsibility or accountability for the future. Humanity is a mere pawn in the cosmic football game between God and the Devil. This has created a false dependency, weakness of spirit and crippled humanity from taking action. But it has also suited our laziness.

The new Book of Genesis according to quantum theory reads very differently. The universe was not created in some distant past but is an on-going work of ceaseless creativity. The universe is not a static mechanistic world of predetermined prescriptive rules ordained by God but a living breathing flux of change operating via the self-regulating processes of life according to universal law. Moreover, everything is connected to everything else, and every unit of consciousness is seeking unfoldment and fulfillment within this sea of cosmic consciousness that is vastly intelligent and all knowing.

Essentially, every aspect of life is responsible for its own being, its own evolutionary journey and its own participation in the whole. The non-human world does this automatically and in perfect order: there is 100% compliance with universal law. Humanity, however, has been given the gift of free will to join in the creative cosmic dance voluntarily: to *BeCome One* with the gods. But this gift is a double-edged sword and does bestow upon us the choice of non-compliance, of resistance, of going against the flow, of swimming upstream. And this is precisely what we have chosen to do.

We are now out of sync with the system itself. We are now at odds with nature. We are now running our own race contrary to universal law. We are now out on our own – a very dangerous place to be. The problem being, there is nowhere to go, nowhere to hide, nowhere to run to. Universal law means just that - omnipresent, omnipotent and omniscient. God is All There Is. There is nothing else. There is nowhere for an aberrant species to go except into extinction. Many scientists now believe we need to urgently find another home, another planet once we destroy this one. But we will only be taking our aberrant ways with us to destroy it as well. A new way must be found, not a new home!

We are given the right to choose our own reality, but we must be prepared to accept the consequences for our decisions because this is the true nature of the gift of freedom. Freedom does not exist if there is no accountability and accountability means acceptance of the consequences of our behaviour. We need to become accountable for the impact of our behaviour on the whole.

This is the major distinction of the new cosmology. We live in an interconnected whole; we cannot separate and divide pieces of the puzzle as if there will be no consequence just as we cannot divide matter into some finite indivisible particle and take it out of the matrix. Every action, every behaviour, indeed every thought, bears fruit and goes out into the whole like ripples on a pond. Our ripples are tearing the fabric of life apart. The consequences of our actions are destructive. The inevitable long-term effect of our classical separatist world view is there will be no world left. At least not for mankind.

Personally, I believe that in some infantile way, humanity believes it can misbehave, like some truculent spoilt child and daddy (read God the Father) will somehow come and make it all good again. This is the folly of our childish philosophy. There are many Biblical and religious texts that say so: the Second Coming, the Resurrection, the Uplifting, Armageddon and so on in all religions both East and West.

But free will means precisely that: if we wantonly create our own self-destruction then we need to be left alone to do just that. This is the corollary of freedom. We must be allowed to experience the inevitable consequences of our choices so that we can learn from our mistakes. God is not going to come down and save us for that would rob us of our freedom!

More importantly, this is simply not the way life works. Life works through the evolutionary process of ceaseless experimentation where individual species come and go depending on their ability to adapt and flow with the Tao of existence. Those who do not flow or go against the tide eventually become exhausted and extinct. This is just a law of nature not some form of punishment. The universe is objective and impartial. Humanity overstates its stake in the game because of its deluded sense of self-importance.

Humans once believed the Earth was the centre of the universe and that the sun and all the stars revolved around us! We still believe we are the only intelligent species both on the planet and in all the galaxies. We live in a totally myopic world of self-delusion and grandeur that is unfortunately incorrect. We simply cannot comprehend or imagine a world without humanity. Yet, it is a very sobering thought.

In the Teaching of Don Yuan by Carlos Castaneda, Don Yuan explains that one should always walk with Death on one shoulder to reinforce reverence for life and remind one of one's impermanence and mortality. Similarly, I believe we need to live with the awareness that we are not the centre of the universe, nor essential and are currently facing extinction as a species. We need to wake up and start to take personal responsibility for the state of the world.

For it is not only quantum physics and science that tells us we are all connected. Mystics of all persuasions tell us about this oneness and that we are the world; the world is us. There is no division, no separation; everything is one. Each of us is personally responsible, each of us is accountable; every single one of us is currently creating our personal and collective future. What will it look like?

This all depends on whether humanity can live in harmony with universal law – something which currently we simply are not doing. Because of our immature world view, we continue to behave like the spoilt child expecting to be able to misbehave but escape the consequences of that behaviour. This is classic narcissism. Traditional religion fosters a psychological dependency upon religious intermediaries: priests, rabbis, gurus and so on which is exactly what the religious establishment wants. One must remember that most religious doctrines have a sociopolitical basis in that they are designed to keep the populous under control.

As Karl Marx is so often quoted: religion is the opiate of the masses. Over the last several thousand years, the Church and the State have combined to keep the people sedated and in bondage. The established elite exists in both and have a vested interest in keeping the masses asleep. Traditional religion is designed to keep people very much in their comfort zone of compliance and obedience to the status quo. And fearful.

However, modern science teaches us that change is the order of the universe not the status quo. We need to learn to flow with that change and not become anxious by the fear of change. Human beings like stability and resist change. Yet, it is this very resistance that causes the problem. Once we accept the inevitability of change and realise that change occurs in very stable and orderly patterns, we can learn to ride these waves of probability without becoming anxious. Obviously, this requires skill and discipline which is the whole thrust of *Tao Tuning*.

We need to learn to be comfortable in the unknown rather than always trying to force the situation back to a false stability that is regressive and dangerous. Often, we merely need to be able to await the right time for action and be prepared to sit with the circumstances of our matrix; yet this is what so many people simply cannot do, preferring to try to force the fulfillment of their inner wants and desires.

To be comfortable amidst discomfort because it is not scary; it is not some form of punishment for not being good enough. It is simply the process of change which is ongoing and eternal. We best get used to it.

Chapter 19

The New Cosmology

The number one, fundamental difference between the traditional, classical, established world view and the one we need to embrace is taking personal accountability and responsibility for our lives.

Humanity needs to come of age, emerging from the dependency of childhood and accepting the sovereignty of adulthood. As children, we naturally depend upon our parents; as adults, we take responsibility for our lives. Traditional religion robs the individual of their sovereignty teaching that the individual is dependent upon both the intermediary and the prescriptive rule to ensure salvation. In other words, we must follow the rules and accept our dependency. The new philosophy teaches us we alone are responsible and must take charge of our lives accepting the accountability for our actions.

This is a far more difficult but rewarding path. We can no longer go cap in hand to God; we can no longer just pray and hope everything will be OK; we can no longer do what we like and then say 3 Hail Marys to be forgiven for our sins. We can no longer go to Church on a Sunday but spend our lives erroneously. We need to learn to ride the Tao of our destiny. We alone determine our fate, choose our path, create our future. We are the writer, producer and main actor in our own story. This requires training and skill; this is the very purpose of our lives, of being human.

To deny this responsibility keeps us trapped in a false reality. One cannot change what one does not own or acknowledge. The first step in any reckoning is acknowledgement. We must firstly acknowledge that it is we who are creating our lives - not some mythical deity. We must also recognise the patterns of our aberrant behaviour. One does not simply get on one's board and ride that 5-meter wave: that would be foolish and suicidal. We need to accept that humanity has gone down a 2,000-year detour which has taken us to a dead-end.

We have all inherited genetic and cultural erroneous cues. We no longer know what it means to be a natural being. This is the legacy of the fall and the misinterpretation of the Garden of Eden. (Please see *Personal Sovereignty* for more on this concept in detail.) We have all allowed our negative ego to usurp control and lead us on this merry ride of deception. We each have deep ingrained habits, behaviours, beliefs and patterns that are false and need rectifying. There is much work to be done, much clearing out of the old before we can plant the new seeds of personal growth.

It is very much like an old and overgrown garden that is full of weeds. We need to pull out the weeds, tend the earth and fertilise the soil before we can plant the new seedlings. To heal oneself of the past one needs to process the untruth. The personal growth, self-development, positive psychology and new age movements are all variations on this path. Yet a path that must be trod nonetheless. Which path you take does not matter; that you choose a path and stick to it does. You must be committed and persevere. You need to rewrite your story; you need to redefine who you are at the core of your being.

Humanity has erroneously defined itself at both the collective, species level and at the individual personal level. Tinkering at the corners will not suffice; we need to totally redefine our being. This is the path of enlightenment where one fully realises one's oneness with the whole; not in some academic, artificial way, but fundamentally at one's core. This is not book-learnt catechism: there are no rules to recite and justify our existence. Your spirituality is your living, breathing relationship with life. It must be real; it must be passionate, and it must be 24/7.

Religion is not a hat or garb you don on Sunday and then take off to do your misdeeds on Monday morning when you go to work. Religion is your attitude to life: to your family and loved ones, to your friends and work colleagues, to your work and play, to your money and finances, to your health and daily practice, to yourself and to the planet. The oneness of life is just that! Modern science tells us that we cannot divide; that we cannot take pieces out of the puzzle; that we cannot take ourselves out of the manifestation matrix and pretend we are an objective and remote observer.

We are an integral part of that matrix: we are the dominant variable. You do not go to a Church of whatever description or faith - you are the Church. Your body is your temple and your soul is your conduit to God, Goddess, All That Is. The only path out is in. You are the only intermediary: the conversation is intimate, the dialogue direct. No two people can have the same relationship with the divine for we are all on our own sacred journey. Our lives, our paths, our wave, our personal Tao is as unique as our character, face and fingerprint.

To commence one must fully embrace and accept one's uniqueness and the responsibility and freedom that uniqueness bestows: this is the real gift of life. We are not some form of cookie cutter clone; we are not predetermined robots and we certainly are not a freak chemical accident of biology. We are sparks of consciousness; we are holographic points of light containing the whole within our very being. We are interconnected and interwoven with the whole. We emerge from universality into individuality and return over and over again. It is the dance of the dialectic: being one and being whole are another of those yin/yang continuums that go on into eternity.

The ocean surfer, the wave, the board and the sea become one in the ride. The cosmic surfer, the personal Tao, cosmic consciousness and the universal Tao become one in the journey of life. One must learn to move into and out from this unity at will. This is real meditation where one becomes still, where the egoic mind ceases its dominance and rational linear thought stops, where one enters the silence and *BeComes One* with the Divine. One learns to hold this posture so that one can swim at will in divine consciousness. One can only really enjoy the ocean by learning how to swim. One can only really enjoy the journey of life by learning how to swim in the cosmic ocean.

For it is in this practice that one learns to relax, to let go, to accept and to flow. It is in this union that one learns to trust, to acknowledge, to understand the beneficence of the universe. It is in this discipline that the petty ego ceases its control! Until one learns and practises this discipline daily, one cannot really be free from the personal negative ego and the collective negative ego of humanity.

We are all victims of tradition, of the past, of the collective unconscious, of our upbringing, of a legacy that traps us into the status quo. In many ways, we reject our uniqueness. We all want to be the same, to fit in, to not be different. We want to be accepted.

Moreover, we want reality to be solid, fixed and predictable; we want to live in a mechanistic universe run according to predetermined rules. We crave surety and stability so that we do not have to think or make too many decisions. But quantum theory has taught us that the world simply does not operate that way: it is malleable and deals in probabilities rather than certainties. Many of the original quantum physicists at the beginning of the 20th century had to radically redefine their personal philosophies and world views as a result of their discoveries. Einstein, Niels Bohr, Louis De Broglie Erwin Schrodinger, Wolfgang Pauli through to David Bohm all experienced deep inner psychological turmoil in coming to terms with the paradoxical and fluid nature of reality that was being demonstrated by the sub-atomic world. All eventually experienced a profound spiritual transformation triggered by this strange new world.

The classical texts of Taoism also speak in this strange paradoxical language of '*neti neti*' which means not this, not that. The mind seeks security via definition, clarity and absolutes. The classical world view provides surety via the mechanistic model and rational linear logic of objectification and certainty. Both modern science and ancient mysticism, however, disagree with this absolute, telling us the world simply does not operate that way. Rather it is fluid, malleable, in a permanent state of flux and change.

Learning to consult the I Ching requires a completely different mindset, not just learning another linear language. We now know reality is not composed of solid material objects which interact mechanically but is a sea of wave-like probability patterns with tenancies to occur in the time/space continuum, where one can never be certain nor measure the precise location coordinates of anything. Moreover, these probabilities are interconnections in a complex web of relationships displaying paradoxical characteristics that defies linear logic.

It is extremely frustrating for a westerner brought up in mainstream classical education to retrain the brain to function in this algorithmic way and it takes many years of discipline and study, but this is not academic or book learning: it must be experiential just as the atomic physicists had to experience this paradoxical nature of reality firsthand as they conducted their experiments.

Think of your own life. We all seek order and stability to make our lives work. We all want comfort, security and success. We all want the best life has to offer. But so often this eludes us because we want the simple answer – we want the world to operate logically and mechanically like a good Swiss watch where cause and effect are neat and precise.

Unfortunately, life just does not work this way and it is a part of humanity's arrogance and folly that it wants to impose its rules upon the world it inhabits. Life will not be contained nor is it predictable. But is this not the joy and excitement of life – that it is unpredictable, that it is always new, that we need to learn to flow with the tide of the Tao?

Life is a glorious adventure and must be lived on its terms not ours! We need to accept the paradox of life and the wave-like quality of our existence. Interestingly, the more we resist and attempt to force an erroneous world view on life, the less secure our reality becomes, for we are basically out of sync with universal law. The only true way to create peace, stability and order in our lives is to live in harmony with the Tao. We need to learn to flow rather than adopt a fixed and rigid standpoint. The more we want to hold onto a static position the more we lose our hold on reality. There is a Zen saying that the more one tries to hold water in the palm of one's hand the more one loses it.

As Lao Tzu said, so many thousands of years ago:

> 'Watch your thoughts; they become words.
> 'Watch your words; they become actions.
> 'Watch your actions; they become habit.
> 'Watch your habits; they become character.
> 'Watch your character; it becomes your destiny.'

We need to do a complete about turn; we need to begin to look at reality from a completely different point of view and come to terms with a more fluid, malleable context. In many ways, this is disconcerting and terrifying for the egoic mind craves security, stability and constancy. We fear change! But as we embrace this paradigm of change, as we relax into the probability patterns and holographic nature of reality, we do actually become more secure because we realise that the change is orderly and does follow seasonal patterns. We do not fear the coming and going of the 4 seasons because we know they are an intrinsic part of nature and follow their own patterns. We do not freak out when a deciduous tree loses all its leaves in autumn, thinking it is dead. We know this to be a part of its annual life cycle. Everywhere in nature and in life there are these seasons, cycles, patterns and rhythms. They are a fundamental characteristic of the wave nature of reality.

Tao Tuning is learning to live one's life in harmony with these rhythms and cycles just as a good farmer sows, plants and reaps in tune with the annual seasons of nature. Some people go further planting according to lunar cycles and so on. So, this way of living is not strange or revolutionary. Indeed, most indigenous, native societies live in harmony with the cycles of the earth and understand this concept. It is just that modern, western human under the influence of the classical world view, the egoic mind and living divorced and disconnected from nature, has lost this perspective. After the Industrial Revolution, with the advent of both urbanisation and the dominance of machines, western society became more separated from these natural cycles and more dominated by the mechanistic model of creation.

The goal of the ancient mystics was to become one with life, to live in total harmony with nature, to learn from its cycles and its being. For them there was no divorce, no separation, no machine. Everything was consciousness and this consciousness permeated reality and guided its expression and manifestation. Similarly, quantum physics, fuzzy logic, string theory and complexity theory are once again teaching us that reality is not set in stone, that life is not linear and logical but a ball of pulsating energy patterns that we interact with and create our future as we go along.

But before we can plant these new ideas and concepts into our taoic mind we need to weed the false beliefs that we have been operating on for so long. If one thinks of a garden full of weeds, one cannot just plant the new seedlings without first weeding the bed and preparing it for the new planting. Moreover, as anyone knows weeds are extremely difficult to eradicate. Erroneous beliefs and habits take perseverance and commitment to be replaced by new fresh ideas particularly when these are radically different and difficult to comprehend. Far safer and easier to stick with the status quo of traditional wisdom even if that is wrong.

Humanity needs to learn a completely new way of living. I personally believe this will be a major quantum shift in understanding and modus operandi whereby we do become a new species in evolutionary terms. Life will force us to adapt whether we like it or not. Planet Earth, our home, will demand a more harmonious and holistic relationship with humanity based on mutual respect, trust and acknowledgement. Our current trajectory simply cannot continue on its current path without major catastrophe.

Humanity is fast approaching the limit of its permissible zone of variance and is on a collision course with the planet and life itself. The choice is whether we adjust willingly and voluntarily, before it is too late, or whether we stubbornly wait until we are forced to mutate by some major global cataclysm which will probably result in far fewer humans living on the planet who will then go through the mutation process.

The fundamental premise of *Tao Tuning* is that life is conscious and operates under the divine benevolence of the universe, meaning life always wants what is best for each individual unit of consciousness. Life does not suck, is not hard and does not fight us. However, life will guide us on our path by warning us when we get lost or go off our path. At first, this warning is gentle and cooperative but if we insist on ignoring these messages from life, they become more severe until we collide with an unfavourable reality.

This is all about learning to speak the language of life: of being constantly alert, aware and in a perpetual dialogue with one's destiny. This is certainly not a set and forget, auto pilot, mechanistic universe where we simply choose a path and then go to sleep. We need to work cooperatively with life, co-creating our destiny, riding our wave, our personal Tao and manipulating the manifestation matrix that becomes our future. This is an incredibly intricate skill especially if one wants to keep within the bounds of Implicate Order. Bohm argues that the universe is in a constant process of transition from Implicate to Explicate Order: Implicate Order being the non-manifest ground of being from which the manifest world of Explicate Order comes.

Our daily lives are a continual process of moving from ideation to expression. We have an idea, whether that is as mundane as a shopping list or as complex as Relativity Theory. We all have these desires, hopes, aspirations - the things we want to achieve or bring into our lives. The basic difference between the successful and the unsuccessful person is that the successful one brings these ideas into the daily reality of their lives more efficiently, elegantly and with greater ease while the unsuccessful person struggles viewing life as hard, unyielding and difficult.

It is not unreasonable to suggest that everyone wants a more successful life especially if we do not define success in monetary terms. Success can be family, love, service to humanity, career, artistic expression – whatever! This is the beauty of life that we all get to define exactly what we want our lives to look like. We all get to fulfill our own individual life purpose. We all get to express our innate unique individuality. I believe the purpose of life is to spontaneously express god. Not god with a capital G, as some mythical being in a remote heaven, but the divine principle of creation which is the Tao.

Life is the most glorious smorgasbord of opportunity to Be who we are: to go into our inner selves, discover that inner essence and express that law as radiant joy by becoming more of who we are: to not shrink from our magnificence and grandeur but to give full expression to our own unique creativity. However, as in any smorgasbord, one must exercise prudence and discipline. One cannot eat everything; nor can one achieve everything. One must exercise moderation; one needs to be able to limit one's desires and aspirations so that they become meaningful, take shape and form in the material world.

This limitation is the definition of who we are. We are not boundless creatures. We need to know and understand the limits set for us and work within those boundaries. This is the wisdom of knowing one's destiny, of working with one's fate, of consciously choosing precisely what one wants to experience and create and then focusing on that creation exclusively. It is often said that the most successful people know how to limit their desires and to focus on their outcome singularly and obsessively until achieved.

An essential characteristic of the manifest universe is this process of limitation: by attuning to the inner law of our being we know who we are, what is right for us, what are the limits set for us by our fate and our destiny and then squarely focusing on that and not becoming distracted. Unsuccessful people tend to swing wildly from one endeavour to the next without achieving anything concrete. It is essential to know who you are, what is right for you and to be content with this definition.

Too often, especially in this age of social and mass media, where we are continually bombarded by external influences telling us what to think, who to be, how to behave, what is chic or in or the latest fashion, we lose track of who we really are. We need to listen and pay more attention to the small, quiet voice from within and shut out the turbulence and noise of the outer world. This is how we turn around: self-time. Spending time on one's own, getting to know oneself, being at peace with one's inner being and learning to acknowledge that inner law. But in a noisy, fast paced world of conformity and stress this is the very thing we avoid.

The first thing one must do is to establish an intimate relationship with oneself. To not be afraid to spend solitary time with no television, radio, music, iPhone, internet, world wide web but with you. To discover who you are, what you like, what are your preferences, what are your inner desires, dreams, hopes and aspirations, what makes you tick. To *BeCome One* with yourself! To not feel guilty or awkward or that there is something wrong with you because you are alone. To make it a conscious choice to spend quality time with your inner being.

This first step is a sine qua non, without which it just does not happen. Awareness begins with self.

For it is only by quietening the outside noise that we can then hear the inner chatter of the egoic mind. And this is where the challenge and the fun begin. To become aware of the thinking mind; to discern its patterns; to know precisely how your negative ego works. We all have our own patterns of thought and because this a plane of duality we each exist on our own personal yin/yang continuum of positive and negative. To know oneself is to know the positives and the negatives; to know oneself accurately, exactly as one is without any sort of self-deception or illusion. To be capable of being brutally honest without going down in a screaming heap, without becoming myopic, subjective and despondent.

This is a very fine line, but one one must walk if one would become enlightened. We need to know the truth of who we are. We need to know how our negative ego operates: what are its favourite patterns, fears, doubts, conceits and arrogance. We need to know the weather patterns of our own moods so that we can catch the storm before it becomes full blown. This work requires years of processing; years of weeding and perpetual attention and awareness. One must dive into the ocean of one's neurosis but be able to surface at will without contamination. One must know one's own trigger points and the things that press one's buttons.

We all have them yet choose to live in blissful ignorance pretending we are more perfect than we are. Denial, justification and excuses are the staples of the negative ego, and your negative ego has had control for most of your life, so it is not going to give it up easily. You need to use your mind to outsmart your mind. You need to cease the chatter, the internal dialogue. You need to learn to use your mind in a completely new and different way where intuition, insight, gestalts of awareness, spontaneous knowing and trust are paramount and linear, logical reasoning and analysis are just a tool to be used sparingly and only in certain circumstances.

The goal is not to get rid of your ego but to befriend it, to heal it, to make it whole and transform it back into the positive assistant it was designed to be. Your egoic mind is but one aspect of your multidimensional being; it is not the entirety of your consciousness or your intelligence. Your ego is not very intelligent at all but operates with extremely limited software. In its rightful place it is a dutiful servant, but like so many things when in the wrong place, it has become destructive, overworked and unreliable. It cannot be trusted to guide you through life. The ego is not your guiding mechanism – the inner law of your being, your personal Tao is the only rudder to set your course by. And to do this you need to be able to listen to and trust its message.

This discipline requires time, perseverance, patience and tenacity for we often hear but do not heed. Whether it is that impulse to take the umbrella when it is sunny and then we get caught in the rain; whether it is that prompting to do or not to do, as the case may be, that we ignore only to regret it later. Whether it is that inner knowing not to trust someone that we discount and then fall prey to their manipulation and dishonesty. The inner warnings and knowing are invariably there.

We have all had these experiences countless times. We have all heard and ignored or even disobeyed the inner voice of our being. We have all gone against our inner conscience. We have all allowed the negative ego to overrule the voice of wisdom!

There are many voices clamouring for attention. How do we know for certain which one is which – is it my ego or my Tao, is it my intuition or wishful thinking? How do I know? Like anything, it requires attention; learning to distinguish the various voices; learning to trust the inner voice of our being; having the courage to travel the path less travelled; having faith in ourselves. Quite often, this means going against the crowd, against the traditional view, against the established protocol, having the strength to back oneself when everyone around you is telling you, you are wrong.

As one pays attention, as one reduces the noise, as one weeds the negative fears and doubts, gradually clarity returns. One becomes less cluttered in one's mind and stillness regains control. The more one meditates the easier it becomes; the less hold the egoic mind has on one's consciousness.

Remember, we want our minds to be still like a clear pond reflecting the beauty of the world without interference. If the surface is choppy and turbulent, stirred by conflicting emotions, the reflection becomes distorted and unclear. One makes erroneous decisions and bad choices. One loses one's way and forfeits the favourableness of the situation; one is no longer on the wave riding the energy and momentum of the universe. One needs to paddle really hard relying only on one's own energy. This is why so many people experience life as a struggle and hardship because they are not flowing with their destiny but have gone AWOL and operate on their own steam. This is not a pretty place to be!

It is obvious that what I am describing here is almost a foreign and alien state of being. First and foremost, we need to distinguish this from the old religious connotations so often associated with these concepts. Meditation is not so much a religious exercise as a neurological process of brain gym. We are not practising anything because a dogma tells us to. We are not doing anything in order to earn salvation in another afterlife. This is most definitely not about repeating mantras and following just another set of prescriptive rules.

We are doing these things because it makes our lives work better. We are not accepting religious dogma, ritual or false promises – we are learning from cutting edge scientific wisdom. We are not rejecting any part of our being - all are essential components of an enlightened life. We are not even using the term enlightened in any religious context. We simply mean a life full of light, joy and happiness, not darkness and despair.

It is essential to remember that this life is not a dress rehearsal, is not a means to an end, is not a punishment for sin, is not in any way to be sacrificed for some mythical promise in an afterlife. Life is the gift and is there for its own sake. It is the means and the end.

We need to turn around completely and begin to live our lives from a radically new perspective – one that has not been tried before en masse. Down through the ages there have been many mystics, saints, prophets and sages in every age, culture and tradition that have alluded to this exalted state. They have been the harbingers, the way showers, the guides and scouts pointing to a new way of being. But it is now time for humanity to make the transition, for us a species to attain a critical mass or threshold of migration.

And once again we need to turn to science to guide our journey. We know evolution is the key characteristic of life; we know life evolves through mutation and change. We know species come and go but that the glorious adventure of life continues through the process of adaptation to ever changing environmental circumstances. We know species become stronger through this Darwinian adaptation.

Humanity is deluding itself if it thinks it is not susceptible to this same process. We must evolve; we must adapt; we must mutate. Science teaches us that those individuals with the stronger gene or characteristic that most meets the current environmental demands win, grow and prosper whereas the individuals who do not adapt die out. To be sure this often happens gradually and takes time and may not be immediately apparent. But sometimes whole species, like the dinosaurs, just disappear en masse quite quickly because of some cataclysmic event.

We are now in what has been termed the sixth great period of extinction and the most serious and destructive event since the asteroid that wiped out the dinosaurs. The difference being that this extinction event is being caused not by nature or some interstellar cataclysm but by human activity. The planet is losing up to 100 species every day and it is estimated 50% of the world's species will be extinct in the not-too-distant future. This extinction is a direct consequence of capitalism and colonialism where this classical western world view geographically expands across the planet dominating and usurping less powerful ideologies that are more in harmony with the natural flow.

A large part of the egoic neurosis is the insatiable quest for economic growth that is fast devouring the biodiversity and wilderness of the world. We need to understand that the western world view and collective negative ego operate through the international agencies of debt and trade that promise false riches to poorer third world countries in exchange for their natural resources and wealth. So, we export our pollution and the destruction of their natural estate for a supposed better life. Nowhere is this more pronounced than in China and India, the 2 most populous nations.

The classical western world view is taking over the world via the dominance of capitalism as a socio- economic system. Yet, all we are doing is literally trashing the world. There is now so much pollution and waste that an ocean Garbage Patch stretches from the West coast of America all the way to Japan. The western world produces 1.3 billion tons of Municipal Waste a year. We are drowning in our own waste.

We have now moved into the Anthropocene Age where the overriding determinant of the environment is human activity upon the planet. This is the age of awakening: humanity has declared war on the environment and nature stands ready to fight back. But exactly how nature will react is uncertain. However, one thing is abundantly clear: the rhythms and cycles of nature that have nurtured humanity for hundreds of thousands of years have been severely disrupted to the extent that the patterns of probability are now stacked against humanity.

It has taken over 4 billion years for these patterns to stabilise so that they support human life on planet Earth; it has taken humanity a little over 50 to create chaos so that the chi of the Earth is no longer stable. In other words, we are entering unchartered waters where we can no longer rely upon the beneficence of the universe. We must stand accountable for what we have created and the forces we have unwittingly unleashed. The Earth has been mobilised to protect itself. Mankind has become an aberrant species causing too much havoc, disruption and destruction. The greater forces of life must respond and take over.

It is not too farfetched to imagine any number of scenarios where humanity stands in peril. Our current trajectory pits us directly against nature and we have disrupted the very rhythms and cycles we need to rely upon for our continued survival. It is not my intention to go into depths about climate change or global warming, however, in terms of *TaoTuning* and being able to have this intelligent and direct communication with life, it is clearly a matter of global warning.

The planet, our home is warning us: cease and desist; stand down from your current stance and change your attitude. The message is abundantly clear and needs no debate. Nor do we have the luxury of the time to indulge in that frivolous exercise. We need to take the warning seriously. There are currently 7.5 billion people on the planet, and it is estimated that we are operating at 50% over the Earth's ability to sustain that number!

Thus, the really interesting question becomes do we heed that warning? Do we engage in an intelligent and meaningful dialogue with Gaia as a superior consciousness and our host to address this issue or do we plunder on regardless? This is no longer a rhetorical question nor a fringe or alternative heresy. The United States Defence Chiefs now view an unstable environment as the number one threat facing our future. We need to get serious, and we need to do it fast. The actual steps humanity takes to rectify the pollution, the waste, the global warming, the extinction rates, the destruction of the rain forests and the shrinking biodiversity are not the subject of this book. The ability to heed the warning, to realise we have passed the permissible zone of variance and are now on a collision course with nature, with the Earth and with Gaia as a living consciousness is.

For it goes to the very heart of the matter. *Tao Tuning* is not just some esoteric or academic argument. Nor is it pertinent just for the individual. It is relevant for humanity; for humanity is also on its own path, has its own collective Tao, must adhere to its own inner law. As previously mentioned, the most important thing about a world view is that it defines the individual's relationship with that world. The current predominant world view on the planet is the classical western egoic view of linear logic and separatist elitism. It is this world view that is directly responsible for our current predicament and the wholesale environmental destruction it is unleashing on the planet via the colonial expansion of rampant out of control capitalism and conspicuous consumption.

It is this world view that is erroneous and destructive. It is this world view that is the root cause of the problem and must be amended and this needs to be done individually, one by one, for each of those 7.5 billion people. To be sure, some ethnic minorities do still exist within a more holistic and harmonious paradigm, but this is statistically negligible.

In Darwinian terms, those individual members of a species that can mutate and adapt survive. Those that cannot become extinct. I am asserting that the necessary gene, characteristic or attribute that each individual member of the human race needs to survive is this radically different world view. I call this Singularity Consciousness where one knows all life is One. The evolutionary process does not need 7 or 10 billion aberrant humans causing chaos on the planet. A few million attuned beings will do!

Several million or even 1 billion enlightened souls who are living their lives harmoniously, intelligently, conscientiously and gratefully. People who are committed to living their lives in harmony with the natural flow; who are not needlessly raping the Earth. People who are able to dance in the dialectic and embrace their divinity as well as their humanity. People who are accountable for their behaviour and their actions and who live responsibly, aware of their impact upon others – not just other humans but all of life including the Earth. People who willingly and graciously accept their role and duty as custodians of life on planet Earth. People who care; people who are healthy, harmonious and happy.

People who will restore the Garden of Eden!

This now becomes a very personal question. We can easily lose 6.5 billion people. We can easily be rid of the waste, the pollution, the greed and the malice. We can easily adopt a more sophisticated and spiritual world view and socio-economic system that is less rapacious and suicidal than current western capitalism. We can easily inherit a new Earth by becoming the new human.

It is your choice! It is a very personal and solitary choice for you cannot make it for anyone else even your closest loved ones. Moreover, no one else can make it for you and no God, Saviour or Christ is going to come down and save you in some mystical and nonsensical rapture.

You need to give up the childish fantasies. You need to wake up from your indolent slumber. You need to take stock of your actions and ascertain exactly where you are at on your spiritual journey. Are you listening? Are you alive, awake, aware? Do you know your story? Are you on your path? Are you riding your wave, your personal Tao? Are you being true to the inner law of your being? Are you sincere? Do you totally get the immense privilege and honour it is to be alive and a resident of planet Earth? Do you take your responsibility seriously? What precisely are you doing to solve this planetary problem? As David Suzuki once said: you are either a part of the problem or a part of the solution. On which side of the line do you stand, for it is that line that will determine the survivors.

The problem is that we do not take the issue seriously to heart; we do not own the problem and make it our own. We see it as something the government or the greenies, the United Nations or the United States must fix. It is always out there in the too hard basket and what difference can I make anyway. The individual feels powerless in the face of the enormity of the problem, plus the change and sacrifices needed are just too great. So, we slumber in our ignorance and avoid taking personal responsibility.

But in the end, this is an individual change and an individual choice. Evolution operates one member of a species at a time. Those individuals who mutate survive to reproduce and form the new species; those who do not die out. As I emphasised in *Personal Sovereignty*, the essence of this mutation is the taking of personal responsibility and accountability for our lives and the consequences of our behaviour on the world. The days of feeble dependency and childish fantasy are over. This mutation goes to the heart of being human and being a mature human adult: willing and able to act responsibly, being capable of making our own personal decisions in an intellectually and emotionally mature way. Not seeking shelter behind ancient myths and texts that cripple our decision making and make us beholden to false gods who deprive us of our sovereignty.

The earth is 4,600 million years old. It took 4,000 million of those years for evolution to stabilise the planet's biosphere – the rhythms and cycles of nature so that biological life could exist. In other words, evolution worked on the mineral, geological and atmospheric levels creating the cocoon we now know as our home. It then took another 600 million for evolution to work on the cellular and biological level developing the fauna and flora of the Earth – the delicate, intricate and complex biodiversity that sustains all animal and plant life within that cocoon. The water cycle, the oxygen/carbon cycle, the shifting sands and ocean currents of wind and water, the cycles of the moon and so on that all contribute to the natural rhythm and flow of mother nature.

We live within this womb - this biosphere - never stopping to truly appreciate its natural wonder and now we have tinkered with its interconnections so severely that we have torn holes in its delicate fabric – the garment that protects, sustains and nourishes us.

It is only in the last 2 million years that evolution has moved into the genome of creating the human genus which evolved into homo sapiens approximately 200,000 years ago in Africa. There have been 7 homo species: Heidelbergensis, Rudolfensis, Abilis, Floresiensis, Erectus, Neandererthals and lastly sapiens. All the other homo species are now extinct. It is of note that homo erectus was an extremely successful species lasting almost 2 million years before suddenly becoming extinct about 70,000 years ago because of natural cataclysm. Homo sapiens is the only surviving species of the genus Homo.

So, we can see that the evolutionary thrust of change and mutation continues on regardless. Because of our egoic arrogance and foolish pride, modern human thinks itself to be beyond this evolutionary process but unfortunately this is just wishful thinking. Life moves on inexorably and homo sapiens will mutate into another species of the genus Homo whether we like it or not. It has happened before, and it will happen again.

What is important to realise is that this evolutionary thrust has moved from biological and anatomical development and mutation into behavioural and neurological change. Recent sequencing of gorilla chimpanzee and bonobo genomes confirms that the difference between our genome and these species is less than 1%. Genetically and biologically, we are the same. What distinguishes the modern human is brain size and brain neurology.

In general, there is a correlation between brain size and intelligence and human brain size has increased dramatically in its evolutionary journey. Primate brains on average are double the size one would expect for another species of equivalent stature, but human brains are approximately 3 times the size.

Moreover, human brains have reorganised themselves away from visual perception towards other tasks centred around planning, communication, problem solving and other more advanced cognitive functions. The modern human brain is the largest and most complex of any living primate. It is also significant that brain growth increases most rapidly in times of dramatic climate change such as those facing modern human today. Neuroplasticity proves that the brain grows and reshapes itself structurally dependent upon cognitive function. Like any muscle those areas of the brain we use grow and develop.

Thus, the evolutionary process, for humanity at least, has moved away from anatomical or biological mutation to cerebral and neurological development. We will not be sprouting new limbs or changing our body, but we will be changing and developing our brains and our minds. The important point to grasp is that no species is immune from the evolutionary process no matter how invulnerable we may like to believe we are. Part of the immaturity of youth is the belief in personal immortality and invincibility. Part of the immaturity of the collective negative ego of modern human is its belief in being above and beyond the processes of nature.

Precisely because we have created this separatist world view where humanity stands apart from nature, we believe that somehow, we are immune from the natural order. It is this erroneous belief that allows us to tinker with the rhythms and cycles of the delicate biosphere that supports and sustains us without acknowledging the inevitable consequences of our aberrant behaviour.

The point being it is precisely a shift in this cognitive understanding that is the next evolutionary development. Homo sapiens will mutate into another species – one that is more in harmony with the natural order of the world in which it lives and one that understands its place in the Infinity of Being. The lessons learnt from quantum physics combined with the impending catastrophic climate changes on the planet will force this evolutionary quantum leap.

As already mentioned, the importance of a world view is that it defines the relationship between the species and its environment – it defines its place in the world. Homo sapiens has erroneously defined that place. Remember, the key to *TaoTuning* is arriving at a central and correct position by being in the right place which means adopting the right attitude to what is occurring in one's life: acknowledging and accepting the matrix within which one lives. Not being in denial of what is; not seeking shelter in childish excuse and justification; not sticking one's head in the sand and pretending everything is alright.

Taoism, like science, deals with the reality of what is: the 'physis' of existence. 'Physis' means the endeavor to perceive the essential nature of all things which was the quest of ancient Greek philosophy in the sixth century B.C., and it is here that humanity took its disastrous detour two and a half thousand years ago, for there were 2 schools of thought in this philosophy – the Milesian and the Eleatic. It is essential to understand exactly how and where these 2 schools differ and why it has had such an overwhelming influence on the historical development of modern culture.

The Milesians, like the ancient Indian, Chinese and Aztec philosophies, viewed the world as being alive, divine and an organic whole. Moreover, they believed in a world of perpetual change, flux and development that arose from the dynamic interplay of the web and flow of the seasonal cycles created through the dialectic opposites of the manifest world. However, they viewed these opposites as two hands of an essential unity which they called the Logos. This term can be viewed as the divine principle very similar to the term Tao. It basically refers to the Oneness of creation.

What is important is that this Divine Principle or Logos existed within creation and was not separate from it. On the other hand, the Eleatic school taught that this Divine Principle existed outside of the created world and was viewed as a personal God who stood above the world and directed its workings. Thus, we had the beginning of the prescriptive rules regulating life on planet Earth and the personified God existing in Heaven. This split between spirit and matter later led to the belief in an inanimate world that was not divine, nor alive and became the basic foundation and building block of the future classical western world view.

This view held that this Divine Being, because it stood apart from the world, was constant and static and beyond change. Change was merely an illusion of the material world, not an integral part of the evolutionary process. The concept of the atom as the basic building block of matter grew out of this philosophy. In other words, there must be some indestructible and constant substance that was beyond change and that God had used to construct the mechanistic universe. Once the world had been created by God and put into motion there was no further change that was not an illusion of our limited human perception.

Western science then spent the next 2,500 years searching for this indivisible and indestructible atom only to discover in the end there was simply no such thing, and the world did not operate according to Greek philosophy or Newtonian physics. The 'physis' of the Western world was wrong! Our understanding of the true nature of reality was erroneous and has led us into dire straits threatening our very existence.

It is essential to grasp that the classical western world view is just one of many views that have existed down through the ages in many societies and cultures. In the final analysis, it was just the opinion of one school of thought and in particular one or two individuals within that school: namely Parmenides, Leucippus and Democritus. Even amongst the Greeks there were those who disagreed with their view.

We no longer live in ancient Greece and both the world and humanity have moved on. We certainly would not be happy giving up our modern conveniences to live in the physical world that existed over 2,000 years ago, and neither should we be living with a philosophy that was enunciated back then. Humanity has matured and our scientific understanding or 'physis' of the world within which we live is profoundly different to that of the ancient Greeks. It is time to move on and formulate a more modern and appropriate world view based in that scientific knowledge and emotional maturity.

The problem is that the established order has a vested interest in keeping humanity asleep. The state and the church have combined to form and protect the status quo, the entrenched wisdom and the accepted world view. Look at the difficulty great minds like Galileo, Leonardo, Columbus, Einstein and so on had in changing our ideas of how the world worked. All mavericks and radical thinkers are viewed as suspect, fringe, alternative and wrong. Yet, change we must and far better to proactively make those changes willingly and voluntarily before we are forced to by a hostile fate.

If we examine any of the major issues concerning global warning: pollution, the burning of fossil fuels, deforestation, agribusiness, and the military-industrial complex, it is obvious that the divide or debate is always between the concerned few and the entrenched establishment who have a vested interest in maintaining the status quo for as long as possible while they rape the earth. It is always a choice of short-term gain and profit for the few as opposed to the long-term well-being of the many. We are effectively robbing the future rather than enriching it.

Environmental destruction is basically an abuse of the 'common' – those things that make life worth living: fresh air and pure water, wilderness areas and nature. The issue is that the capitalist economic system places no monetary value on these rare and precious assets and so they are exploited and raped. Even the ancient Greeks who formulated our world view understood the intrinsic value and sanctity of nature establishing their philosophy schools in gardens and nature. They understood that nature was to be respected, honoured and 'followed' in the sense of taking one's cues and guidance from it.

As the world becomes more urbanised, with over half the world's population now living in cities or urban areas, we become disconnected from nature and its rhythm and cycles. So, it is not just the attack on the common and wilderness, it is also that humanity has lost its appreciation of and its ability to live in harmony with this chi of nature. When humanity depended upon the ebb and flow of the seasons to plant and sow its crops, there developed a oneness, an intimacy and a profound respect for the cycles and grandeur of nature. As we have become divorced and disconnected, the ravage of nature passes unnoticed.

The essence of *Tao Tuning* is that one lives in harmony with nature and that nature is not seen as purely the physical world in which one lives: meaning the flora and fauna of the Earth. Nature is much greater than that for it includes the unseen world as well: those spiritual realms that surround us and within which we have our being. Remember, it is one's ability to have an emotionally and intellectually mature relationship and conversation with nature that is the essence of Taoist wisdom.

When humanity split the world into spirit and matter it placed nature on the side of matter making it inert, inanimate, dead and unfeeling and placing God or the divine on the other side of spirituality. Nature was there to be dominated and exploited: at the service of man rather than man being the divine husbandman and custodian of nature. In the Taoist sense, nature is far more than inert matter – it is a living, breathing whole that encompasses the entirety of life. Modern nuclear physics and other recent scientific discoveries now validate this oneness of nature that is imbued with transcendent and divine consciousness.

It is not just that man depends upon nature for air, water, food and physical sustenance but also and more importantly for his spiritual nurturing and nourishment. The more urbanised and disassociated from nature humanity becomes the more unwell, neurotic and anxious we also become. As science dissected, measured, categorised and exploited nature we robbed it of its divine essence and chi. The classical western world view sees nature purely as a physical resource to be exploited for our own purposes rather than existing in its own right and having its own meaning and purpose.

Once again, we have usurped the superior ground of domination making nature beholden to human rather than appreciating that human is a part of nature just like any other species on the planet. We are a part of the whole and not apart from it. The mystic and the nuclear physicist alike understand this dilemma of the observer and the observed and that one cannot disconnect the two. It is much like a tree especially a young sapling or plant – if one pulls it out of the earth it will wither and die, for it has lost its rootedness in the earth from which it draws nourishment and sustenance. Similarly, as humankind has uprooted itself from the ground of nature from which it exists, it is fast losing vitality and vigour and becoming unwell both physically and mentally. Part of this unwellness is the emotional neurosis of the negative ego.

Chapter 20

Gaia

If we return to the fundamentals of Taoism: the one became two – the yin and yang of the manifest world, meaning Heaven and Earth. These are not opposites but complements. The Earth is just as important and divine as Heaven. It is not that one is spiritual or alive and the other is not: both are necessary and complementary aspects of the One.

In our disassociated state, we have put spirituality in the temple or church (which is always a building) and relegated nature to a position of servitude and slavery. Nature and wilderness are something to be feared and dominated via a mechanistic and ruthless science. Nature is not to be trusted and certainly not something to be followed and have an emotionally mature relationship with!

This dysfunctional relationship with nature has been a dominant characteristic of the western mindset particularly since the seventeenth century which interestingly is also the advent of the Industrial Age and the supremacy of the machine. It is the machine more than anything else that has allowed humanity to rape the Earth. Humanity uses machines to mine, to fell, to move, to build, to destroy and to conquer. Before the advent of machines humanity could not really wreak havoc on the planet. Since the dominance of the machine age, wholesale environmental destruction and pollution have followed humanity into every corner of the globe. Today, both science and technology are predominantly used for destructive and harmful purposes and to wage war on nature.

Modern humanity is basically at war with nature! Every other civilisation, culture and society throughout history understood the importance of nature in the life of humanity developing a philosophy of deep respect, profound appreciation and reverential awe. They built a working partnership of cooperation and longevity ensuring sustainable environmental practices. Their spirituality was always in nature, not in a building. Their rituals and deities were primarily nature based rather than being in some remote heaven. We view these pagan practices with suspicion and distain.

Humanity understood its oneness with nature. Taoism puts it this way: *'those who follow the natural order flow in the current of the Tao'.* Epicurus of ancient Greece said: *'he who follows nature is in all things self-sufficient.'* As mentioned, the genus homo is approximately 2 million years old, so humanity has existed in harmony and cooperation with nature for a long, long time. Machines have been around for three hundred years, but it is really only in the last 50 or so that the wholesale and wonton destruction of the planet has occurred. It is entirely probable that within the next 50 or 100 years, machines will totally destroy what little habitat remains.

This is a folly of the grandest order. It is short-sighted, selfish and arrogant but more importantly it epitomises the neurosis of the negative ego and the pernicious hold it has on the human psyche. The essential prerequisite and sine qua non of becoming an adept Taoist or cosmic surfer, being able to attune to the inner law of one's being and ride the wave of one's personal Tao in harmony with the Tao of the Universe and live one's life in harmony with the Oneness of creation, is to establish this intimate and correct relationship with nature.

To become central and correct, the first priority is to examine one's ecological footprint on the Earth. By engaging honestly in this introspection, one will discover whether one is still in an antagonistic and dysfunctional relationship with nature, whether one is merely weak and ambivalent or whether one is truly committed to developing a personal philosophy that is cooperative, non-harmful and deeply ecological. One must come from a deep and profound respect and reverence for nature as the manifestation of God, Goddess, All That Is.

The closer we are to nature, the closer we are to the divine. To exist in that state of oneness one must first appreciate the oneness of the world. The divide between spirit and matter, between heaven and earth, between human and nature must be healed. One must be moved by a divine appreciation of the sanctity of life and that means for every living creature and that all of nature is alive. Every cell, every particle, every wave, every aspect of creation is a spark of divine consciousness and has equal right to life as we do.

This is the big one, for we still believe that our life – whether that be the life of humanity or our own individual, personal, biological life takes precedence and has more validity than other beings, other species and even other humans. We still live within the premise that my views, opinions and attitudes are more valid, right or correct than someone who disagrees with me. Other world views, other religions, other philosophies, other cultures, other systems etc. are somehow lesser than mine.

We still believe it is OK to destroy nature for our collective and personal gain. We still believe it is OK to go to war and kill in the name of our socio-economic system which is ultimately just one person's opinion. We need to understand that no human has more validity, right or precedence than any other. All life is sacred, and every living being has a right to life whether that be human, animal or plant but most particularly the planet.

The Earth is a living being - her name is Gaia - and she has a divine consciousness that far surpasses that of any individual human or that of collective humanity. For humankind to embark upon this war with nature is to declare war upon its host, mother and home. Whether we will acknowledge it or not, our collective wonton behaviour is slowly but definitely killing the Earth. We are most certainly causing serious injury.

Where the Earth is loved, she is most beautiful. One has only to view the scar of deforestation or an open cut mine or any of the other grossly polluted places on the planet with sensitivity and emotional maturity to sense the injury and pain being inflicted upon the Earth by human greed and rapacious activity. One cannot flow with nature and condone this behaviour. One cannot survive the impending doom and destruction if one has one foot on either side of the line. Each person must make a sovereign choice.

To flow is to be one with nature: to cultivate a harmonious reverential attitude. This is true religion – not to be confused with a hierarchic establishment that does not practise what it preaches. And this awe and wonder is not to be found in any church or temple but only in the wilderness of nature. As humankind destroys what little wilderness remains, we forfeit our ability to seek sanctuary in the bosom of mother nature. We are effectively robbing Gaia of her bounty and ability to sustain and nurture us.

One must of necessity spend time in nature. One must spend time alone with oneself. One must develop that ability to listen, to hear the sounds of silence, to be able to communicate with the All that Is. This requires dedication, commitment and practice just as developing any meaningful relationship with anyone requires time and perseverance.

To begin, one must examine how much time one spends inside particularly with the ubiquitous monitor of television, computer or smart phone. Can one just exist? How much time one spends in grace and gardens? How much one communicates with plants and animals? How much one can exist in silence?

Moreover, one must begin to know one's own story – not the one handed down by tradition, not the one told by your negative ego, not the one sold by the establishment but the one that is authentically you, the one in harmony with your inner being. To do this one must turn off the external noise and listen to the sounds from within. To achieve this is much easier in nature for it is here that the Tao will talk to you, whether that is verbal or not does not matter. You do not hear with your rational mind but with your heart and your soul.

Your inner being will communicate via the living I Ching – the gestalt of awareness: you will just know what is right for you, what you need to do, what is your path. You will silently attune to the law of your being. You will gradually become central and correct. It is never dramatic; it is not exuberant or showy. It is not egoic! The negative ego craves drama and to be the centre of attention. Your soul seeks solitude and silence. As you cultivate this practice, the essence of your being takes over control and the dominance of the negative ego wanes. There is no violent battle, no exertion of vain will power.

Your inner knowing, moral compass, conscience and inner law assert their power wordlessly, elegantly and majestically. There is no fight. The negative ego withdraws to its rightful place as custodian of physical survival and messenger of sensory perception leaving the higher octave of discernment and decision making to the conscious mind. Your consciousness becomes a hologram of intuitive awareness, gut feeling, spiritual insight and rational logic working together synergistically and harmoniously to deliver the best solution, the optimum path for you to travel.

Your neurotic, restless, egoic mind becomes silent in the tranquillity of nature. The chi of mother nature, the embrace of Gaia stills the anxiety and nurtures the soul. Slowly, imperceptibly, one is healed; one becomes strong; vigour returns, and one regains one's vitality, enthusiasm and natural excitement for life that one knew and had as a child before the split.

Even Christ said, *become as a little child if you would enter the kingdom of heaven* – not the mythical Christian heaven of another life but right here, right now! Owning your life, knowing your story, being yourself, attuning to your inner being of innocence and love. Becoming who you truly are – unadulterated pure consciousness stripped of your baggage, of your background, of the trappings and accumulation of the negative ego. Putting aside the basket of possessions, both material and psychic, that you have accumulated to bolster your insecure ego.

In that state of oneness and innocence one does not need those heavy weights and burdens – one travels light and thus one's footprint on the Earth is also light. Those who need the most toys are the ones who create the most havoc on the Earth. Excessive and conspicuous consumption are the fuel for the capitalist system that is causing the damage.

There is nothing wrong with satisfying one's personal needs; there is nothing wrong with living graciously, elegantly and joyously but one does not need to overconsume, and one does need to be frugal and prudent if one is not to inflict injury upon the Earth. The Taoist treads lightly satisfying one's needs but no more. It is not about being seen and it is not a race to the top (or the bottom). It is about being oneself and being content with who one is and one's lot in life.

Most importantly it is cultivating an attitude of gratitude and reverence: giving thanks for the wonders of life and the gift of it all.

TaoTuning is a diametrically opposite way of living one's life. We are taught to take our cues from outside: to listen to and fit into societal norms, traditional values, accepted mores, religious precepts, cultural customs and the conventional world view. We are expected to fit in: to be the same as everyone else and not question or cause waves upon the ocean of humanity. Family, education, peers, advertising, social media and all the other numerous influences that bombard us daily conspire to keep us within the bounds of normality.

Psychologically, we all want to fit in, to be accepted, to not be the odd person out. Everyone wants to disappear into the woodwork and if we do want to stand out it is usually our negative ego that craves the attention of others. We live a life that is very much directed from without. Many of us hardly know ourselves. We surround ourselves with significant others who tell us how to behave and what to be.

Tao Tuning, on the other hand, is an attunement to the inner law of one's being: a going within to discover who we really are and build a genuine and loving intimacy with ourselves. This is not to be confused with vanity that is still of the ego and is merely concerned with posturing and what other people think, so I present an image to the world. Developing a genuine intimacy with oneself is a very private affair that has nothing to do with another.

Tao Tuning is building that solitary path upon which one can be true to the inner self. To thine own self be true! It begins with honest introspection and coming to know oneself: what one likes and dislikes; what are one's preferences; what brings you true joy; what feeds and nourishes your soul. For to be on your path is the royal road of excitement and fulfillment. Doing what you love is the only path to success, but first one must discover what truly brings you joy. For the interesting thing about this journey, that distinguishes it from traditional religion, is the fundamental precept of joy and happiness. Most religious doctrines, because they are based in the belief that this life is either a payment for sin or a preparation for the next, preach a life of suffering, penance, sacrifice and renunciation. Life on planet Earth is always fraught with loss, pain and hardship. We need to suffer to prove our worthiness to enter the kingdom of heaven.

Tao Tuning preaches that this life is it – this is as good as it gets, and it gets as good as you want to make it. Joy, happiness and excitement are the indicators that you are on the right path. Doing what you love, doing what brings you great joy, fulfillment and satisfaction means you are fulfilling your life purpose. Life is not meant to be hard; we do not need to suffer. Suffering is merely a message that we are off our path.

We do not need to trek to the Himalayas to find our path. We do not need to seek a guru or master to find our enlightenment. We do not need to suffer to prove our worthiness and be accepted by God. What we do need to do is to go within, become acquainted with our inner being and learn what brings us great joy. This joy is the message of our soul that that activity is right for us.

This is not indulgence or hedonism; this is the way of the Tao, the path of least resistance. What is an unhappy animal or plant – one that has been abused or neglected by us perhaps. The universe is a joyous place. The energy or chi of the Tao is based in happiness; life is to be celebrated not borne in suffering. Yet, most of us feel guilty when we enjoy ourselves.

Yes, we are here to create and to work and to achieve significance. We are all here to contribute, but we can only do that by discovering our soul purpose and the only way you will truly find that is by paying close attention to your emotions and moods. It is not about being myopic, spoilt, emotional or moody. It is most definitely not about being neurotic and needy, but it is about honouring the self and we can only do that by honouring and acknowledging our emotional body.

In the traditional split between mind and matter, the rational, linear, logical mind takes over and the emotional body is pushed to the rear. We suppress how we feel and only acknowledge what we think. But the rational mind will not lead you to your destiny; you need to feel your way. You need to hone your emotions so that they are not the whining of your victim but the call of your hero. Qualities like courage, impeccability, strength, determination, perseverance and tenacity may not be readily understood emotions but joy, excitement, enthusiasm and curiosity are.

Tao Tuning is that ability to pay heed to what is going on within rather than what is going on without. And what is going on within is not just thought; it is the matrix of moods, emotions, thoughts and feelings; it is the gestalt of all of you, not just one small part – the thinking brain. You need to befriend your entire being. You need to be able to communicate articulately and intelligently with all the various components and parts of your larger self.

We have come to define ourselves as our egoic mind – the thinking brain. But we are much more than that. Normal verbal communication with other human beings traditionally relies upon language and language is a function of the rational mind. Once one embarks upon this solitary journey of silence and stillness one learns to use other methods of communication and perception. One senses, one feels, one intuits, one has insights and gestalts. Being becomes multifaceted and multidimensional. You become much more than your thinking mind. Your definition and appreciation of yourself changes dramatically.

Moreover, as one cultivates this holistic sense of self, you become more self-reliant and self-confident and so less needy of outside validation and support. The main reason we turn to outside input is that we lack the strength and conviction of ourselves to respect and trust our own navigation enough to not need any other reinforcement.

This does not mean we become pig-headed, self-willed, precocious, stubborn or foolish. What it does mean is that we possess the mechanism, capability and intelligence to form our own opinions, make our own decisions and choices and determine our own destiny. Remember, decisions determine destiny! And remember also, that this process involves all aspects of your being: your rational mind, your gut feeling, your intuition, your higher consciousness. You must be able to attune to all of these separate inputs putting them together synergistically in your own gestalt of awareness.

And the ultimate determinant, criteria or benchmark that you use is joy. If the decision feels right, it will be light, easy and bring you joy. If the decision is wrong, it will feel heavy, ponderous and be associated with reluctance and dread. Right decisions nurture our soul and feed our journey. Wrong decisions stall the wheels of motion and bog us in the mire.

This is such an elegant and simple system. Your conscience is not programmed by any set of predetermined or prescriptive rules. There are no commandments that need to be obeyed or followed. Your conscience is the inner law of your being that knows infallibly what is right for you, what is your path, what is the next step on your journey to lead you to your destiny.

But you must be able to hear, to listen to and to follow its promptings even when what it says is radical and opposed to the status quo of the traditional world. You see your inner being does not really care about what others think. Your inner being is not fixated on other peoples' opinion. Your inner being is not timid, lame, crippled or frightened.

Your inner being is a valiant and noble spiritual warrior that wants to follow its path and fulfill its destiny come what may. So often, we hear the story of remarkably successful people who just know their destiny, who have the courage to follow their dreams, who do not allow the world to hinder their advance and who do achieve their goal. And sadly, too often, there are those who are cowered into submission.

Tao Tuning is nothing more and nothing less than being able to be true to the self. Easier said than done and this book is nothing more than an offering of ideas, concepts and thoughts to trigger your own personal exploration of this essential and exciting topic. In the end, there is no higher quest. Every great story of human endeavour and victory boils down to one strong and valiant individual who was able to follow the calling of their heart and be true to themselves.

In the end, there is no more satisfying and fulfilling destiny than to have lived your life fully, authentically and nobly. It is not about what you achieve on the stage of the world; it is about what you achieve in the quiet of your own bosom. For within are all the challenges, all the temptations, all the excuses to be weak but also all the dreams, all the opportunities to be strong. What you achieve, out there in the world of human, will merely be an out-picture of your inner journey. And what truly inspires others to their greatness is not your external achievement but your inner battle.

We all love the hero. All of drama and the essence of storytelling down through the ages and in every civilisation and culture is about the courage of the hero who overcomes their inner inertia and fear to conquer their mountain.

Modern Hollywood fiction is all about the super-human: the superman, spiderman, 007, Jason Bourne and so on. We all crave to be transported out of the petty self that imprisons our real nature. And that real nature is far larger than who you presently are. That prison is the neurotic shell of your negative ego clinging to the need to be accepted, to fit in, to conform, to play small. But the real hero is not the Hollywood fantasy of superhuman physical feats. The real hero is the genuine and humble being who is able to honour their inner being and follow their truth.

Your true nature wants to express your divine magnificence; wants to achieve your destiny; wants to be all you can be; wants to play large. Pain and suffering are nothing more than the constriction of the egoic shell tightening its grasp around that magnificence. Joy and happiness are the fruits of its fulfillment.

TaoTuning is one way to experience that joy. But you must find your own way – one that is right for you. You can call it what you will. If you listen attentively to the voice of your heart and soul, you will find what is right for you. If you pay attention to your innermost dreams and heed what gives you the most joy, you will find your path. If you follow your passion, you will be strong and conquer. If you are true to yourself there is nothing else that matters.

Gaia needs spiritual warriors who will stand up and be counted, who will speak their truth and find a new way of treading lightly upon the earth. Humanity needs brave souls who will forge a new path of creativity and harmony and lead us into a grand and glorious future. As David Boem stressed this is all that is left now – there are no other frontiers or fights worth fighting for. We must be vigilant to form the new human consciousness by becoming the new human on planet Earth.

Chapter 21

Paradigm Shift

The modern world we live in today in the developed countries is almost unrecognisable to that of yesteryear, and we do not need to go too far back. AI, smart phones, computers, the world-wide web, airplanes, bullet trains, extreme urbanisation and other recent technological developments have totally transformed the way we live and more importantly who we are as human beings. We are almost a different species to that of our grandparents. The world has changed and moved on.

So too, in the next 50 years and by the end of the 21st century, life will be unrecognisable to us yet again. The process of evolution is speeding up – we now inhabit a world of exponential change. Things are happening faster with less of a cushion between idea and manifestation. One of the positive functions of time is to serve as a buffer or delay between the inner process of ideation and the outer process of manifestation, particularly while humanity grows up, becomes more responsible and masters this manifestation process.

Imagine if every thought or feeling you had became immediately apparent upon the projected screen of your daily life. We would simply not be able to cope; there would be chaos in our lives. Every fear, every doubt, every angry intention, every negative thought operating in real time. No; we do have the luxury of the buffer so that we can reflect and make sure that is what we want in life.

But that cushion, that buffer is decreasing, and the process of life is speeding up as we enter the new age. Gaia, the Earth, is also on her own evolutionary journey through the Milky Way, through the cosmos and through the universe. We are entering unchartered waters or regions of space and life is changing. The descriptive rules of life are changing, and we need to catch up. It is pointless burying your head in the sand, playing the victim and lamenting that it is unfair. It just is and we need to acknowledge the change in pace. We are all aware of the speed up. We all feel it in our lives.

So, the changes will begin to accelerate. Once upon a time change moved very slowly. Life hardly changed down through the ages and it was frustrating. Now the rapid pace of change is becoming exponential and will become even more so as we move into the future. The point is this change will be either creative or destructive dependent upon our perspective, orientation, belief structure and attitude. In other words, whether for good or ill your personal life will definitely accelerate. So, you need to be on the right path for you. There is no point being on a bullet train if it is going the wrong way.

In these days of accelerated change, it is imperative that you do this inner work of introspection precisely because the luxury of the buffer is no longer there. What you think and feel becomes more immediately apparent in your daily life. Instant karma! While learning to surf small waves, one has the luxury of learning, of changing one's stance and position and so on. But if riding a 5-metre wave, one no longer has this opportunity – things are just moving too fast with too many variables operating. One just needs to get with the movement and ride that wave. If one hesitates or doubts one will fall off.

Spiritually, we have entered a new era where everything has become accelerated. We live in a time of monumental change, and we need to get on our metaphoric surfboards and be able to negotiate the cosmic waves of change that are bombarding the planet as it moves through new regions of space. The extreme weather changes: storms, droughts, floods, winds, cyclones, fires and so on are just harbingers of this new era. We have unsettled the delicate ecosystem of our life-support system and best be prepared for the coming ride of our lives. The only problem is no-one will be able to sit this one out. Each and every human being alive on the planet today has signed up for this one and it is going to be exciting. It is going to take all your courage, wisdom, agility and strength to negotiate the cosmic currents of change that are now sweeping the Earth. Whether you will be dumped in the white waters of chaos and mayhem that will wash across the globe or be able to successfully ride the waves of change is entirely up to you. But time is running out for the decision and the preparation. We need to get ready.

It is vitally important to understand *The Temple of Understanding* and alter your perspective and attitude. It is absolutely essential to build your own personal paradigm and world view that is in harmony with the theme of these changes. The basic problem with the negative ego is that it inhabits an extremely limited space with a very narrow view or perspective. Humanity is incredibly immature and myopic viewing everything from its own narrow and limited perspective.

But there is a much larger cosmic story going on here that does not just pertain to humankind or even the Earth. This is not just about global warming or humanity's affects upon the ecosystem. It is rather an evolutionary journey of life itself. We need to get out of our comfort zone of ignorance and arrogance and realise there are cosmic forces of gigantic proportion working here and we need very quickly to get on board lest we just get left behind. Say life no longer needs humanity. Say humanity has strayed so far from its true path that it can no longer play its part in this cosmic drama. What if we have written ourselves out from the script?

This is also the available option of free will and personal sovereignty! Life is all about probability patterns and outcomes that are primarily determined by the attitude and expectation of the observer. We have learnt that both the individual and the collective human exist very much within the context of the observed. We are not separate from the field of existence but are firmly rooted and have our very being in it.

But we are refusing to cooperate. We are choosing to go our own way. We have become an aberrant species. We do live within the erroneous meta-paradigm and mechanical world view that simply does not allow us to participate in this cosmic process of galactic change. One is either in or out of the flow; there is no in-between. You cannot have your cake and eat it. You must make a sovereign choice and that is either to be a separated being, existing in your own shell of egoic isolation or become connected to the whole and learn to flow.

The world is polarising. We see it everywhere: politically, economically, socially and spiritually. We are all taking sides; choosing our positions; adopting our attitudes and crystalising our behaviours. What is your position? Where are you at in this process of change? And if your answer is one of ignorance or default then you have not consciously chosen and thus are not sovereign. Personal sovereignty demands that we make a consciously aware and emotionally mature decision, not just a passive posture of paralysis. If you do not think for yourself and consciously explore this emerging reality, others will think and decide for you. You will be part of the herd heading for the precipice.

Going to the beach is not enough. Putting your big toe in the water and deciding it is too cold is being weak. You need to go in the water and get wet. Furthermore, you need to go catch some waves if you want to experience being one with the flow. Unfortunately, we have become a spectator species preferring to watch others live their lives rather than go out and live our own. Witness the glossy magazines, the celebrity watching, the Hollywood paparazzi, the preoccupation with the rich and famous, spectator sports, social media and so on. The forces of collectivity are gradually suffocating and strangling any remaining individuality. The herd is gathering momentum and muscle and if you do not stand clear you will be trampled underfoot or carried along by the collective madness.

You need to travel the road less travelled. You need to honour your individual uniqueness and cherish your inner spirit. You need to become a spiritual warrior upholding your own inner truth. As I have previously mentioned, this is a journey that must be made solo. No matter how close you may be to another, each has their own journey to tred, their own truth to express. We each must make a personal and sovereign choice. We each must be true to our own inner voice, or the journey will not be authentic and will not sustain you through the coming crisis.

We need to stop watching other lives and focus on our own. We need to stop idolising others and glorify ourselves. We need to stop unfavourably comparing ourselves with others and remain true to our own inner nature. We need to stop living our lives through a monitor and a social media app and start living in the now.

Now is the time of training and preparation. Now is the time of discipline and practice. Now is the moment of your being. We need to get good at making our own decisions – this is the path of *Personal Sovereignty*. We need to get good at living our lives in harmony with the flow – this is the path of *TaoTuning*. We need to change our paradigm, world view and attitude to one of inclusivity and respect for all life – this is the path of *BeComing One*. These three disciplines are the foundation stones of the Temple of Understanding. You need to start building your own temple of Truth.

One of the true scientific marvels of our time is weather forecasting. With the use of satellites and other means we are now able to predict with a high degree of accuracy the coming fronts, storms and patterns that will create the weather in the immediate future. And if that prediction is for storms or other forms of bad weather, we need to take precautions and to take shelter. We need to get our house in order and batten down the hatches.

Spiritual or cosmic storm clouds are brewing on the horizon, and you are going to need to take shelter in a robust dwelling – you need to build your temple, now! This temple may not be physical, but it needs to be able to shelter you in the coming psychic storm. We have discussed the wave-like nature of reality and the need for a polarised tension to fuel the wave like the terminals of a battery. The polarisation process that is going on all over the world is just another of these yin/yang continuums that we have been discussing and is necessary to drive the immense wave of change sweeping the planet. Remember, opposition is a necessary prerequisite to union.

We need this extreme polarisation to fuel the wave, to drive the momentum and energise the change process. But this polarisation will also bring instability, unusual patterns and unexpected events. We need to be prepared as in the approach of any storm front. Those who are wise and adequately prepared will ride out the storm to safely catch the wave of change generated by the storm. Those who are ill-prepared will suffer the consequences and onslaught of the front. They may not be able to ride the subsequent wave of change precisely because they will be floundering in the white water.

Do not miscalculate the coming upheaval and disruption. The wave of global change is upon us, and it is time to take shelter by building your own temple of understanding. I only offer these thoughts to provoke your own inner discussion and reflection. You may take and or discard whatever works for you. These are not prescriptive measures but merely catalysts to stimulate your own process of building.

But build you must, and you must begin by evaluating your own belief system, meta-paradigm and world view. What are your beliefs? Are they grounded in reality or superstition and religious fantasy? Have you done the necessary homework and introspection to even know what they are? Are they yours or just hand-me-downs from parents, teachers and intermediaries? Are you authentic or just a carbon copy?

You need to clean up your script to ensure the story is genuine and authentic. You need to know your purpose and the deeper meaning of your life. You need to be able to engage in that emotionally intelligent discussion with your higher self and your soul. You need to determine precisely where you are going as a sovereign individual, or you will just be drawn along with the herd especially when the panic sets in and everyone is looking to each other for reassurance and guidance but like lemmings are merely running for the cliff.

In *BeComing One* we will examine how you do this work: how you clear your system of the blockages to the flow and become one with your own self and your own creation: the story of your life. Learning how to flow with the greatest and most exciting wave there is – you.

About the Author

Author, entrepreneur, business owner, environmentalist & keen gardener, Adrian Emery has devoted his life to creating a new philosophy called *LifeWorks* based on understanding the laws, principles & codes that make life work easily, effortlessly & successfully. Life is a gift & we are here to enjoy life & be successful: it is our birthright.

Adrian founded & developed several hugely successful health/vegetarian cafes & restaurants along the Eastern seaboard of Australia during the 70's, 80's & 90's, eventually publishing *The Art of Nourishment* in 1995 which encapsulated the ideas, philosophy & recipes developed over that period heralding the concept of cooking with love.

In 2001, he became a management consultant specialising in executive mentoring teaching others how to build businesses based on spiritual principles & harmonious team structures. His fundamental premise is that a happy employee is a productive employee & that culture precedes performance.

In 2010 Adrian was awarded the CSIA Customer Service CEO of the Year for bringing customer service excellence to the strata industry where he co-built a multi-million-dollar national company with 11 offices & over 180 employees.

Adrian is also a gifted personal counsellor & accountability coach, having developed a coaching modality called *TaoTuning* designed to assist others to find their life purpose or ikigai & attune to the flow of their inner destiny & fate, establishing their life on the firm foundation of cosmic principles.

Adrian has now retired to *Sennikatan*, a spectacular garden built over the last 50 years to demonstrate we can regenerate the Earth, to write & prepare others for the coming planetary transition to a new world. With his partner, Marianne, he has also created **rusticspirit** as a spiritual retreat for guests to come & experience the stillness.

To learn more about Adrian's work or follow him -
website: adrianemery.com
facebook: adrianemery.author
instagram: adrianmoranemery
youtube: Adrian Emery
blog: adrianemery.com/blog

If you have enjoyed this book please leave a review on Amazon on my Author page: www.amazon.com/author/adrianemery

Printed in the USA
CPSIA information can be obtained
at www.ICGtesting.com
CBHW022029010724
10982CB00003B/29